*QUICK*STRATEGY™

A Proven Method to
Focus & Guide
Your Business in
Rapidly Changing Markets

By

Bruce R. Robinson

authorHOUSE®

i

This book is a work of non-fiction. Names and places
have been changed to protect the privacy of all
individuals. The events and situations are true.

ISBN: 978-1-4140-0203-3 (sc)
ISBN: 978-1-4140-0204-0 (e)

Library of Congress Control Number 2003097429

Print information available on the last page.

This book is printed on acid-free paper.

1stBooks - rev. 10/23/03

To My Wife, Ellen

Preface

This book gives business leaders a comprehensive guide to direct their business strategy in rapidly changing markets. It not only explains the theory of business strategy, but it also gives actual case studies applying the theory and relating strategic planning to managers' day-to-day decision making.

Unlike many academic discussions on the subject of strategic planning, this book is written for business leaders who are looking for a quick method to direct their business strategy without sorting out the vague concepts and incantations of consultants and academics.

In the 1950's, a collaborative study centered in Boston, MA with the involvement of a number of large U.S. corporations tried to identify those business characteristics that led to high financial returns on investment.

The study looked at a number of business variables including level of capital investment to sales, research and development, and selling expense to sales, etc. If you were a participant in the study, you could access this data to help you understand how your business could improve its return on investment. To many, the most striking outcome was that businesses in market leadership positions always seemed to generate much higher returns on investment.

Kenneth R. Andrews in his book, The Concept of Corporate Strategy, published by Richard D. Irwin in 1971, followed with a concept that strategy was a match between a company's strengths and weaknesses and the environment in which it did business. The market leaders in the earlier study clearly had overwhelming strengths and few weaknesses, giving rise to their market position. However, Andrews gave us little insight into how to apply his concepts to the variety of environments in which we do business.

Michael E. Porter's book, Competitive Strategy: Techniques for Analyzing Industries and Competitors, Free Press 1980, taught us that the structure of the industry determines the state of competition within that industry and establishes the basis for a company's strategy. He defined five forces that he claimed would determine the average profitability of the industry. He emphasized the importance of choosing the right industry and, within that, the best market positions to maximize financial returns. That's good for stock pickers, but difficult to apply by those of us who are trying to run a business.

Various professors at major business schools and consulting firms have more recently emphasized "Core Competence" and company "Capabilities" as the basis for strategic planning. The problem I have with core competence or capabilities in today's fast moving business environment is what to do with my core competence and capabilities when the market shifts and they don't lead to a performance or price advantage in the eyes of my customers.

This book is written in a personal style based on the author's 27 years of first-hand experience as a business owner, company president, and head of corporate development at several large diversified companies*. It begins with three case studies that show how the *Quick*Strategy™ methods are useful in reducing complex business strategies to a two-page summary. These case studies are followed by an in-depth analysis of strategic planning concepts. It concludes with a step-by-step guide to the use of the *Quick*Strategy forms that describe your markets and market strategy. The author demonstrates a practical knowledge of what is necessary to develop winning strategies.

---

* The author has also taught as adjunct faculty in several Graduate Business Schools.

Acknowledgements

The author wishes to express his appreciation to the executives of the profiled companies in the case studies for their cooperation in developing these cases with respect given to their need for anonymity in cases one and two: Michael McConnell and Andrew Broom of Eclipse Aviation in case three.

The author thanks his colleagues, Bob Bellemare and Jon Brock of UtiliPoint International Inc. for their diligent support in testing a variety of fast foods for Case #1 and their help with early drafts. The author also thanks Nick Kaufman, Paul Loch, Peter Murphy, Mark Robinson, Phil Whisenhunt and Brent Stacey for reading and providing valuable comments on early drafts.

Special thanks to: Ken Silverstein for editing the first drafts of this book and Lee Ann Watkins for putting the manuscript into its final format and with Sandy Stacey editing the final draft.

The author thanks George H. Gage, Sr. Vice President of Planning at EG&G Inc. for introducing him to the concept of market driven strategic planning. George and his staff were able to put the essence of a strategic plan on a one-page format (they called it a Form K) that became the common basis for managing hundreds of strategic initiatives in this high technology conglomerate.

Strategic Plans Then and Now

THEN:

In the past, strategic plans were often lengthy analyses of markets, company capabilities and opportunities that were usually performed over many months by expensive outside consultants or corporate staff. They asked people running your business operations lots of questions about their business and often called customers to ask similar questions. Each year, the completed strategic plan was introduced to boards of directors and senior management with great fanfare and ignored by all for the rest of the year.

NOW:

"*Quick*Strategy is different."

It is a real time management tool that lets people who run businesses react quickly to changing markets and stay ahead of competition.

Contents

Introduction

*Quick*Strategy™ Introduction

In the past, as a president of several high technology companies and director or vice president of corporate development in large diversified corporations, I took up to three months every year to prepare detailed strategic plans that were allegedly used for directing our business operations. Too often the efforts were used to satisfy the demands of investors and boards of directors; they did not work.

Today, we must continuously update our business strategic plans to survive rapid changes in our markets. We then must quickly relate those changes to the day-to-day direction of our business. I have seen telecom service-related businesses go from $50 million to $5 million in annual revenue in less than one year. I have helped owners of small manufacturing companies fight bankruptcy after losing their homes, their jobs, and years of hard work because they failed to adapt to rapid market changes. I have sold an Internet services business for millions of dollars that vaporized a year later. I have acquired environmental service-related businesses that lost their markets overnight when a federal government agency changed their policy. Real time strategic planning, once a luxury of large business, is now a necessity for the survival of your business, no matter what its size.

Fortunately, *Quick*Strategy techniques outlined in this book and our online support system at www.quickstrategy.com give you a proven technique that has been developed over the last ten years. It will help users focus and guide their businesses in today's rapidly changing markets. This approach will give you the strategic planning capabilities available only to large corporations in a fraction of the time and at a cost you can afford. This book and www.quickstrategy.com provides:

- FAST RESULTS: A functioning strategic plan in less than one week;
- CONCISE PLAN FORMAT: An easy to use two-page format focuses strategic concepts and details tactics necessary to implement your plans;
- MANAGEMENT FOCUS: All *Quick*Strategy plans lead to measurable outputs, keeping management focused on strategy driven results;

- ADAPTABLE: Real time Internet updates and shareware keep plans continuously updated to reflect current market conditions; and
- ON-LINE SUPPORT: Affordable technical and research support gets you started and keeps your plan current.

This proven approach to strategic planning will get your business positioned in its markets in a way that will significantly improve its chances of success and survival.

What Drives Rapid Change in Our Markets?

There are no guarantees of success and survival in this rapidly changing world. From large corporations to small businesses, we see changing market conditions and competition devastate even the best-managed businesses.

What is behind all of this rapid change? Why is it harder to survive in business today? *Quick*Strategy gives you a better understanding of the three forces that will quickly change the size and shape of your markets: Market Alternatives, External Factors (Externalities), and Saturation. Let's look at some recent examples of each of these:

- Xerox corporation started the copy machine revolution in the early 1960's and then came to dominate the market. Forty years later, it has only a fraction of this market, having lost market share to low-cost competitors from around the world. In addition, market alternatives like personal computers with gigabyte memories and scanners are chewing away at total copy machine demand as paper documents are replaced with e-mail and electronically stored documents that are printed on demand.
- Eastman Kodak, meanwhile, soared to financial success with secret silver halide photographic processes over the last sixty years, but then saw its market shrink in the last few years with the introduction of digital camera technology—a market alternative that opened the photographic market to a whole new set of competitors.
- IBM has built its business around large mainframe computers, only to face the onslaught of small personal computers and decentralized processing that shook the company's core strategy in the 1990's. Only 24 percent of IBM's revenue now comes from mainframe (large) computers. According to an article in the *International Herald Tribune* May 14, 2003, "The erosion of IBM's mainframe business has been far slower than many experts expected." In 1991, one Silicon Valley commentator predicted that the last mainframe would be unplugged by 1996. IBM's competitors insist that the long-predicted demise of the mainframe is close at hand. Microsoft Corp. says its new Windows Server 2003 operating system can replace mainframe applications in corporate data centers. At Sun Microsystems, Inc., Don Whitehead, director of the company's mainframe replacement business, said his company had nearly 1,000

customers who moved from IBM's mainframes to Sun's Unix technology in the last several years. In spite of this competition, IBM just introduced a new mainframe computer, code name "T-Rex." Will IBM, with new products, be able to meet these challenges from market alternative technologies?

- Utilities were once thought to be the safest investment because they could count on consistent revenue and profit based on government regulation of their industry. Now, many utilities are losing money and some are even filing for bankruptcy, largely because the market has been deregulated and companies have miscalculated the impact of these externalities.

- Demand for new cell towers peaked in 2002 as major market areas were saturated and required no additional installations.

- Airlines were growing every year. They had plans to continue growing passenger revenue miles by at least three percent a year. But they are now facing bankruptcy with fewer passengers and declining revenues per passenger mile. All of this is driven by market externalities like September 11-related terrorist threats and SARS virus fears.

- Large regional banks are fighting for their lives as nationwide banking mergers create superbank competitors with international reach and access to a wider range of banking services. More recently, on-line banking services provide comparative interest rate data permitting customers to shop for the best available loan from a wide variety of loan sources. This was not possible until the government permitted interstate banking, an externality to the banking market that dramatically changed the competition.

- Small retail outlets and local restaurants are facing the onslaught of national chains offering more products and lower prices. Local hardware stores fall apart when Lowe's or Home Depot enter an area. Meanwhile, local drugstores vaporize when large Rite Aid chains move into the area and Wal-Mart targets small towns, replacing the entire community retail infrastructure. A clear market alternative to the local paint store is a purchase at one of the national chain home improvement stores.

- Fast-food burger sales have peaked, as 61 percent of the U.S. population is now overweight. McDonald's, for example, lost money for the first time in its history. It is now being sued by obese customers and demonized by diet-conscious consumers in the press.

Is a food market saturated when the consumers are too fat to eat any more product?

- Seven years ago, my partners and I acquired a $40 million engineering business from a large conglomerate. It was losing $1— $3 million a year. We looked at each business segment in the company. The management described over sixty segments, many of which were operating in markets where market alternatives had long since replaced their product or service. Some segments were declining as customer demand was saturated and there was no opportunity for recovery. By looking at each segment and eliminating those that were poorly positioned, we were able to immediately turn a profit and grow the remaining business segments.

From this handful of examples, you can see how market alternatives, externalities, and saturation are the forces that rapidly change the size and other characteristics of your markets, sometimes leaving well-managed businesses with no alternative but to close their doors. *Quick*Strategy techniques will let you anticipate these changes to your markets and give your business a better chance for survival.

Why Are We Facing Such Fierce Competition in Today's Markets?

In the 1970's, as president of a small electronic instrument company in upstate New York, I set prices based on a multiple of costs to support the necessary R&D, administrative expense, selling expense and overhead. I generally knew our competitors' prices and kept within a reasonable distance of them, *but most of our customers were not aware of our competitors' prices.* We managed our business with little competitor information and our customers purchased our products based on trust in our sales force and product quality. As long as our prices were not, in their judgment (based on limited information), excessive, they were happy. Those days of operation in an information vacuum are gone.

The Internet has made vast quantities of competitive product information available to all competitors and customers and they can monitor changes in prices and product performance daily in many markets. At any moment, your competitors can look at your prices as well as your costs and think they can do better.

Look at the airline industry: Southwest Airlines operates at a cost of 7.3 cents per passenger seat mile versus the 11—12 cents per passenger seat mile for the major air carriers. Herb Kelleher, co-founder of Southwest Airlines, examined the costs of the major air carriers and knew he could offer lower prices by changing the way services were provided. The other major air carriers (with high fixed costs) responded to Southwest fares by creating pricing models that also offered selective low fares but were too complicated for most passengers to understand. Today, consumers can sort out prices on the Internet and pick the lowest available airfare from all carriers and the best routing. As such, the major air carriers can no longer hide in their complex pricing models and charge some passengers several times the discount fare to make up for their excessive costs. Instant availability of competitive information forces airline competitors to aggressively price their products and reduce costs if they are to survive.

In selling products or services to the government, we once operated under cost plus contracts: pricing based on our cost plus some reasonable profit (usually limited to 5—10 percent of selling price). Today, the government purchasers have extensive information available to them at their fingertips from other government agencies making similar purchases. They are also aware of government (GSA) auditors who are continuously monitoring government purchases for consistency between agencies. Where we once could charge three times the salary of contract support personnel to the federal government, now we are lucky to get two times their salary[*]. Today, we are asked to bid fixed prices for hardware procurements. If we win, then our competitors can find out our pricing through freedom of information privileges. They, then, are ready to bid a lower price the next time around. The government has made us more aggressive competitors by using available electronic information on product price and performance to obtain the best possible price for products and services it procures.

Continuous on-line procurement and shipment of products to large retailers and manufacturers has significantly reduced the inventory carrying costs of large retailers and manufacturers. How can a small retailer or manufacturer compete if they have a wholesaler or middleman adding their costs and profits to products and services? Wal-Mart monitors daily its sales by product codes while also procuring and distributing replacement products. My local hardware store orders new products weekly by taking a physical inventory or responding to customer complaints.

I recently talked to an engineer who develops Radio Frequency Identification chips (RFIDs) to put into each product in company or retail store inventories. The stores can use radio frequency signals to remotely activate the chip's code to tell where the product is and the quantity on hand at any time. This chip, when imbedded into the inventory, will automatically tell how many parts are loaded on a truck for delivery and how many of each part was delivered. Eventually, these chips will be in every item in a store. You will then wheel your shopping cart to a checkout area and insert your credit card. Each chip will then signal the code of the product purchased and your bill will be automatically calculated and charged to your card; no cashier is needed. This is not twenty years away; it is in test markets today. If you don't know what management tools and information technology your competitors are using, then they will destroy your business.

The Internet and proprietary data services can tell us more about you and your company than ever before, even if you are a private company. We can tell you how many people each competitor employs, what they owe, their major customers, payment history, product pricing, and performance information without leaving our researchers' offices. Your competitors can also get this information on your business. I can log onto web sites like

---

[*] The two to three times multiplier on direct employee salary covers the other employee costs including FICA, medical and dental insurance, other benefits, administrative support, sales, marketing, and overhead expenses.

Epinions.com and find out what your customers like and dislike about your products. Where is the line on confidentiality? After all, governments, banks, and public corporations (in many cases) must publicly report information and industry surveys. When your competitors know your every move, they will react aggressively to hold their market position or take away your market share if they see a weakness in your business.

Finally, globalization has created fierce competition in areas previously thought to be sacrosanct. Many manufacturing jobs were exported outside the U.S. in the last twenty years. It is hard to find a piece of clothing not manufactured in Asia. Now, we are facing globalization of our technology production jobs like software development, routine engineering design, and laboratory testing. A division of one of the companies I worked with recently faced a new competitor with a next-generation software solution to replace their outdated software product. When I met with the new competitor in an effort to evaluate the possibility of acquisition, I found there were only three people in their office. They subcontracted all software development to India with over 100 software engineers engaged at a fraction of the cost of U.S. software engineers. Their new venture was funded by a U.S. venture capital fund that, ironically, raised much of its capital from labor union pension funds. The ability to manage technology and production on a global basis has been revolutionized in the last ten years by immediate access to information. There is no safe haven for U.S. industry; your competitors will use the lowest cost resources available globally to aggressively compete with your business.

There is one common thread to the above scenarios describing the new highly aggressive competitive environment you face in your business today: instant access to information. It is driving down prices by making consumers aware, improving operating efficiencies, reducing costs, driving out unaware competitors, moving production and design to the lowest labor cost markets, and keeping your competitors aware of your every move. *Quick*Strategy is designed to give you a standard way of evaluating and compensating for a continuously changing competitive environment. You must know your competitors and their every move to position your company for survival in today's high-speed business environment. You are facing fierce competitors in every market today. Because the information highway gives you no place to hide, you must properly position your business to compete.

Strategy is Positioning

We define business strategy as **"the art and science of meeting your competitors on the market battlefield under advantageous conditions."**[♦] To accomplish this, you must define the market battlefield, position your business relative to your competitors, and react to those forces changing the size and shape of the market battlefield. (*Some have suggested the expression "market battlefield" is too coarse a description of the competitive business environment. If you agree, now is the time to put this book down and sell your business as you will not survive in today's businesses without engaging in a battle against your competitors.*)

As you will see in Chapter 4, we define the market battlefield by precisely defining the product or service offered to a specific set of customers to satisfy a well-defined customer need. We identify the factors affecting the size and overall characteristics of the market battlefield in terms of market alternatives, external forces (externalities), and saturation. We define the competitors as those businesses that directly compete to satisfy the defined customers' needs with products or services closely related to those offered by your company to the market.

Only when you have defined your market battlefield and your competitors' relative positions can you develop a strategy and position your business to meet your competition under advantageous terms. With *Quick*Strategy, we offer a methodology that lets you easily and continuously monitor a changing market battlefield and changing competitive positions. You can then react rapidly by repositioning your business to survive and flourish.

[♦] An obvious corollary to this definition is if you cannot meet your competitors on the market battlefield under advantageous conditions, retreat from the battlefield.

How to Most Effectively Use This Book

This book is organized in three distinct sections. The first section introduces you to the concepts of *Quick*Strategy through three case studies, which are stories about three businesses that are analyzed using *Quick*Strategy methods. The second section, starting with Chapter 4, provides the theoretical basis for the *Quick*Strategy approach to business analysis and management. The third section in Appendices A and B provides you with step-by-step directions to help you use the two *Quick*Strategy forms: The Market Battlefield Summary Form and The Strategic Plan Summary Form. These two forms will be your guide to successful strategic management for each segment in your business.

Many of us who are busy running businesses have read enough by now and will go directly to the *Quick*Strategy forms in Appendices A and B to start filling them in for our business, stopping to read the directions only as we run into trouble. After all, we seldom read directions when we buy a new appliance or piece of software—we don't have time.

For the theorist, professor, or consultant who may differ with my approach to the basic planning concepts outlined above, you should go to Chapters 4 and 5 where I develop the theory of *Quick*Strategy in more rigorous detail. This will at least give you more ammunition to use in critiquing my model.

For the rest of you, I suggest you read the next three chapters describing actual cases where I have used *Quick*Strategy methods to help unravel complex business situations. Read these chapters like a mystery; enjoy the unraveling of the business situations and contemplate the potential for developing alternative strategies. There is no single right answer to strategic planning. In your different interpretation of each case study, you should bring your own experience to bear on potential winning strategies while assimilating the basic concepts of *Quick*Strategy without the boredom of rigorous textbook descriptions. Then proceed to at least skim Chapters 4, 5 and 6 on the underlying theory before going to Appendices A and B to apply *Quick*Strategy methodology to your business. If you get stuck or want to use our on-line support services, go to www.quickstrategy.com to register your book purchase and to obtain our staff support.

Chapter 1

CASE #1:
The Albuquerque Turkey Burger

I was introduced to Tony Romero[*] in early 2003 by an investment advisor friend who described Tony's need to raise capital for a new fast-food chain in Albuquerque, New Mexico. I met Tony one Saturday morning at the Owl Café on Juan Tabo Boulevard just off the I40 interstate expressway. I listened to his story while enjoying a cup of New Mexico piñon coffee, a specialty of the Owl Café.

Tony, an enthusiastic 34-year-old chemical engineer with a recent MBA from the part-time program at the University of New Mexico, wanted to leave his engineering job and launch his own fast-food business. With the precision of a chemical engineer, he had developed a tasty recipe, complete with secret seasonings (it worked for Colonel Sanders!), for a turkey burger that he believed would take a significant share of the $40 million a year (his number) Albuquerque fast-food burger market.

His turkey burger creation had almost half the calories of the equivalent beef burger and half the fat content. All he needed was the capital to get his first restaurant started and the world would beat a path to his door and make us all rich. Tony said, "After all, we only needed to capture 10 percent of the local market to be overwhelmingly successful and have a $4 million/year business." He would call his new fast-food restaurant "Albuquerque Turkey Burger" as a tribute to his hometown and because its unique flavor comes from New Mexico ingredients.

Tony and his investment advisor pointed out that the national opportunity to franchise Albuquerque Turkey Burger was enormous with over 750 million burgers sold each week in the U.S. They also knew the market was waiting for a low calorie and low fat alternative to the conventional fast-food burger as more Americans were trying to reduce their dietary intake of saturated fats. Turkey burgers could be produced in low fat versions to satisfy this consumer demand. In addition, they believed turkey was 25—30 percent lower in cost than comparable beef products. Lower fat and lower price with unique flavoring no burger lover could resist—a winning combination. I was assured we could not go wrong.

---

[*] Fictitious name; any resemblance to persons living or dead is purely coincidental.

Although their primary reason for meeting with me was to explore my interest in an investment in "Albuquerque Turkey Burger," I told them they would need to develop a complete business plan before they could attract the required capital to finance their business. I volunteered to apply my "*Quick*Strategy" methodology to analyze the market opportunity and help them focus their activity on specific strategic objectives. They could then use this material as a basis to develop their financial plan and determine their capital needs.

I suggested a test of the product, complete with secret seasonings, to determine if it passed the "smell test." I was not going to waste time on market analysis if the product was a dud. To determine if the recipe was easily assembled, I suggested he give me the basic recipe and some of his secret sauce. I would purchase the remaining ingredients and test the recipe in my home with assistance from my wife, Ellen. I did not tell him Ellen had worked in the commercial food industry and was once an assistant to James Beard, cooking icon of American cuisine.

Tony provided me with the following recipe:

- ¼ pound of ground turkey, either skinless white meat or skinless dark meat
- 1 Hatch green chile, medium hot, roasted, seeds and skin removed
- 1 tsp. Tony's secret sauce
- 1 slice low fat Monterrey Jack cheese (optional)
- ½ tsp. vegetable oil for cooking
- Salt and pepper
- One hamburger bun, baked per Tony's recipe and toasted

I was to form the ground turkey into a specific size patty and cook in the vegetable oil according to Tony's strict timetable. Partway through the cooking process, I was to add the slice of Monterrey Jack cheese and the chile strips to the top of the patty. The bun was to be toasted while cooking the turkey; then add the secret sauce to the Albuquerque Turkey Burger when I put it on the toasted bun, just before eating.

Ellen and I purchased both the skinless white meat and skinless dark meat ground turkey at the local Whole Foods Market along with the other ingredients, except the Hatch green chile. Like most New Mexicans, we had an ample supply of roasted Hatch green chiles in our kitchen.

Although New Mexico produces more chiles than any other state with over 35,000 acres under cultivation, Hatch, New Mexico is the most famous chile growing area. The chiles it produces are six to eight inches in length and green in color when fresh, ripening to a bright red color with age. They range from mild ("trainer *chiles*") to medium to hot in taste and are roasted at farm stands throughout New Mexico in the fall, adding their spicy aroma to the crisp cool New Mexican air. According to Tony, these chiles actually do add a unique flavor to the above recipe.

On a snowy New Mexico Saturday afternoon in our mountain home between Albuquerque and Santa Fe, we cooked according to Tony's Albuquerque Turkey Burger recipe and carefully tasted our preparation. It was wonderful, warm, with just the right amount of seasoning and uniquely Southwestern in its flavor. The dark meat version was judged best, but I guess the high fat version of any burger tastes best. Both light meat and dark meat versions were judged to be worthy enough to invest more of our spare time in this project. We were starting with a good product.

I called Tony and told him we were excited about his product and would begin analysis of the market opportunity for turkey burgers in the Albuquerque area. Recognizing the need to do some local research, I called Jim Hale, the Director of Project Development and Business Assistance at Technology Ventures Corporation. Jim is also adjunct faculty at the University of New Mexico, Anderson School of Management. I asked if he knew any graduate Business School students interested in working with me on the project. He recommended several students. I met with them, selecting the team that would collect local fast-food burger market information.

The first step in developing *Quick*Strategy with Tony was to define the "market battlefield" to know who and what we were up against before we developed a strategy. We started with a definition of the product or service to be offered. We then identified the customers, customer needs, competition, and factors affecting the shape and growth of the market. How will Tony focus and deploy his business resources against competitors? That is the essence of developing a winning *Quick*Strategy initiative.

Defining the Product Market

The target market is fast-food burgers. While this market today is beef burgers, we believe conditions will change: customers will move from beef to turkey burgers—a primary market opportunity. As such, we consider the turkey burger a direct substitute to the beef burger rather than a market alternative. Typically, burgers are sold with a side order of potatoes, usually fries, and a soda or other drink such as a milkshake, coffee or milk. We found there were 128 fast-food stores in the Albuquerque area selling burgers. Although individual burger prices ranged from 99 cents to over $6 per burger, our research indicated that typical "combo" meals including potatoes and a drink sold for $3.49 to $5.02. A competitive offering from Albuquerque Turkey Burger must, therefore, be a burger sold with a side of fries and a soda or other drink with the combination selling in the range of $3 to $5.

Customers

With more than 556,000 people in the Albuquerque area and with the average consumption of burgers at three per capita per week (according to food consumption stats), there could be more than 1.5 million visitors to burger outlets in the Albuquerque area each week. Unfortunately, we were unable to determine how many burgers were consumed in fast-food outlets versus other types of restaurants. According to national surveys, the majority of customers are likely to be repeat buyers of burgers from shops within a five to ten-mile radius of their office, home, or shopping area. There are also transient customers stopping at the off ramp locations on the freeways that transition through Albuquerque. Although there was not enough time to profile each customer, it is generally accepted that fast-food buyers tend to be concentrated in the under-35 age group. They have made up their mind to purchase a burger and have less than ten minutes to spend purchasing their lunch or dinner. I guess that's why they call it "fast food." We define the customer as a "burger buyer" at a fast-food outlet.

Customer Needs

Our initial survey found that customers of fast-food burger shops expect fast service, less than a ten-minute wait, and convenient location near their home, work, or shopping area. They expect consistent quality and cost-effective menu selections. They tend to be repeat buyers from a pre-selected menu, i.e., a "Combo Meal" such as a Big Mac, medium fries, and a 16-ounce soda for $3.49. Many are drawn in by the quality of the fries or side dishes and drinks as well as the burgers. McDonald's customers are alleged to have as much loyalty to their fries as their burgers. In many situations, we found convenient in-store access to market alternative products like chicken, fish, or salads was important when burger buyers were traveling with non—burger consumers.

Competitors

The graduate students working for us to survey the Albuquerque market identified 128 fast-food outlets for burgers. We were surprised to find a local New Mexico chain of stores; Blake's LotaBurger has the largest number of outlets in the Albuquerque area and slightly more than McDonald's. That does not necessarily lead to a larger share of the burger market as each Blake's outlet sells fewer burgers than each McDonald's outlet. The chart below shows, however, the Albuquerque market is unique compared to the national averages where McDonald's has a 43 percent market share, Burger King has an 18 percent and Wendy's has 13 percent. It is clear that McDonald's does not have the market presence in Albuquerque that it has nationally while Burger King and Wendy's have a market presence more closely aligned to their national position.

ALBUQUERQUE, NM: FAST-FOOD BURGER MARKET DATA

Company	Share	Number of Stores	Avg. Annual $/ Store	Total Annual $ Revenue	Mkt. Share
Blake's LotaBurger	23%	30	$500,000	$15,000,000	12.0%
McDonald's	22%	28	1,600,000	44,800,000	35.8%
Burger King	17%	22	1,100,000	24,200,000	19.4%
Wendy's	11%	14	1,200,000	16,800,000	13.5%
Sonic	10%	13	900,000	11,700,000	9.4%
Bob's Burgers	6%	7	Est. 460,000	3,200,000	2.6%
Carl's Jr.	4%	5	1,100,000	5,500,000	4.4%
Other Small FFRest.	4%	5	Est. 400,000	2,000,000	1.6%
WhataBurger	3%	4	Est. 400,000	1,600,000	1.3%
Total		**128**		**$124,800,000**	**100%**

Note: Average Annual Revenue $/Store in preceding chart is from national chain data, where available. Privately owned store revenue was estimated.

With each store offering non-burger market alternatives such as chicken sandwiches, salads, and tacos and many stores offering breakfast items, we found it difficult to identify the exact dollar sales attributable to burgers or even burger combo sales. We did find that Blake's LotaBurger focuses primarily on burgers, with limited sides, only one non-burger sandwich (chicken), and only recently introduced breakfast items. They had 70 outlets in New Mexico in 1995 and averaged $400 to $500 thousand per outlet (pre-breakfast product introduction). McDonald's averages $1.4 to $1.6 million per outlet each year but has a more diverse menu and at least 24 percent of sales revenue ($330,000 to $360,000) is from their breakfast offerings. Burger King's outlets average $1.1 million per year with 13—14 percent ($143,000 to $154,000) from their breakfast menu. Wendy's company-owned outlets average $1.34 million in annual revenue, franchised outlets $1.164 million (average $1.2 million), and does not have a breakfast offering on its menu. Carl's Jr. average annual per store revenue is $1.1 million and Sonic $900 thousand. Data on the other suppliers was not readily available and we estimated revenue based on store visits, size and menu.

Growth in average revenue per unit varied widely among the major burger competitors. From 1990 to 2001, Wendy's average unit sales rose 48 percent, Burger King's 14 percent, and McDonald's 8 percent. This may indicate a trend toward higher quality burger products or just an increase in the variety of offerings at Wendy's.

These revenue and growth numbers may be seriously impacted by a price war initiated by Burger King. In 2002, it shifted 11 items on its national menu to 99 cents. McDonald's followed by dropping prices on 8 items to $1 each. Blake's recently matched these two major suppliers with 99-cent items for a limited time period.

Does this price war indicate the level of price competitiveness in the burger market? Is this shifting to a more price-driven market, i.e., the customers are primarily interested in price? What we do know is the financial losses it has created for burger franchise owners have reached a crises level. One of Burger King's largest franchise operators sought Chapter 11 protection in early 2003 and 16 Albuquerque Burger Kings were recently shut down when the franchiser was unable to pay its franchise fee.

Wendy's has had a limited small portion 99-cent menu for 13 years, but has focused on higher priced menu items in its promotions and keeps its average combination sale prices higher than either McDonald's or Burger King; typical burger combo meal (burger, fries and soda) prices at McDonald's are $3.52 whereas Burger King's price is $3.70. Meanwhile, Blake's LotaBurger's price is $4.23 and Wendy's is $5.02.

Historically, the top four competitors were differentiated in the burger market by unique product offerings through variations in preparation, toppings and side orders. McDonald's was focusing on price and fast service while Burger King was concentrating on "having it your way" and flame-broiled burgers. At the same time, Blake's and Wendy's were zeroing in on fresh preparation and quality ingredients.

When Burger King launched the 99-cent price war last year, it said it was in response to a sagging overall market for its products. That meant that McDonald's and Blake's were forced to respond to sustain their market share in a relatively flat to declining overall market. Albuquerque Turkey Burger's entrepreneurs should be asking why McDonald's and Burger King have little or no revenue growth in the last three years along with eroding profit margins, while Wendy's has sustained growth in the last three years as the higher priced, high performance based competitor and average sales per store have grown from $1.042 million in 1997 to $1.199 million in 2002 (15 percent).

Overall revenue from the major burger suppliers has grown modestly at best in the last five years and we suspect that much of that growth has been gained by adding menu items rather than growth in burger sales. The following table shows growth trends in the major national burger chain revenue:

TOTAL SALES REVENUE: LARGER FAST-FOOD BURGER SUPPLIERS ($000,000)

Company	2002	2001	2000	1999	1998
McDonald's	$41,343est	$40,630	$40,181	$38,491	$35,979
Burger King		8,500	8,700	8,500	8,200
Wendy's		6,890	6,412	5,994	5,528
Carl's Jr.		1,784	1,990	1,892	1,149
Sonic	2,205	1,971	1,774	1,596	1,437
TOTAL		**$59,775**	59,057	**$56,473**	**$52,293**
% Growth		**1.2%**	**4.6%**	**8.0%**	

Note: *Revenue figures are based on total international revenue and much of the expansion in recent years has been in the international market for the large chains. Also note that McDonald's has the largest percentage of their business in foreign markets, with 43% market share in the U.S. and Burger King with 18% U.S. market share. McDonald's U.S. revenue may be only half of the amount shown above. Note: Only 2001 and 2002 data available for Sonic, 10% sales growth was assumed for prior years.*

There are many factors cited for the slowing growth in fast-food burger revenues:

1. High fat/high calorie concerns
2. Poor economy
3. Price wars
4. Rapid growth in "healthy" market alternative outlets
5. Move to "quick casual" restaurants
6. Location saturation

Concerns about high fat and high calorie content have led to highly publicized lawsuits against fast-food burger chains. Plaintiffs accuse the suppliers of making them obese and susceptible to diseases such as heart disease, high blood pressure, and diabetes. The recently published New York Times bestseller book, Fast Food Nation, exhorts the unhealthy nature of the fast-food burger market. An article in *USA Today* dated May 8, 2003, said the number of obese adults in the U.S. has grown from 13 percent of the population in 1962 to more than 31 percent today. This has resulted in an estimated 300,000 deaths associated with extra weight and obesity. The article also points out that people need 2,200 to 2,500 calories per day and many eat 1,500 calories at a fast-food outlet lunch. The burger chains are reacting with more low fat alternatives to their burger offerings such as grilled chicken sandwiches, salads, and veggie-burgers. They are also changing to healthier oils in their cooking processes.

The poor economy, with unemployment hitting six percent this year, leads to more cautious discretionary spending and directly impacts all fast-food outlets. More customers take lunch from home or eat breakfast at home versus stopping at a fast-food outlet. This trend should improve modestly in the next few years as the economy rebounds.

Price wars among the major players have hurt the entire industry. Burger King initiated the price war last year allegedly to gain share from its major rival, McDonald's. McDonald's responded with a vengeance. Most of the smaller players in the burger market responded in order to maintain their market position. However, Wendy's did not directly respond to the industry-wide price cutting. Burger King initiated this price war shortly after its U.K.-based parent company, Diagio, PLC, announced it was selling the Burger King operation. The clear intent was to give Burger King's parent company a boost in revenue to maximize the price obtained in the sale of the parent business. With 91 percent of the company units franchised and Burger King charging a flat fee to each franchise based on its revenue, cutting prices is a quick way to boost revenue and fees to the parent company. However, the increase in revenue and profit at the parent company level comes at the expense of the franchise operations' profits by cutting their price on higher margin menu items. Now that Burger King has been sold to U.S. investors, they may increase prices back to normal levels and the rest of the industry seems poised to follow.

The rapid rise in market alternative fast-food shops has cut into the fast-food burger market. This year, Subway fast-food sandwich shops surpassed McDonald's in the number of stores in the U.S. Although each store has lower revenue than McDonald's (est. $300—$500 thousand compared to $1.6 million), they have become a clear winner in outlet growth in the fast-food sector with a promotional emphasis on low fat, healthier food. Although they are not necessarily a healthier fast-food market alternative to burgers, Kentucky Fried Chicken grew at 33 percent and Taco Bell at 15 percent. That's compared to eight percent for McDonald's during the 1990 to 2001 time period. When a fast-food customer heads toward a burger outlet, they are likely to pass a number of tempting market alternatives along the way, significantly affecting the purchaser's decision process.

Some industry analysts indicate market alternatives such as the "quick casual" restaurant market is growing at 20 percent per year. Such establishments include new restaurants like Chipolte Mexican Grill (part owned by McDonald's), Cosi, and Panera Bread. They offer higher quality food but, like fast-food restaurants, they still have no table service. The average customer spends $6 to $8 per check versus $3 to $5 in a fast-food burger outlet. Many customers of these restaurants say they are spending more to stay healthy. ("Quick casual" is a type of restaurant as defined above.)

There is hardly a busy intersection or off ramp in Albuquerque that doesn't have multiple fast-food outlets. Gas stations, large retail outlets (like Wal-Mart), airports, and schools have co-located fast-food outlets. It is reasonable to assume that all of the best available sites are taken and opening new sites will require paying a premium for good locations or locating in lower traffic areas. One family that owns a chain of fast-food restaurants told me they have made more money on real estate appreciation than on business operations because good locations are no longer available.

Given the above factors affecting the market for fast-food burgers, successful entry into this market will require a well thought-out analysis and strategy. There is no clear gap in product offerings, each competitor has strengths and weaknesses, and Albuquerque Turkey Burger will have to fight hard for a winning position in this market and be prepared to defend their position vigorously.

Individual Competitor Analysis

McDonald's:

McDonald's is the clear market leader in the fast-food burger market but is alleged to be in severe turmoil. It is said to have 43 percent U.S. market share compared to its nearest competitor, Burger King, with only 18 percent market share. Meanwhile, the next nearest competitor, Wendy's, has only a 13 percent market share nationally.

It (MICKY D's) also has a lower market share of the Albuquerque market. On a comparable national per—store basis, they have lost 2.1 percent in revenue in 2002 and 1.3 percent in 2001. It is opening 800 restaurants in 2003 but closing 400—550. It lost money in the last quarter of 2002 for the first time in the history of the company. What is the problem at McDonald's?♦ Has it lost its strategic focus or has the market drifted away from their product offerings toward market alternatives?

Historically, McDonald's market leadership position was based on extensive promotion, especially to young people (every month it is estimated that 90 percent of children between the ages of 3 and 9 visit a McDonald's in the U.S.), price leadership, fast and efficient service, clean and well-lit facilities, broad menu choices, and more locations than any competitor. Their old message was: "We love to see you smile," "You deserve a break today," or "McDonald's is your kind of place." What is the new message? It was the American family's fast-food restaurant that you could always count on for consistent product quality and fast service at a fair price. The market is waiting.

It is clearly struggling to hold its market position. In 2002, it revamped kitchens in order to serve hotter food, added 40 temporary items like chicken flatbread, put eight items including the Big-n-Tasty burger (normally a $1.99 value) and McChicken sandwich (normally $2.89) on the $1 value meal menu, and closed a number of outlets. Furthermore, it has changed to healthier oil for cooking French fries, partially in response to lawsuits claiming that its high-fat food caused health problems. Critics argue its message and menu have been scattered.

♦ What happened to the concept that the market leader should have the highest return on investment?

On top of all of this, a recent University of Michigan study suggests that McDonald's now has one of the lowest national ratings in U.S. fast-food establishments for service and quality of food. Their menu has been identified as unhealthy and outmoded. As one customer was quoted, "they have lost touch with what customers want."

The stock market has recognized the problem at McDonald's and its stock has dropped by 50 percent in the last six months to a seven-year low. One stock analyst from a major investment house was quoted as saying: "With no fundamental visibility and currently improper long-term strategy, in our opinion, we continue to recommend that investors avoid McDonald's stock."

Recognizing the problem, McDonald's has recalled Jim Cantalupo to become its chief executive and he has committed to return the restaurants back to basics. Ray Kroc's vision of consistent food and service has been lost while its brand has been made more vulnerable than ever. What will Jim Cantalupo do to return back to basics?

He and his crew are committed to a new brand vision: "Our customers' favorite place and way to eat." But is new vision without improving service and product quality at every restaurant putting the cart before the horse? Cantalupo has committed to shifting more resources toward local promotions and reinvesting in local store marketing, but has to also focus on the basics of service and product quality.

McDonald's has had little or no growth in the Albuquerque market even with menu expansion. Here, they appear to be the low price leader in the most commonly purchased burger combo meal ($3.52) even before the introduction of the $1 value priced items.

With 28 stores in the Albuquerque area and annual sales revenue estimated to be $1.6 million per store, McDonald's has the most revenue of any competitor in the market, $44.8 million. We estimate that more than half of that revenue, or at least $22.4 million per year, comes from burgers or burger combos in the Albuquerque area.

Even with all of McDonald's current problems, we must evaluate its market position carefully, as it is the market leader and is committed to hold that position.

What are the company's strengths? It has the most recognized brand name in the industry and the lowest prices. Even though its per store sales revenue has dropped slightly in the last few years, it still is the clear market leader with more than twice the market share in dollars of its nearest competitor in the Albuquerque market. It is the price leader in the combo burger offering. It has some of the best outlet locations in the area and highest per store revenue.

What are McDonald's weaknesses? Its service has suffered dramatically in the last few years. Its outlets often offer slow service and are not as bright and clean as they once were. Its product quality has slipped with offerings often old and cold, prepackaged where they should be fresh and hot. (Note: the company recently announced it is investing heavily in revamping kitchens to keep food hotter.) It has no clear product image and the $1 value meal takes away from the notion of value and degrades its brand. Furthermore, it does not offer the range of low fat alternatives supplied by other competitors.

In summary, McDonald's is the clear market leader but is in turmoil with no clear strategic direction. However, it is a well-entrenched and well-financed competitor and well positioned in the burger market for a comeback. Taking on a competitor with the size and market position of McDonald's is a real challenge. However, there are lessons to be learned from McDonald's current market dilemma that may help us position Albuquerque Turkey in the burger market. Don't forget to address the basic needs of the customer!

A lunch hour visit to McDonald's on Menaul Boulevard in Albuquerque with my business associates Bob and Jon showed us how hard McDonald's is trying to improve its image. Unlike many McDonald's outlets, this unit had no play area for children and most of the customers were adults. There were 12-13 people working during the lunch hour time period and it seemed like semi-organized hysteria in the food preparation and service area. They took five minutes to deliver meals to Bob and me and over ten minutes to deliver Jon's. I ordered a double chile cheese burger combo meal for $3.17, Bob ordered a ¼ pounder with cheese and chile, medium fries and 16 oz. drink for $4.20, and Jon ordered a double ¼ pounder with chile and cheese, large fries, and water for $5.00 (all prices included tax). The food seemed to be prepared just before delivered, the burgers were hot, fries hot and tasty, and drinks were as expected. The facility was neat and clean, service friendly; better than most McDonald's Jon and Bob have recently visited. The lines were short inside the store, but the auto pick-up window was backed up to about ten cars. The inside restaurant was about 1/3 full with about 30 people seated. Service was a lot slower (over ten minutes) for Jon when he ordered a special preparation, but fast (five minutes) for standard product. Nothing about the food was outstanding, but it wasn't as bad as many customers have recently reported to the press.

McDonald's Menu January 2003 (Albuquerque Sample)

McDonald's Combo Meals (sandwich, medium fries, and medium beverage)

Menu Item	Price $	Menu Item	Price $
Big Mac Combo	3.49	Big-n-Tasty Combo	2.99
Double Cheese Burger Combo	2.99	Chicken McGrill Combo	4.29
Crispy Chicken Combo	4.29	Filet of Fish	3.49
Quarter Pound Beef Combo	3.69	Green Chile Double Cheese Burger	2.99

McDonald's Sandwiches

Menu Item	Price $	Menu Item	Price $
Big Mac	2.29	Big-n-Tasty	1.00
Cheese Burger	.95	McChicken Sandwich	2.89
Crispy Chicken Sandwich	2.89	Hamburger	.85
Quarter Pound Burger	2.59		

Note: Add 35 cents for cheese

McDonald's Salads

Menu Item	Price $	Menu Item	Price $
Caesar Salad	2.49	Chicken Caesar Salad	2.99

McDonald's Desserts

Menu Item	Price $	Menu Item	Price $
Fruit-n-Yogurt Parfait	1.99	Ice Cream Sundae	.99
McFlurry	1.99	Ice Cream Cone	.99
Apple Pie	.79	Cookies	1/.39, 3/.99

McDonald's Breakfast

Menu Item	Price $	Menu Item	Price $
Bacon, Egg & Cheese Biscuit	1.89	Egg McMuffin	1.89
Hash Browns	.89	Hotcakes & Sausage	1.99
Sausage Biscuit	.89	Sausage Biscuit w/Egg	1.89
Sausage McMuffin	1.29	Steak & Egg Cheese Bagel	2.69
Breakfast Burrito	.89		

McDonald's Happy Meals (sandwich, fries, cookies, drink, promotional toy)

Menu Item	Price $	Menu Item	Price $
Hamburger Happy Meal	2.39	Double Hamburger Happy Meal	2.79
Cheese Burger Happy Meal	2.59	Double Cheeseburger Happy Meal	2.89
4 Chicken Nuggets Happy Meal	2.89	6 Chicken Nuggets Happy Meal	3.29

McDonald's Drinks and Sides and Chicken Nuggets

Menu Item	Price $	Menu Item	Price $
4 Piece Chicken Nuggets	2.69	6 Piece Chicken Nuggets	2.99
Medium Fries	1.39	Large Fries	1.69
Super Size Fries	1.99	Bottled Water	1.29
Medium Soda	1.00	Large Soda	1.29
Super Size Soda	1.49	Milk, 1%	.89
Shake	1.69/2.11	Coffee	.79/1.49
Side Salad	1.00		

The above menu shows the diversity of McDonald's product offerings along with the $1.00 value pricing recently introduced to their menu. A news announcement from McDonald's' headquarters in Oak Brook, Illinois, February 18, 2003 stated, "McDonald's franchisees have decided to stop discounting the big burger (Big-n-Tasty). The franchisees have voted to remove the premium hamburger from the Dollar Menu and replace it with a double cheeseburger; they may continue to sell the Big-n-Tasty burger at a higher price."

Burger King:

Burger King is number two in the U.S. market for fast-food burger restaurants. It has over 11,450 restaurants worldwide and 8,146 in the U.S. Its U.S. sales last year were $8.6 billion or a little over $1.1 million per restaurant, compared with $1.6 million for McDonald's and $1.2 million for Wendy's. It has 18 percent market share nationally and 19 percent of the Albuquerque market. However, all is not well at Burger King.

First, the number of restaurants in the U.S. has declined in the last three years from 8,293 in 2000 to 8,248 in 2001 to 8,146 in 2002, with annual unit sales flat at $1.03 to $1.05 million. (Note: this includes start-up units, so it is lower than the typical unit average of $1.1 million.) Second, an estimated 20 percent of its 7,568 franchised restaurants are having financial difficulties. Sixteen of the Albuquerque franchised restaurants were recently closed for failure to pay royalties. The company has engaged a restructuring firm, Trinity Capital of Los Angeles, to help franchisees work through their financial problems. Third, they initiated a price war with McDonald's that they cannot sustain.

As number two in the market, it has been following along behind McDonald's with menu changes and additions while expanding overseas. Instead, it should have focused on offering and building its brand in its largest market. It seems to have entered the price war with McDonald's more to pump up franchise royalties to enhance the parent company valuation than to improve their market position. Now that Burger King has been sold to a U.S. investment group, it may get back to basics and focus on its unique product offering and improved service and quality to rebuild their brand.

Burger King's unique position in the market was once based on its "flame-broiled" burger, the Whopper. It enhanced its market position and differentiated itself effectively from the leader with its "Have it your way" campaign launched in 1974. Compared to McDonald's standard prepackaged burgers, Burger King let you select the toppings you wanted on your burger at the time of order. It was early to spot the trend toward healthier food by offering a salad bar in 1983, chicken sandwich in 1989, and one percent milk in 2000. It has since dropped the salad bar and tried to copy the McDonald's Big Mac with a product it called Big King, which has been upgraded to King Supreme. Its latest attempt to attract the diet conscious buyer is with the introduction in 2002 of the BK Veggie sandwich. Its menu, however, looks similar to McDonald's—with prices and product offering options showing little differentiation.

Burger King Menu:

Burger King Burgers

Menu Item	Price $	Menu Item	Price $
Whopper	2.19	King Supreme	2.09
Double Whopper	3.19	Double Cheese Burger	1.99

Burger King Sandwiches

Menu Item	Price $	Menu Item	Price $
BK Veggie	2.09	Chicken Sandwich	2.89
BK Fish Filet	1.99	Chicken Tenders	1.99

Salads, Sides and Drinks

Menu Item	Price $	Menu Item	Price $
Chicken Caesar Salad	3.08	Fries	1.39/1.69/1.99
Onion Rings	1.39/1.69/1.99	Soft Drinks	1.09/1.29/1.49
Orange Juice	.96	Coffee	.74/.84
Milk	.74	Ice Tea	1.09/1.29
Shakes (Vanilla, Choc, Strawberry)	1.59/1.99	Hot Fudge Brownie	1.39

Ninety-Nine Cent Menu

Menu Item	Price $	Menu Item	Price $
Nestle Toll House Cookies	.99	Apple Pie	.99
Hershey Sundae	.99	Whopper Jr.	.99
Chili	.99	2 Tacos	.99
Baked Potato	.99	Chicken Tender Sandwich	.99

Kids Meals

Menu Item	Price $	Menu Item	Price $
Kids Hamburger Meal	1.99	Kids Cheese Burger	2.19
Kids Chicken Tender Meal	2.79		

Combo Meals (sandwich, medium fries, medium drink)

Menu Item	Price $	Menu Item	Price $
Whopper Combo	3.59	Double Whopper Combo	4.09
Chicken Whopper Combo	5.19	Whopper Jr. Combo	3.19
Chicken Whopper Jr. Combo	4.09	Chicken Sandwich Combo	4.09
Bacon Whopper w/cheese	4.09	Chicken Club Combo	4.69
BK Fish Filet Combo	4.09	Chicken Tender Combo	3.99

> I visited Burger King's outlet on San Mateo Boulevard in Albuquerque with my business associates, Bob and Jon, for lunch. We found the facility to be a little tacky compared to other fast-food burger facilities; service was six to ten minutes, depending on items ordered. There was a little confusion on the numbering of orders and getting to the pick-up area to pick up our orders, but we were able to customize our sandwiches to our tastes. Bob and I ordered the Whopper Jr. with chile and cheese, fries and a drink; we noted that the cost was about 80 cents lower than at other local fast-food burger outlets. The food was hot and the green chile strips were a pleasant surprise, although they were not hot enough for local tastes. They also had extra chopped chile topping available at the condiment counter. Jon ordered the Whopper Combo meal with large fries. The food was not bad, but nothing to get excited about, either. The operation had three service people working the counter and car window, and three people in back doing food preparation. It did not look as clean as other fast-food restaurants we visited. The seating area was about 1/3 full and the car drive-up service was busy throughout lunch. We concluded that we liked the charbroiled flavor, but the rest of the food and the atmosphere were average in quality and the service seemed confusing.

It is also trying to emulate McDonald's programs to attract more children to its outlets by teaming with Disney on movies and including promotional toys with its kids' meals. Although it remains a significant player in the fast-food burger market, the new owner of Burger King will be busy in the next year getting its franchisees out of financial trouble and repositioning its products in the market.

Burger King's strength is in its established product line of flame-broiled products and its good restaurant locations established over the last 49 years, along with low price offerings. It still has loyal customers, but has copied McDonald's pricing and menu to the point of minimizing its brand differentiation.

It is weakened further by customer perception that its service and product quality have diminished over the last few years. The financial instability of many of their franchise operators has also taken a toll.

In the last few years, Burger King has been a follower in the market, copying anything that works for its rivals. It may try to emulate any successful operation initiated by Albuquerque Turkey by copying its product offering. Franchisees (7,568), however, may resist menu changes and the new owners are focusing the business on its core products and improving their financial performance.

Wendy's:

Wendy's is Wall Street's favorite fast-food burger chain. It has consistently grown earnings in the 12 to 15 percent per year range, although it claims 2003 may be slightly less. (In fact, early 2003 per store sales were off a little more than expected.) Compared to McDonald's and Burger King, it has delivered for its shareholders. It has focused on the domestic market, growing the number of outlets for its products at an average rate of 4 percent per year over the last five years and increasing net sales per outlet 3.7 percent per year over the same time period. Even in the last few years when the market leaders' average sales per outlet were declining, it managed to grow average sales per outlet in excess of 2.5 percent per year. This has resulted in total revenue growth averaging 6—7 percent while McDonald's and Burger King have had little or no revenue growth.

Why is it more financially successful than the market leaders with only 13.1 percent of the domestic market compared to 61 percent for the two market leaders? What happened to the concept of market leaders enjoying higher profit margins than smaller competitors?

One answer may be in keeping with its brand focus. While the leaders have lost market focus or focused on the wrong market segment, Wendy's has kept its product and market focus. It focuses on the more mature customer with more discretionary dollars to spend and more concern for product quality than the younger customers sought by McDonald's and Burger King. There are no children's playgrounds at Wendy's. Their founder's concept of made-to-order hamburgers and fast, friendly service has earned Wendy's the position as quality leader in the fast-food burger market.

It has used independent market research to sharpen its product focus, introducing "Garden Sensations"—a new line of fresh salads in 2001 in response to low-fat alternatives demanded by their more mature customers. It has a low-priced menu, but has dodged the current discounting war by limiting it to baked potatoes, chicken nuggets, Junior Bacon Cheese Burger, and a Frosty Dairy dessert rather than discounting their premium products. It has focused on pick-up window service, earning the number one rating for the fastest pick-up window service and overall performance by *QSR Magazine* in 2001.

It has also concentrated on lunch and dinner as well as late evening diners. It has no breakfast food offering, reducing its potential per store annual revenue by $150,000 to $300,000 compared to the market leaders. To meet its more mature customer needs, it has recently extended its pick-up window hours to 1:00 A.M.

Their stated four key operating strategies are:

- Exceeding customers' expectations
- Creating the Wendy's difference through marketing
- Growing their restaurant system aggressively but responsibly
- Creating a performance-driven culture

Its strengths are clearly illustrated by stock market analysts who rave about Wendy's performance saying they have stuck to the basics: high product quality, speed of service, late night business at the drive through, focus on low-calorie alternatives and avoidance of the price wars. Its weaknesses are hard to identify unless you think the lack of children's toys or play areas is a failing.

Its menu reflects its orientation toward quality with their most commonly sold combo meal 42% higher than McDonald's and 36% higher than Burger King.

Wendy's Menu:

Burgers

Menu Item	Price $	Menu Item	Price $
¼ lb Classic Single Hamburger	1.99	½ lb Classic Double Hamburger	2.99
¾ lb Triple Classic Hamburger	3.99	Big Bacon Classic Hamburger	2.99
Jr. Hamburger	.80	Jr. Cheese Hamburger	.90

Cheese, .40 extra

Sandwiches

Menu Item	Price $	Menu Item	Price $
Chicken Breast Fillet	2.99	Spicy Chicken Fillet	2.99
Grilled Chicken Fillet	2.99	Chicken Club	3.49

Salads

Menu Item	Price $	Menu Item	Price $
Chicken BLT Salad	4.29	Mandarin Chicken Salad	4.29
Taco Supremo Salad	4.29	Spring Mix Salad	3.29

Sides

Menu Item	Price $	Menu Item	Price $
Fries (med./Biggie/Great Biggie)	.99/1.29/1.49	Bacon & Cheese Baked Potato	1.99
Broccoli & Cheese Baked Potato	1.99	Sour Cream & Chives Baked Potato	1.99
Large Chili	1.69		

Kids Meals

Menu Item	Price $	Menu Item	Price $
Hamburger Meal	1.99	Cheese Burger Meal	2.29
4 Piece Chicken Nugget Meal	2.69		

$.99 Menu

Menu Item	Price $	Menu Item	Price $
Jr. Bacon Cheese Burger	.99	Jr. Cheese Burger Deluxe	.99
5 Piece Chicken Nuggets	.99	Small Chili	.99
Medium Fries	.99	Small Frosty	.99
Side Salad	.99	Caesar Side Salad	.99

Drinks

Menu Item	Price $	Menu Item	Price $
Soft Drinks (sm./med./large)	.95/.99/1.29	Ice Tea	.95/.99/1.29
Milk	.75	Coffee	.75
Hot Tea	.75		

Combo Meals (sandwich, medium fries, and medium soft drink)

Menu Item	Price $	Menu Item	Price $
Classic Single Combo	3.79	Classic Double Combo	4.99
Classic Triple Combo	5.99	Big Bacon Classic Combo	4.99
Grilled Chicken Combo	4.99	Spicy Chicken Combo	4.99
Chicken Breast Fillet	4.99	Bacon Swiss Burger Combo	4.99
Chicken Bacon Swiss Combo	5.49		

A lunchtime visit to Wendy's: One of my business partners, Bob (president of a utility consulting firm), and I went to Wendy's on Menaul Boulevard in Albuquerque for lunch. We had to wait in line a few minutes to place our order and then wait another few minutes for its preparation. The staff was efficient and friendly with two behind the counter; several others were visible preparing orders and several more out of sight in the food prep area. They made us Green Chile Cheeseburgers, an order of fries, and a drink for about $4.35—$4.50. The burgers were freshly grilled and wrapped in foil to keep them hot. The fries were in a cardboard container and hot when served. The drinks were average in size. The coffee was hot with real dairy creamers. The burgers were on a 4-inch bun, still hot and fresh, about ¼ inch thick and tasty. The chile was medium hot and added a pleasant kick to the flavor. The bun was not smashed like we find at many other fast-food burger restaurants. The fries were hot and crispy but had little flavor. The restaurant was neat and clean and we estimate they sold 150 to 200 lunches in the time we visited. There were plenty of extra seats in the restaurant, as most customers seemed to take out their orders. The flow of customers was continuous with the line always three to ten customers long. Although they feature four salads, we only saw two ordered during our lunchtime visit. No children's toys or special incentives were available. It was a well-run and efficient business with good food prepared quickly and efficiently in a clean, friendly environment. No surprise here.

Summary: Wendy's Old Fashioned Hamburgers started with the idea that cooked-to-order hamburgers stand out when compared to prepackaged and reheated food sold by the major competitors in the market. The market has confirmed its product quality is superior to the major competitors' and verifies this every day by paying higher average prices for their products.

It has focused on the basics of fast, courteous service with high quality products aimed at mature buyers willing to pay for quality, and it has worked. Its advertising program "Where's the Beef" of a few years ago highlighted its emphasis on product size and quality and attracted customers to their performance position in the fast-food market. It still holds that market position and it shows in their financial results.

Blake's LotaBurger:

Blake's LotaBurger is a New Mexico based fast-food burger chain founded by Blake Chanslor in 1952. It has more Albuquerque outlets than any competitor, with 30 outlets compared to 28 for McDonald's and 22 for Burger King. We estimate it has only a 12 percent market share, however, because its per store annual revenue of $500,000 per year is much lower than the market leaders. We were not able to confirm current revenue numbers and based our estimate on a 1998 interview with the founder.

Headquartered in Albuquerque and run by Blake's son Ron, Chanslor sums up the secret to his success in one word, "LotaBurger." He is quoted as saying, "It's a whole different hamburger. We might not be the cheapest and we might not be the fastest," he says, "but we think we are the best."

"I don't mind waiting," says one loyal Albuquerque customer. He's been eating at Blake's for 20 years; his mom and dad took him to Blake's as a child. He can count on their burgers being fresh and will taste good by his standards.

The reason for the 5—10 minute wait at Blake's is that each burger is slapped on the LotaBurger grill when the customer places his/her order. Blake Chanslor says he is a stickler for freshness, and he won't allow heat lamps or pre-wrapped burgers.

Even though Blake's has drive-up windows, it only lets you place your order from your car. You then have to sit in the parking lot for ten minutes while your food is prepared. It's fast food New Mexico style, kind-of fast.

A lunchtime visit to Blake's on Menaul Boulevard in Albuquerque with my associates from UtiliPoint International, Bob and Jon, told us a lot about LotaBurger. There were six employees, all middle-aged women: one working the grill, one working the counter, one working drinks and fries, one working the drive-up window and two in the back doing food preparation. The facility was clean and pleasant with new seats (yellow) and a cheerful environment. However, only one of the food preparation people was wearing gloves. The LotaBurgers were cooked on a large flat griddle (to order) from high quality "Angus" ground beef, each patty about 5" in diameter and ¼ inch thick. The 5" buns were placed on the grill, so that one side was slightly toasted. Toppings for the standard LotaBurger included lettuce, pickle, onion, mustard, and optional chopped green chile or cheese. Served in about 10+ minutes, Jon ordered the seasoned fries and I ordered the standard fries. Bob and I ordered the LotaBurger with Chile and it was a good quality burger on a fresh bun with mild chile topping. My fries were marginal in both crispiness and texture, cold with little or no flavor. My coffee was acceptable, but only available with non-dairy powdered creamer. Jon's double meat LotaBurger green chile cheeseburger was also good and his seasoned fries were also marginal. I was tempted to get a vanilla Coke, as they will add flavors to soft drinks. In the time we were there from noon to 1 P.M., we saw about 50 customers, all adults (they had no kids' toys or other attractions), and no particular enthusiasm among the clientele or workers.

Although Blake's LotaBurger has expanded its menu over the years to include hot dogs and chicken, turkey and BBQ sandwiches, it is still primarily known for its burgers. Blake's adds a New Mexico flare by adding green chile or jalapeno peppers to any of its sandwiches for 15 to 30 cents. Its menu is smaller than most of the competitors as seen below with little emphasis on low-fat alternatives to its LotaBurger and only recently adding breakfast items to the menu.

Blake's LotaBurger Menu:

Burgers

Menu Item	Price $	Menu Item	Price $
LotaBurger	2.39	Double Meat LotaBurger	3.34
ItsaBurger	1.99	Double ItsaBurger	2.74
KiddyBurger	1.29	Double Meat KiddyBurger	1.70

Hot Dogs

Menu Item	Price $	Menu Item	Price $
Hot Dog	1.29	Corn Dog	1.29
Chile Dog	1.59	Cheese Dog	1.59

Sandwiches

Menu Item	Price $	Menu Item	Price $
Chicken Sandwich	2.99	Turkey Sandwich	2.99
BBQ Sandwich	2.99		

Sides

Menu Item	Price $	Menu Item	Price $
Small Fries	1.19	Large Fries	1.49
Onion Rings, Large	1.69	Seasoned Fries, Large	1.49
Chile Bowl	1.85	Chile Pie, Fritos w/chile/cheese	1.85

Combos

Menu Item	Price $	Menu Item	Price $
LotaCombo	4.98	ItsaCombo	4.18
Chicken Tender Combo	4.69	Kiddy Meal Combo	3.05

Drinks

Menu Item	Price $	Menu Item	Price $
Soft Drinks (small/med./large)	1.09/1.19/1.39	Hot Chocolate	.75
Shakes (Van/Choc/Straw)	1.39	Coffee	.75

Extras

Menu Item	Price $	Menu Item	Price $
Green Chile	.30	Jalapeno Peppers	.15
Cheese	.30	Bacon	.40

Blake's strength is in its local appeal to customer tastes and its large number of outlets—more than any other fast-food burger supplier in the Albuquerque area. It also supplies large, fresh, made-to-order burgers. Its weaknesses are slow delivery of its products, good to average burger quality, and poor quality sides.

Summary: Blake's is a laid-back New Mexico experience at a pace its customers have accepted. Some say that its burger quality is not what it once was, but it continues to have a loyal local customer following. It furthermore adds stores and new outlets each year. We learned the importance of good location and local market presence in our study of Blake's.

Sonic Drive-In Restaurants:

Sonic is a truly differentiated service from other fast-food burger outlets. It believes that good old-fashioned hamburgers and milkshakes delivered to your car by (roller skating?) carhops a la 1950's beach movies is an enjoyable experience. The name "Sonic" came from its original slogan: "Service with the speed of sound." At Sonic, you pull into a drive-in stall, place your order through your own personal ordering station, and it's delivered made-to-order by a carhop at your automobile window. With 13 outlets in the Albuquerque area and 9.4 percent of the local market, it is a significant player in the fast-food burger market with growth driven by menu expansion—it has the largest number of menu items of any competitor—and new outlets. Nationally, it is growing corporate-level revenues at 11.9 percent and profits at 18 percent by adding new outlets and menu expansion. They have grown same store revenue by 3 percent in 2002 at a time when McDonald's same store revenue is declining.

What is its secret to growth in this highly competitive market? It's not by following competitors or listening to fad dieters. What we found is a complete lack of interest in the current low-fat, low-calorie market segment. It offers a 929-calorie burger with 66 grams of fat, a country-fried steak sandwich with 748 calories and 56 fat grams, and a 582-calorie chicken sandwich. You can top off its items with a selection of 16 flavors of milkshakes and malts or 5 sundaes. It doesn't have just hot dogs; it has foot-long hot dogs with cheese (666 calories). You will never leave a Sonic drive-in hungry. It promotes special milkshakes, sundaes, and sodas targeting people with an appetite for calories and a fun eating experience.

Its nostalgic presentation is appealing to the more mature market, and the in-car dining is appealing to groups and family diners as it minimizes the effort getting into and out of a restaurant. (This may also appeal to some diners that are getting heavier on Sonic's high fat, high calorie menu.) It boasts one of the highest levels of customer loyalty through repeat business of any fast-food chain. It has clearly carved out a successful niche in the fast-food burger market. Can we conclude you should bring on the calories and bring on the fun if you want to make money in the fast-food burger market?

A visit to the Sonic Restaurant on Eubank Boulevard in Albuquerque with Tony verified the notion that Sonic has produced a great product at competitive prices. We found in-car dining was a pleasant lunch experience when the weather is nice. The Sonic burger was hot, thick and wrapped in a foil material to keep it warm. The fries were hot and crispy and the variety of drinks unique. The chile on the green chile cheeseburger was hot enough to make a difference, but not too hot. The service, from time of placing the order to receipt of food, was seven to ten minutes with every item freshly prepared. Prices were between $4 and $5 per meal. The carhops don't ask, but we felt a tip was appropriate and tipped at the normal rate. This is an extra 10% to 15% cost to those patrons with a conscience but, with a full parking area, it looks like many people find prices acceptable.

The Sonic menu had to be condensed to fit in this book, but as you can see it offers more items than any competitor in the market.

Sonic Drive-In Menu

Burgers

Menu Item	Price $	Menu Item	Price $
Sonic Burger	2.04	Cheese Burger	2.39
Super Sonic Cheese Burger	3.44	Bacon Cheese Burger	2.89
Green Chile Cheese Burger	2.69	Jr. Burger	.99

Chicken Sandwiches

Menu Item	Price $	Menu Item	Price $
Chicken Strip Dinner	4.59	Chicken Strip Snack	2.99
Breaded Chicken Sandwich	2.99	Grilled Chicken Breast Sandwich	2.99

Toaster Sandwiches

Menu Item	Price $	Menu Item	Price $
Chicken Club Toaster	3.69	Bacon Cheddar Burger	3.09
BLT	2.39	Country Fried Steak	2.99
Grilled Cheese	1.49		

Hot Dogs

Menu Item	Price $	Menu Item	Price $
Ex-Long Coney	2.59	Regular Coney	1.79
Corn Dog	.99		

Kids Meal

Menu Item	Price $	Menu Item	Price $
Jr. Burger	2.59	Regular Coney	2.59
Corn Dog	2.59	Chicken Strips	2.79
Grilled Cheese	2.59		

Sides (regular, large, Sonic size)

Menu Item	Price $	Menu Item	Price $
Tater Tots	.99/1.49/1.69	Tater Tots/Cheese	1.34/1.84/2.34
Tater Tots w/chile/cheese	1.69/2.29/2.94	French Fries	.99/1.49/1.69
French Fries w/cheese	1.34/1.84/2.34	French Fries w/chile/cheese	1.69/2.29/2.94
Onion Rings	.99/1.49/1.69	Ched R'Peppers	1.99
Mozzarella Sticks	2.19	Fritos Chile Pie	1.99
Tacos	1.29		

Drinks (13 Different Drinks Listed on Menu)

Menu Item	Price $	Menu Item	Price $
Drinks(sm/med/lg/Rt54)	1.04/1.19/1.39/1.54	Orange Juice (med/lg)	1.39/1.79
Milk	.79	Coffee	.69

Shakes & Malts (regular/large) **(16 Items Listed & Desserts)**

Menu Item	Price $	Menu Item	Price $
Shakes & Malts (reg/lg)(16)	1.79/2.29	Sundaes (5 types listed)	1.79

Breakfast

Menu Item	Price $	Menu Item	Price $
Toaster Sandwich on a stick w/sausage/ham/bacon	1.99	Breakfast Burrito	1.49
Pancake on a Stick	.99	Fruit Taquitos	1.29
Wacky Packy Kids Breakfast	2.59		

Combos (sandwich/medium fries/medium drink)

Menu Item	Price $	Menu Item	Price $
Burger Deal	3.89	Super Sonic Deal	4.79
Coney Deal	4.49	Chicken Sandwich Deal	4.49
Chicken Toaster Deal	4.99	Bacon Toaster Burger Deal	4.99

Chicken Wraps (chicken in a tortilla)

Menu Item	Price $	Menu Item	Price $
Chile Cheese Wrap	1.99	Grilled Chicken Wrap	2.99
Chicken Strip Wrap	2.99		

Sonic's strengths are in providing high quality, high-calorie food with a minimum effort to the customer. You don't have to get out of your car. Its selection of side orders, drinks and desserts is the largest in the industry.

Sonic's weakness is that it does not offer a low-calorie, low-fat menu and can be a negative experience in bad weather when you are forced to eat in your automobile.

Summary: Sonic has a successful strategic formula and is focused on customers wanting a different experience than the typical fast-food drive-through or sit-down restaurant. It demonstrates that there is a large percentage of the population that want good tasting fresh food delivered in quantities that satisfy their appetite and with a variety of add-on items that make each meal unique and enjoyable.

Carl's Jr.:

There are five Carl's Jr. fast-food hamburger restaurants in the Albuquerque market that we estimate have a 4.4 percent market share with $1.1 million annual per store revenue based on their national average data. It is a Santa Barbara, California-based chain with 308 franchised units and 541 company-owned units that has been in business since 1941. With only 19 international units, its company data is representative of U.S. store performance.

It is a relative newcomer in the Albuquerque area within the last three years and offers a large variety of charbroiled burgers and chicken sandwiches with a western and southwestern flavor. It also offers a few low-calorie, low-fat menu items if you can get past the 900-calorie burger and 700-calorie chicken sandwich offerings. It has recently announced the addition of a six dollar guacamole bacon burger special to its menu as a "tasty alternative for burger lovers" at $3.95. This southwestern-style burger features a charbroiled beef patty topped with guacamole, two strips of bacon, two slices of Pepperjack cheese, Santa Fe sauce, red onions, tomato and lettuce on a seeded bun. We estimated the six dollar guacamole burger may contain over 1000 calories, a fast-food burger record. However, like the market leaders, it is experiencing a slowdown in same store sales. Last year, it lost 1.5 percent in same store sales even with the addition of several new items to their menu.

The menu below shows how they emphasize variety in their sandwich selection with limited sides and drink selection.

Carl's Jr. Menu:

Char Broiled Burgers

Menu Item	Price $	Menu Item	Price $
Six Dollar Burger	3.95	Super Star Burger	3.09
Double Western Burger	3.75	Bacon Cheese Burger	3.75
Sourdough Bacon Cheese Burger	2.99	Western Bacon Cheese Burger	2.69
Famous Star Burger	1.69	Chile Burger	2.99
Ranch Bacon Cheese Burger	2.99		

Char Broiled Chicken Sandwiches

Menu Item	Price $	Menu Item	Price $
Western Chicken	3.49	Bacon Swiss Crispy Chk.	3.49
Charbroiled Chicken Club	3.59	Charbroiled Santa Fe	3.29
Charbroiled BBQ Chicken	2.99	Spicy Chicken	2.99
Chicken Strips 3/5/9	2.89/3.99/6.49		

Sides

Menu Item	Price $	Menu Item	Price $
Fries (sm/med/lg)	1.29/1.39/1.79	Crisscut Fries	1.69
Onion Rings	1.69	Fried Zucchini	1.69

Desserts

Menu Item	Price $	Menu Item	Price $
Strawberry Cheese Cake	1.49	Chocolate Cake	1.09
Chocolate Cookies	1.29		

Breakfast

Menu Item	Price $	Menu Item	Price $
Breakfast Sandwich	1.99	Breakfast Burrito	1.99
Sunrise	1.79	Biscuit Sunrise	1.79
French Toast Dips	1.39	Breakfast Quesadilla	1.19
Biscuits and Gravy	.99	Chile Cheese Omelet	2.39
Scrambled Egg Breakfast	2.19		

Drinks

Menu Item	Price $	Menu Item	Price $
Soft Drink (sm/med/large)	1.19/1.39/1.69	Coffee	.79
Milk	.79	Orange Juice	.99
Shakes (Van/Choc/Straw)	1.69/1.89		

Salads and Fish

Menu Item	Price $	Menu Item	Price $
Charbroiled Chicken Salad	3.39	Garden Salad	1.49
Fish and Chips	3.69	Carl's Catch Fish Sandwich	2.29

Carl's Combo Meals (sandwich, medium fries, medium drink)

Menu Item	Price $	Menu Item	Price $
Six Dollar Burger	5.39	Super Star Burger	5.09
Double Western Burger	4.99	Sourdough Bacon Cheese Burger	4.69
Western Bacon Cheeseburger	4.39	Famous Star Burger	3.89
Chile Burger	5.99	Chicken Western	4.99
Spicy Chicken	3.19	Chicken Strips (3pc/5pc)	4.39/5.49

I visited Carl's Jr. on Menaul Boulevard in Albuquerque with my business associates, Bob and Jon. This was a new operation taken over from Burger King and renovated for Carl's Jr. The traffic was light with no wait; the facility was clean and new. The service was fast (under six minutes) for fresh charbroiled burgers.

Bob had the chile cheeseburger, I had the sourdough bacon cheeseburger, and Jon the six-dollar guacamole burger. We all had fries. The burgers were fresh and well presented without being smashed in a paper wrapper. Jon's six-dollar burger was too big to eat by hand and he had to use a knife and fork. The fries were hot and crispy, but with little flavor. The drinks were standard from a serve-yourself dispenser. There was nothing bad about the facility, food or service, but nothing that overwhelmed us except the size of the six-dollar burger.

Bob's Burgers:

Bob's Burger is one of the smaller fast-food hamburger chains in Albuquerque with only seven restaurants and 2.6 percent market share. It is important because it focuses on the local market's southwestern taste in food and has a fairly limited menu. We found nothing impressive about its relatively small facilities, speed of service or product quality. There were no low-calorie items on the menu. However, half of its burger menu features southwestern flavorings. Little financial information was available so we could only estimate their revenue and cannot comment on their growth.

Bob's Burgers Menu

Burgers

Menu Item	Price $	Menu Item	Price $
Ranchero Supreme Burger (green chile)	1.90/2.60	Old Fashion Burger	1.50/2.20
Red Chile Burger	1.50/2.20	Patty Melt	2.80
Taco Burger	1.30	Tortilla Burger	1.40

Hot Dogs

Menu Item	Price $	Menu Item	Price $
Foot Long Chile Dog	2.35	Chile Dog	1.40
Foot Long Hot Dog	2.15	Hot Dog	1.30
Corn Dog	.99		

Sides, Other Items, & Drinks

Menu Item	Price $	Menu Item	Price $
Fries	1.25	Chile Fries w/cheese	1.50/1.80
Frito Pie	1.55	Taquitos (3)	1.85
Taquitos Boat	2.40	Steak Fingers & Fries	3.90
Chicken Nuggets (4pc/6pc)	1.20/1.55	Grilled Cheese	1.55
Soft Drinks(sm/md/lg/giant)	1.00/1.10/1.30/1.50	Coffee	.65
Bottled Water	.65		

Combo Meals (small and large)

Menu Item	Price $	Menu Item	Price $
Ranchero Supreme	4.15/4.90	Old Fashion Burger	3.75/4.55
Corn Dog	3.25	Chile Dog	3.65/4.70
Nuggets	3.45/3.90	2 Taco Burgers	4.45

> A lunch visit to Bob's with several business associates showed us how a locally owned fast-food burger restaurant catering to local tastes can be very successful. They were very busy in their smaller than normal facility. No tables were empty and the drive-through was busy during the entire lunch hour time period. Their secret was hot spicy southwestern-style food. Not just a little hot, but very spicy hot served to order in about ten minutes. Their combo meals sold for $4 and were freshly prepared with good ingredients. Their burgers were ¼ inch thick and just off the grill; their fries were crispy and fresh. One of my associates ordered the chile fries with his large (5") chile cheeseburger and they were a goopy mess of fries covered in melted cheese and salsa. He loved them! The restaurant was reasonably clean with six workers, all visible from the counter. The food preparers wore gloves and service was courteous and friendly. My associates said it was the best of the fast-food restaurants we have visited. This may be more because of their addiction to hot chiles than anything else, but it works for Bob's in Albuquerque.

Bob's competitive advantage is its focus on spicy southwestern food that fits the Albuquerque market. Its disadvantages are it doesn't offer much menu variety, has limited facilities, and its service is slow. Further, it has no low-fat, low-calorie items on their menu, with prices in about the middle of the market. It also does not offer any breakfast items on its menu.

Its customers rave about the green chile cheeseburger and many remain loyal to this small chain of fast-food restaurants. Tony should study it more closely to evaluate sales volume and customer profile as it may attract customers most compatible with the Albuquerque Turkey products.

Bruce R. Robinson

WhataBurger:

Founded in 1950 in south Texas by Harmon Dobson, a bush pilot and entrepreneur, this Texas-based chain now has over 500 restaurants in the southern U.S. (Texas, New Mexico, Arizona, Arkansas, Louisiana, Alabama, and Florida). The founder decided that big was better, consistent with Texas "big think." He created a 5-inch bun, compared to the competitors' 4-inch bun and put an extra large ¼ pound burger in each bun. Good quality product freshly prepared and Texas-size portions are what distinguish these restaurants today. It claims to have one of the largest menus and largest number of toppings available from any fast-food burger restaurant.

As a privately owned business, there is little information available about its financial condition, number of franchises versus company-owned outlets, or the average revenue per store. In New Mexico it has eight restaurants, four of which are in the Albuquerque area. We estimate that it does at least $400,000 per store in annual revenue. It may have much higher revenue because of its breakfast menu and 24-hour operation, but it is difficult to estimate. With 3 percent of the fast-food burger restaurants and 1.3 percent estimated market share, this is the smallest multiple outlet competitor in the Albuquerque area.

Its menu is one of the largest in the business. Beyond what is shown in the standard menu, it will custom build your WhataBurger with whatever toppings you specify. Its average price on combo meals is on the high end of the market and just below Wendy's.

WhataBurger Menu

Burgers

Menu Item	Price $	Menu Item	Price $
WhataBurger	2.09	WhataBurger w/cheese	2.39
WhataBurger w/bacon & cheese	3.09	Double Meat WhataBurger	3.29
Dbl. Meat WhataBurger w/cheese	3.69	Dbl. Meat WhataBurger w/bacon	4.09
Dbl Meat WhataBurger, w/cheese & bacon	4.68	Triple Meat WhataBurger	4.49
Trpl. Meat WhataBurger w/cheese	3.69	Trpl. Meat WhataBurger w/bacon	5.48
Trpl. Meat WhataBurger w/cheese & bacon	4.68	WhataBurger Jr.	1.29
WhataBurger Jr. w/cheese	1.59	WhataBurger Jr. w/bacon	1.95
WhataBurger Jr. w/cheese&bacon	2.25	JustaBurger	.99
WhataBurger w/bacon	3.09	JustaBurger w/cheese	1.29
JustaBurger w/bacon	1.65	JustaBurger w/cheese & bacon	1.95

32

Chicken/Salads/Fish and Kids Meals

Menu Item	Price $	Menu Item	Price $
Grilled Chicken Sandwich	2.99	WhataChicken	2.89
Chicken Strips	4.39	Garden Salad	2.19
Grilled Chicken Salad	3.19	Fajitas	2.79
WhataCatch (Fish)	2.19	Kids Chicken Strips (w/fries& drink)	2.79
Kids JustaBurger (w/fries & drink)	2.09		

Sides

Menu Item	Price $	Menu Item	Price $
Fries (sm/med/large)	.89/.99/1.59	Onion Rings (med/large)	1.49/1.69
Green Chile	.30	Jalapenos	.30
Bacon	.33		

Beverages & Shakes

Menu Item	Price $	Menu Item	Price $
Soft Drinks (sm/med/lg)	.89/.99/1.59	Coffee (sm/lg)	.55/.75
Orange Juice	1.09	Shakes (van, choc, straw.) (kid, sm, med, lg)	1.29,1.49,1.89 2.39
Milk	.65		

Breakfast Menu

Menu Item	Price $	Menu Item	Price $
Taquitos	1.39	Breakfast on a Bun	1.39
Egg Sandwich	1.20	Biscuits	.75
Biscuits w/gravy	1.15	Biscuits w/sausage or bacon	1.15
Biscuits w/egg & cheese	1.39	Biscuits w/egg, cheese, sausage or bacon	1.74
Pancakes	1.59	Pancakes w/sausage or bacon	2.19
Breakfast Platter	2.39	Cinnamon Roll	1.39

Combo Menu (sandwich, medium fries, and medium drink)

Menu Item	Price $	Menu Item	Price $
WhataBurger	4.49	Double Whataburger	5.49
Grilled Chicken Sandwich	5.19	WhataChicken Sandwich	4.99
Bacon & Cheese WhataBurger	5.49	3 Piece Chicken Strips	5.39
WhataBurger Jr.	2.89	2 Piece Chicken Strips	3.99

Many customers rave about the quality of the made-to-order, large size WhataBurger and fries, the service to your table in many locations, drink refills are often free, and wide menu variety. Locations are generally clean with friendly, Texas-style service.

The customers complain about the slow service and note that prices are higher than the major competitors.

A lunchtime visit to a new WhataBurger on Wyoming Boulevard in Albuquerque with my business partners, Bob and Jon, and wife Ellen gave us a good first impression of their facilities. They were clean and open with good lighting and lots of windows. They did promote toys for kids but did not offer any special play area for children. Jon ordered the Double Meat WhataBurger with cheese and chile, medium fries and water. Bob ordered the Whataburger Jr. with chile, small fries and an ice tea. I ordered a WhataBurger with small fries and a coffee. Ellen ordered a grilled chicken sandwich. The burgers were made to order and about 5 inches in diameter on a 5-inch diameter smashed-in bun with lettuce, onion, mustard, tomato and additional toppings as special ordered. Each burger patty was hot and tasty but only about 1/8 inch thick. The fries were hot and tasty. The grilled chicken was hot with a spicy barbeque flavor on a smashed-in wheat bun. The drinks were average with good liquid creamers available as desired. The ice tea, water and soft drinks were self-serve. They served us in about four minutes by calling out the number on our receipt. The tables were clean and comfortable. We estimated they served about 50—60 people during the lunch hour from inside or a drive-up window with about seven employees visible behind the counter. But as a new store, this may not be a typical throughput. Only about one-tenth of the seats were occupied at any time and the parking lot about 20% occupied.

In summary, WhataBurger has a loyal following of customers who are accustomed to large portions of food served fresh and are willing to wait a few minutes to get served. It caters to more mature customers, but does offer toys with the kids' meals to attract repeat business from this market segment. Good quality, friendly service, and large portions appear to be working for WhataBurger.

Market Alternatives

To determine the viability of Tony's Albuquerque Turkey Burger versus "beef burgers," we also felt it was important to look at trends in the market alternatives to fast-food burgers. What are market alternatives? In the broadest sense, it is any food product that competes with our product: "fast-food burgers." However, we have to focus on those alternative purchases that most directly compete with fast-food burgers at the time our target customers make their purchase decision. This would narrow the competing market alternatives to other fast-food restaurants or those that deliver product in less than ten minutes. We focused on the fast-food sandwich market alternative, the fast-food hot dog alternative, taco stands, and the fast-food chicken alternative. We intentionally did not focus on the take-out dinner alternative (although many chicken fast-food restaurants also cater to that market segment), as these usually involve a purchase in a higher price range, are ordered in advance, and are usually taken home for consumption. On this basis, we did not evaluate pizza take-out restaurants and Oriental take-out restaurants.

We also did not consider the fast casual restaurants like Chili's, Steak and Ale, Bennigan's, etc., as they usually sell meals at double the average price of the fast-food burger restaurants and offer table service. One way my student assistants looked at a market alternative would be as a restaurant that a customer may drive past on their way to a fast-food burger restaurant and consider an alternative purchase in the $3—$5 price range, mostly finger food, with fast service and consumed on-site or in their car. Although there are a few exceptions, the typical meal at the market alternative restaurants we considered in the Albuquerque market fell in the above price range and is comparable to the leading fast-food burger combo meal prices as seen in the following chart.

Fast-Food Market Alternative Average Meal Prices and # of Stores

Wiener-Schnitzel	Taco Bell	Subway	Quizno's	Blimpie's	Taco Cabana	KFC	Boston Market	TCB	Church's Chicken	Arby's
$4.11	$4.19	$5.14	$7.12	NA	$5.37	$5.29	$6.91	$5.61	$4.65	$5.45
4	19	28	7	6	2	7	3	11	8	10

VS.

Fast-Food Burger Average Combo Meal Prices and # of Stores

McDonald's	Burger King	Wendy's	Carl's Jr.	Sonic	WhataBurger	Blake's	Bob's
$3.52	$3.70	$5.02	$4.79	$4.60	$4.75	$4.23	$4.08
28	22	14	5	7	4	30	7

NOTE: The above tables were based on subjective estimates by students studying each outlet's sales of combo meals and average prices charged per meal. Calculations are based on local price lists and may not reflect choices made by other individuals analyzing this market in other locations. Most combo meal estimates included a sandwich or equivalent entrée, an order of fries or chips, and a medium drink.

The above tables show there are almost as many market alternative fast-food restaurants (105) as there are fast-food burger restaurants (128) in the Albuquerque area.

Why look at fast-food market alternatives? The rise and fall of the total market for fast-food burgers is a direct function of market trends in the fast-food alternative market. For example, as more customers move toward Subway for lunch and away from fast-food burger restaurants, the total fast-food burger market declines. Trends in market alternatives often give us an early warning of future changes in market size and are leading indicators of changing customer preferences. So what are the fast-food market alternatives indicating will happen to the fast-food burger market?

First, we looked at what segments of the alternative market were growing and what was not growing. We found that the only growth in fast-food market alternatives was in Subway sandwiches and tacos while chicken and hot dog offerings appear to be suffering under the same negative market pressure that the fast-food burger market has experienced in the last year. Subway has led the pack in growth. Last year, the sandwich shop chain supplanted McDonald's as the largest fast-food chain in the United States with more than 14,000 franchises. Taco Bell is the leader in fast Mexican food with 64 percent market share. It had three percent same store growth in the fourth quarter of 2002. Church's, KFC and Boston Market all appear to have lower same store revenue in 2002, although it is hard to get exact data from their parent companies. Wienerschnitzel, the market leader in fast-food hot dog restaurants in the U.S., attempted to add burgers to their menu and recently admitted that its "involvement in burger wars just meant casualties" and is beating a tactical retreat. What can we learn about the trends in performance of these market alternatives?

Market Alternative Fast-Food Restaurants that are Growing; Sandwiches and Mexican:

Subway Restaurants

Why has Subway grown so fast? Chicago-based food service consulting and research firm Technomic Inc. says the quick service sandwich sales, which include sales from Subway, Arby's, Panera Bread and Blimpie's, were $14.6 billion in 2001, up from 13 billion in 2000, with sales rising steadily over the last five years. That's a 12.3 percent growth in the overall fast-food sandwich segment. Why?

Subway launched a very successful television advertising campaign a few years ago featuring Jared Fogle, an Indiana man who lost over 45 pounds by eating two Subway sandwiches a day for a year. It successfully resonated with consumers looking for a fast and convenient way to eat healthy.

We also looked at the numbers. Subway plans to add another 800 U.S. franchises in 2003 to its 14,032 outlets. All but one of Subway's outlets is franchised. It is one of the lowest-cost franchises to purchase. It requires only $30,000 to $90,000 of cash investment and is usually located in existing shopping malls or strip mall storefront locations at 1/3 to 1/10 the cost of opening a stand-alone fast-food burger franchise. Its outlets also have average sales of about $350,000 per store but the return on investment is very attractive to franchisees with minimum facilities investment risk. It is a simple operation with no broiling, grilling or deep fat frying, so the number of employees is kept to a minimum and they can concentrate on customer service.

"Have it your way" is carried to extremes at Subway; you can create your own unique sandwich with every visit. However, it is not cheap. The average Subway meal is higher that the average price of the highest priced burger outlet, Wendy's. However, one customer at an on-line website raved about his ability to create his own special sandwich, complete with chopped black olives, although he had to ask for extra olives with each visit. Another customer told how much she enjoyed the fresh ingredients. Its customer loyalty ratings are higher than many of the fast-food burger restaurants as they focus on customer satisfaction, not on frying and grilling.

What we can learn from Subway's growth that is applicable to Tony's Albuquerque Turkey Burger is that customers will migrate to healthy alternative food, if it is conveniently located (Subway has the most outlets in the country), healthy, and of good quality. This migration is taking place at a higher average price per meal than most fast-food burgers.

It also shows us that you don't have to be located on the most expensive real estate in the area. Most fast-food restaurants believe they have to be on a high traffic corner location to be successful. Subway outlets are in strip malls and lower overhead facilities. This keeps the entry cost for franchisees at a minimum. It has also focused on keeping their employee head count to a minimum by reducing the food prep time. Low facility costs and low operating costs mean they can turn a profit even though their volume is 1/3 to 1/4 the sales of the large fast-food burger operations.

Taco Bell Restaurants

Taco Bell is part of Yum Brands, Inc., a publicly traded corporation that also owns Kentucky Fried Chicken and Pizza Hut. Although it is part of a public company, it is difficult to get operating information on the Taco Bell operation. We know that it has outperformed KFC and Pizza Hut in same store growth in the last year and that its system-wide sales have grown to $4.7 billion annually with 6,500 U.S. outlets having a 64 percent market share in the Mexican fast-food segment. Only about 30 to 50 percent of its units are owned by independent franchisees. It also claims that nearly 123 million Americans see a Taco Bell commercial once a week—about half the population—resulting in sales of 4.5 million tacos a day along with other menu items.

Why is Taco Bell growing in the face of an overall slowdown in the fast-food market? First, it is reported to have some of the lowest calorie options in the fast-food market. A regular soft taco is only 170 calories and 10 grams of fat; their chicken soft taco is only slightly higher in calories at 190 and 7 grams of fat. That is half to one-third of the fast-food burger offerings and the nutritionists are recommending their products. However, you can quickly get into much higher calorie options, like the taco salad at over 800 calories, and still tell your spouse you only had a salad for lunch.

Its service is not highly rated and its facilities not the cleanest in the industry. My daughter worked at a Taco Bell in high school and suggested I avoid eating at Taco Bell because of poor food-handling practices. However,

I'm sure that it has improved in the last ten years and this problem could have been store specific.

Most customers, particularly the 18 to 35-year-old male segment, rave about the spicy food and lots of menu options. Taco Bell has made fast Mexican-flavored food acceptable throughout the United States.

What does this mean for Albuquerque Turkey Burger? If you had told me twenty years ago that you wanted to franchise hot southwestern-style food across the U.S., I would have said it would not work. The average U.S. citizen's palate was not ready. Taco Bell has proven that this notion is outdated and we accept Mexican and southwestern flavored foods across the country.

Again, the average meal at Taco Bell is about $4. It is not cheaper than McDonald's or Burger King, so it is not growing by straight price competition. It is reducing its operating costs at many Taco Bells by "multibrand" co-locating. Its parent is combining KFC, Taco Bell and Pizza Hut into the same location to improve unit cash flow and share overhead expenses.

The two fastest growing market alternative fast-food restaurants—Subway and Taco Bell—are growing based on performance and value, not on price. They are offering healthier alternatives to fast-food burgers at a slightly higher price and have shown the importance of controlling costs to make lower revenue operations feasible.

Market Alternative Restaurants with Slow or No Growth; Hot Dogs and Chicken:

Wienerschnitzel, Hot Dogs:

We looked at Wienerschnitzel to see what was happening to slow its average per unit sales volume. This 300 unit California-based hot dog franchise has operations located primarily in the western part of the U.S. Customer reviews vary from rave reviews over corn dogs and chile-topped dogs to "never again" reviews because of stale bread and poor service. Although it focuses on hot dogs, it has tried to compete in the burger market. It has retreated from burgers; however, as burger prices sank to all-time lows in late 2002, even though they are generally perceived as a low price alternative to the larger burger chains. We found you can get a regular all-beef chiledog, fries and a medium soda for $3.37, which is close to McDonald's at $3.23 for a similar meal.

Its standard 99-cent hot dog was a price leader, but is now matched by the hamburger prices at McDonald's and Burger King. Its service is perceived as average, at best, and food quality ranges from good to bad, depending on the franchise and its operators. Its most popular item is its chile cheese dog and chiledog, followed closely by the batter dipped and deep fat fried corn dog that is high in fat and calories. There appears to be no effort to appeal to the low-calorie, low-fat market.

The lesson for Tony and Albuquerque Turkey is that mediocre performance and high fat products don't represent a growth opportunity in the fast-food market today.

KFC, Church's and Popeye's, Fast-Food Chicken Restaurants:

Why has Church's Chicken seen a 4.8 percent decline in same store sales in the last quarter of 2002 and Popeye's a 1.7 percent decline in the fourth quarter of 2002? At the same time, KFC with 46 percent market share in the fast-food chicken market saw an average decline of 4 percent in same store sales growth. Chicken meal prices are comparable to beef burger combo meal prices. The only answer we hear, based on customer reports listed on the Internet, is that it is because of high fat and high calories. A typical KFC three-piece meal includes three pieces of chicken, a biscuit, gravy, slaw and a soda. This meal can be over 1100 calories and 56 grams of fat. There is little or no attempt to provide low-calorie and low-fat chicken alternatives. At one time, chicken producers had convinced consumers that white chicken meat was healthier than beef. Now we know better; it depends on how it is prepared. KFC's parent is lowering costs by combining KFC sites with Pizza Hut and Taco Bell. I don't think this is intended to improve per unit sales revenue, only to reduce operating costs as revenues decline. Given this gradual decline in fast-food chicken per unit revenue, combining brands is the right business move for KFC's parent company.

What can Tony learn from the fast-food chicken market decline? Great locations and great brand recognition does not matter if the consumer shuns your product. If you offer high fat, a dull menu, or high calories, you cannot grow in today's highly competitive fast-food market. Consumers are smart enough to determine whether they are getting good quality and healthy food. You need both excellent product and a healthy appealing menu to grow in this market.

Externalities Affecting Future Market Growth

We need to look carefully at trends in factors outside the market for fast-food burgers that may affect future growth in the market. We call these factors *externalities*. They include factors such as health scares related to E. coli and salmonella, obesity lawsuits related to excess fat and calories, mad cow disease, and a poor economy. Dietary fads such as the Atkins diet may impact future market growth.

What would be the impact of a major burger-borne illness-related incident in the fast food market? This actually happened in California a few years back and several burger chain customers died. This alerted many fast-food burger buyers to the risk of eating improperly handled or undercooked burgers. What if mad cow disease, now isolated mostly to the U.K., was to be found in U.S. meat products? What if the lawyers who won the tobacco suits were successful in their suits against fast-food restaurants, blaming them for the nation's obesity epidemic? What if drought and/or poor feed production drove the price of beef or turkey up by a factor of two? What if the economy went into a tailspin like it did in the late 1970's with hyperinflation and low employment?

What if a large number of franchise owners (like we now see at Burger King) get into financial trouble and banks will no longer lend to this segment and no additional equity is available? How do these externalities, factors outside the direct market for products and services, impact the future business opportunity for Albuquerque Turkey Burger? We looked at the most likely externalities that would affect the growth of Albuquerque Turkey's market.

Obesity and Overweight: According to the U.S. Surgeon General in 1999, 61 percent of adults in the U.S. were overweight or obese; 13—14 percent of children 6 to19 years old were overweight. This problem has nearly tripled for adolescents in the past two decades. Three hundred thousand deaths each year in the U.S. are associated with obesity. Overweight and obesity are associated with heart disease, certain types of cancer, type 2 diabetes, stroke, arthritis, breathing problems, and psychological disorders such as depression. The U.S. Surgeon General's office estimates that obesity-related illnesses cost the U.S. economy about $117 billion in 2000. The USDA states that the anti-obesity campaign of the federal government is in its infancy.

The cause of obesity is easy to calculate. The average American supposedly gained 14 to 16 pounds in the last 8 years, or between 1.8 and 2 pounds a year. Two pounds a year equals an extra 50 calories a day. Since you store about half the calories you eat, you need to reduce your intake by about 100 calories per day to eliminate this weight gain. That is equivalent to walking a mile a day. A typical combo meal at a fast-food restaurant is more than 1,000 calories, half the daily calories required by the average size woman and 40 percent of the daily calorie requirement for an average size male. Fast-food calories and associated high fat content are a real threat to our health.

Litigation against fast-food restaurants is gaining national support and attention. Individuals who claim their obesity-related disabilities were directly related to daily consumption of McDonald's products recently sued McDonald's in New York. This was dismissed, but more cases are in the works as the attorneys who succeeded in winning massive tobacco settlements are now focusing on this issue.

Overweight and obesity issues will remain in the forefront of our concerns over food quality and quantity for the foreseeable future. For Albuquerque Turkey, this could be an opportunity if they provide low-calorie, low-fat products.

Fast-Foodborne Illnesses: Fast-foodborne illnesses capture the attention of the American press immediately and stay in the forefront of the media for weeks following an incident. It is a reality of our times and will continue to be a problem for the industry. It is not just ground beef. Recent studies by the CDC (U.S. Center for Disease Control) showed that salads and coleslaw can cause as many problems with food-borne illnesses as ground beef, but meat, fish and poultry get the most attention.

For example, in July 8, 2002, the CDC was notified by the Colorado Department of Public Health of an E. coli (Escherichia coli 0157) outbreak causing 22 infections between June 13th and 30th, traceable to consumption of ground beef products. Sixteen additional cases traceable to the same products were found in other parts of the country. Of these 38 cases, 11 persons were hospitalized, 6 have hemolytic uremic syndrome (where a toxin enters the bloodstream and may result in kidney failure), and 1 died. Freezing meat products and cooking to a temperature over 160 degrees along with proper food handling can eliminate this risk, but new outbreaks hit the press each year.

Mad cow disease has scared beef-eating consumers for the last few years even though it has, until recently, been isolated to Europe (possibly Canada?)

with no evidence that it has spread to the U.S. British scientists have recently reduced their long-term estimate of potential cases and deaths from 50,000 to 7,000. By the end of 2001, they only identified 113 cases of the human form of this disease, Creutzfeldt-Jakob disease. Because of its long incubation period (10—20 years), we can expect the British to report annual increases in the number of infected people. The junk-science smear campaigns in the U.S. get plenty of press attention, but so far have no basis in fact as the most likely cause of this infection in animals has been eliminated by changes in animal feed. However, these same people caused many apple growers to go out of business with their Alar scare campaign and will probably continue to raise fear in the American fast-food consumer population. This could also make turkey appear to be a more attractive alternative than beef to fast-food consumers.

The Economy: Whenever an industry segment like fast food has a slowdown in revenue and profits, the management is quick to blame the economy. To understand the impact of the economy on the growth opportunity for Albuquerque Turkey, we need to look at specific economic factors that can affect the market for their product. According to the book Fast Food Nation— The Dark Side of the All-American Meal, Americans spent $110 billion on fast food. That is more than we spend on higher education, personal computers, computer software, and new cars. There are several economic variables to watch when evaluating the impact of the economy on fast food. One is the appetite of financial markets to finance growth in the number of fast-food operating units. Two is the impact of inflation on discretionary income as driven by fuel prices. Third is the impact of wage inflation on the industry.

Both McDonald's and Burger King stocks have dropped dramatically in the last year. Why? Because their growth has stopped and their profit margins have eroded substantially during this time period. Any equity investor who has recently read about these problems is less likely to invest in a new fast-food chain. Any bank that has struggled with the financial troubles of 16 Albuquerque Burger King outlets is going to be very careful about lending to a new fast-food restaurant. Poor industry financial performance will have a negative impact on financing a new fast-food chain.

Recently, a television article featured a segment showing the impact of higher oil and gas prices on consumer discretionary income. One consumer was telling how her higher auto gas expense and heating bill has cut into her food budget. She stated that she and her children will be eating at home more often and taking their lunch from home. The growth strategy for Albuquerque Turkey can be impacted by significant declines in discretionary consumer income, an economic variable to watch carefully in the next few years.

The third is the effect of wage inflation on the cost of operating a fast-food restaurant. More than 90 cities in the U.S. have adopted living wage laws that substantially increase the minimum wages in those areas. Fast-food restaurants typically pay close to minimum wages and price their products accordingly. Recently, Santa Fe, New Mexico implemented a minimum wage law to take effect in July of 2003 that would increase the federal minimum wage of $5.15/hour in Santa Fe to $8.50/hour next year and go up to $10.50/hour in 2007. This could double the labor costs in a fast-food restaurant and must be watched carefully as Albuquerque Turkey develops its price structure and staffing plan.

As shown above, externalities can result in opportunity for Albuquerque Turkey or can severely limit their potential growth. Throughout the development of the strategic model and operation of the business, these externalities must be monitored and the business plan adjusted accordingly.

Market Saturation, Impact on Future Growth

How do we define market saturation in service businesses? When the average per store revenue is declining or when the aggregate revenue in the fast-food burger market has peaked and is now declining, these are good indications of market saturation. On top of that, almost two-thirds of all Americans are overweight and are saying, "we just can't eat any more!"

Other less obvious indicators are the rapid growth in low-calorie fast-food market alternatives like Subway and the shift to quick and casual dining to improve the perceived health characteristics of the food we consume, even at higher average prices and with slower service.

The major fast-food burger restaurants grew revenue by 7.9 percent in 1999, 4.3 percent in 2000, 0.7 percent in 2001, and we believe overall revenue in the U.S. declined in 2002. McDonald's recorded its first quarterly loss in the fourth quarter of 2002 and the big players continue to try to solve the problem by price cutting. It is clear that this market is mature and may be flat to declining in the fast-food burger segment for a number of years. Albuquerque Turkey must factor market saturation into its growth plans (the likelihood of the market being 100 percent saturated). There are as many fast-food burger places available as there is demand for outlets.

Putting 37 Pages of Analysis on a One-Page Summary

In the preceding 37-page analysis, we focused on collecting market information that would let us capture the essence of the competitive environment that Tony would face with Albuquerque Turkey. Although experts in the field may argue with the accuracy of some of the information collected, we believe that it is adequate to aid Tony in his understanding of the market and will help establish his strategic direction. You can see from the abundance of market information collected that sorting out the important strategic information from the available information can be an overwhelming task. We capture the essential strategic information on the *Quick*Strategy "Market Battlefield" form on the next page. We will use this perspective later in the book to develop the market strategy that will let Tony favorably position Albuquerque Turkey in the fast-food burger market.

Albuquerque Turkey Burger, Market Battlefield 02/2003

MARKET BATTLEFIELD SUMMARY   *QUICK*STRATEGY™   Form 1.0

1. Product or Service: Fast-food burgers @ $1—$6 selling price. Typically sold as part of a Combination Meal with 1/4 pound burger, medium fries and 16 oz. drink for $3—$5.	**2. Customers:** Lunch or dinner fast-food consumers within a 5—10 mile radius of their work, home or shopping area (90%), or transiting market (10%). Initial market 556,000 people in greater Albuquerque area.

3. Customer Need: Convenient (within 10 miles), fast service (under 10 min.) burgers, sides and drinks, prepared fresh and served warm, reasonably priced ($3—$5 per meal), using quality ingredients, consistently served with emphasis on good taste. Safe, healthy products and clean facility, also.	**4. Market Shape:** Value/Price

5. Market Alternatives: (1) Deli/Sub Sandwiches (+) (2) Tacos (+) (3) Chicken (-) (4) Hot Dogs (-) **7. Externalities: 1.** Obesity litigation (-), 2. Poor economy (-), 3. City zoning laws (-), 4. Fast-foodborne illnesses (E. coli and salmonella outbreaks) (-), 5. Diet fads: Atkins (+/-), high carbohydrate (-)	**6. Saturation:** 100% There is no growth in the number of new customers and there are fast-food burger locations within ten miles of every location in the Albuquerque market.

8. Competitors	Strengths	Weaknesses	Sales $(000) Last Yr./This Yr.	Share (%)
McDonald's (HOLD)	Market leader, most recognized brand, strong child appeal, low price, 28 outlets give it strong market presence	Recently perceived poor quality, poor service and lack of clean facilities. Not tailored to local taste and prepackaged	$44,800/42,000	35.8
Burger King (HOLD)	Number 2 in market with 22 outlets. Strong brand recognition, optional toppings, kids' toys, low price, fresh prep., charbroiled	Slow service and product quality issues	$24,200/22,000	19.4
Wendy's (BUILD)	Number 3 in market, 14 outlets, open late catering to mature market, fresh preparation, high quality ingredients	High price compared to McDonald's and Burger King	$16,800/17,500	13.5
Blake's LotaBurger (BUILD)	Strong local brand recognition, most locations (30), caters to local tastes, fresh preparation	Slow service compared to above and limited menu selection	$15,000/$15,000	12.0
Sonic (BUILD)	Convenient, in-car service, large menu selection, good food quality, fresh prep., 13 outlets, wide selection of add-ons, desserts and drinks	No seating in restaurant, high price Weather-related discomfort Highest calories and fat offerings	$11,700/12,300	9.4
Carl's Jr. (BUILD)	Charbroiled, large quantity in offerings, tailored to southwestern tastes, 5 outlets	Few low-calorie options	$5,500/5,500	4.4
Bob's Burgers	Caters to local tastes, 7 outlets	Small eating area	$3,200/3,200	2.6
Others	Catering to local tastes, 9 outlets	No significant brand recognition	$3,600/3,600	2.9
ABQ Turkey (as planned)	Low calorie, low fat offering	No brand recognition, limited market presence, 1 outlet planned	$0,000/300	

9. Market Size (Sales Revenue $000)					**Total**			$124,800/121,400	100
Year-5	Year-4	Year-3	Year-2	Last Year	This Year	Year 2	Year 3	Year 4	Year 5
105,000	113,000	118,000	122,000	124,800	121,400	119,000	117,000	115,000	112,000

10. Market Maturity MATURE Stage

Strategic Business Unit: ABQ Turkey Burger	Plan Manager: Tony Romero	Date Prepared: February 25, 2003
Company: ABQ Enterprises, Inc.	Strategy Advisor: B. Robinson	Date of Next Plan Review:

Summary Meeting On Albuquerque Turkey Market Information

A few weeks after my first meeting with Tony Romero about investing in Albuquerque Turkey Burger, I met with him and his financial advisor at my Albuquerque office on 600 Uptown Boulevard. I gave him the Market Battlefield Summary above and told him that this will be the starting point for developing his business strategy. It defines the market battlefield in which he must compete for customers. It tells us he is entering a mature saturated market and will have to fight to take business away from existing competitors in order to have a viable business. How he positions Albuquerque Turkey Burger in this highly developed and competitive market and how he attacks these existing competitors will determine whether he has a winning strategy or just another new business failure.

I offered to walk him through each element of the summary to tell him how it was developed and give him the insight he will need to develop his business strategy for Albuquerque Turkey Burger.

We started with the **definition of the product/service in Box 1 of the Market Battlefield Summary**. I explained to Tony that we need to be careful in this definition of the product and service as it not only describes what our product is, but also what it is not. By making this definition too narrow, we would eliminate direct competitors' products: by making it too wide we could be competing against peanut butter sandwiches made at home or $10 hamburgers served in upscale restaurants. What is included in this definition defines the direct competitive products and what is not included will be considered a market alternative to our products.

We focused on *burgers* as the Albuquerque Turkey Burger most closely approximates the flavor, texture and satisfaction a customer derives from a beef burger. It therefore excludes uncooked sandwiches, tacos, chicken and other fast-food alternatives. We limited the definition to *fast-food* burgers, as we knew this is the market segment Tony wanted to concentrate on with his franchise expansion program. We limited the definition to burgers sold in the $1 to $6 range. Most often, these burgers are sold as part of a meal with fries and a drink for $3 to $5. This price range information helps distinguish our product offering from the quick casual and formal restaurant offerings that are priced, on average, two times this amount.

Tony asked how we knew our definition was not too narrow or too broad. I explained, at this point in time, we don't. I told Tony the only way we will know, once he is in business, is by a survey of his customers to see what they were purchasing prior to coming to his business and buying a turkey burger. If most of the customers are coming from Taco Bell or Kentucky Fried Chicken instead of fast-food burger restaurants, we have made a mistake, but industry data indicates there is not a lot of crossover between burgers and these market alternatives. We may pull customers from the cold sandwich and sub market that have left burgers behind for lower calorie alternatives. If so, we will have to open our product definition to include cold sandwiches and the competitors will then include Subway, Blimpie's, etc. Our definition is our best estimate given the data we collected in the market. As more market data is collected, this definition will be refined. It is a continuous iterative process; we agreed with Tony that this is a reasonable starting point in defining the product and service.

We then proceeded to a discussion of how we identified the **Customers as shown in Box 2** of the Market Battlefield form. The definition of the customers is a major factor in determining the size and shape of the market.

Our studies showed that the majority of customers (90 percent) for fast-food restaurants live, work or shop within a 5- to 10-mile radius of the food outlet. There are also a smaller proportion of customers (10 percent) that are transiting the area and may stop at a conveniently located fast-food outlet. The initial market is limited to customers in the Albuquerque area—an area containing about 556,000 people in a 25-mile radius from its center. Tony agreed that these are the initial target customers; however, we also agreed that many customers in the Albuquerque area will not be reachable with just one outlet and that this initial definition may be too broad.

Looking at our definition **of Customer Need in Box 3** of the Market Battlefield form, Tony wanted to know more about how we could prioritize these perceived customer needs. I explained that we could not accomplish a prioritization without actually interviewing customers, a process the established burger suppliers were not going to let us accomplish on their property. However, we can be sure they regularly survey their customer needs. From what we have read from customer opinions on the Internet about the fast-food burger buyer, we would list the following, as priority needs:

1. Convenience: near their place of work, home, shopping area, etc. (5—10 miles).
2. Fast: less than ten minutes from time of entry to food in hand.
3. Warm: nothing seems to irritate buyers more than cold burgers and cold fries.

4. <u>Fresh</u>: an old soggy burger on a mushy bun is a real turn-off; tasteless fries are another common gripe.

5. <u>Reasonably Priced</u>: combo meals in the $3—$5 range are the best sellers; however, 99-cent specials seem to have limited appeal.

6. <u>Quality Ingredients</u>: burger buyers will pay for reasonable quality; they expect good value and know a greasy cheap burger from good quality meat; they know a frozen potato from a fresh potato.

7. <u>Consistency</u>: fast-food burger buyers are mostly repeat customers and they do not want to be surprised as we were at a fast-food restaurant that wrapped the burgers so tightly the buns were smashed down to a fraction of their normal size.

8. <u>Tasty</u>: dry, poorly seasoned and presented fast food does not attract repeat buyers.

9. <u>Healthy</u>: more and more customers are concerned about the calorie and fat content of their food with over 61 percent of the U.S. population overweight.

10. <u>Entertaining</u>: McDonald's and Burger King have done an excellent job of making their sites entertaining for children customers, who also drag along a few adult customers.

11. <u>Clean</u>: many customers have described their last visit to a fast-food burger outlet as a "never again experience" because of the lack of cleanliness.

We have not been able to prioritize these customer needs and agreed that we cannot overlook any of the above needs in such a highly competitive marketplace. We did observe that customers also wanted appealing alternatives to the standard burger fare for members of their family or traveling group not inclined to eat burgers. This has given rise to chicken and fish sandwiches and tacos in many outlets. Tony and I agreed that this diversity of offering issue must be explored in more detail.

The underlying driving forces behind these needs are: less time to prepare and eat meals, more discretionary money for food and entertainment, and more awareness of food quality, health and taste options. We agreed that trends in these driving forces must be carefully monitored to react to shifts in demand.

We describe **the Shape of the Market in Box 4** in the Market Battlefield form. This is the way we indicate whether the typical buyer is either price or performance oriented in their purchase decision. In all of the on-line customer feedback I have reviewed, I found very little concern over excess price. The dismal response to recent price cutting by McDonald's and Burger King is further indication that price is a factor in fast-food purchases but not the dominant factor in customer decision making as long as the price is near their expected price. Wendy's has some of the highest priced burger offerings and is one of the few retailers growing per store revenue.

Customers are expecting good value, with as many price oriented buyers as performance oriented buyers. We all agreed this is a reasonable description of the shape of the Market Battlefield and that Albuquerque Turkey should concentrate on delivering excellent quality product within the price expectations of the market and not focus on being the low price leader against well-entrenched price competitors.

We defined the **Market Alternatives in Box 5** of the Market Battlefield summary. I showed Tony how we need to keep an eye on trends in market alternatives to know whether the overall market for our products is growing or declining as customers move from our product or service, fast-food burgers, to the market alternative products and services.

As shown in this box, we believe the cold sandwich and submarine sandwich market is growing and taking customers from the fast-food burger market. Tony said he believed this was because the Subway promotion, for example, led customers to believe their offering was healthier than food from fast-food burger outlets. His turkey burger was a lower fat and lower calorie choice for burger buyers. I agreed that this is a trend to watch carefully, but we also see the higher calorie and higher fat fast-food burger suppliers (Sonic and Wendy's) growing at the same time.

Mexican flavored fast-food outlets, like Taco Bell, also seem to be growing, although not as fast as Subway. This could be because they are a more interesting alternative to burgers, but it also could be because of a recent and very successful advertising campaign featuring a talking Mexican dog. Fried chicken fast-food alternatives seem to be experiencing declining per store revenue as a result of the awareness of the high fat and high calorie content of the most popular brands' offerings. Hot dog fast-food outlets recently added burgers to their menu and are now withdrawing them from the menu, possibly indicating the lack of growth in their core business.

Overall, Tony and I agreed there is a lot to be learned by continuously monitoring growth in the sandwich and sub market alternative and decline of the chicken and hot dog market alternatives. We also agreed that we couldn't draw any near-term conclusion from the recent growth in the taco business except that it may have come from a great advertising program featuring a small talking dog.

Externalities listed in Box 6 also impact the size and growth characteristics of the market for fast-food burgers. Tony's impetus for turkey burgers was his awareness of the growing number of obese and overweight friends who were regularly eating at fast-food burger restaurants. The public lawsuits in this area and books like Fast Food Nation will have a negative impact on the size of the overall fast-food burger market but should be a plus for a low fat, low calorie turkey burger. The financial turmoil at McDonald's and Burger King will negatively impact the ability of any player in the fast-food burger market to raise capital. We also found that the fear of mad cow disease and beef burger-borne illnesses like E. coli have a continuous negative impact on the beef burger market and should help grow the turkey burger market until they have their first health incident. Generally, Tony agreed we must watch each of these issues to determine their impact on the opportunity for Albuquerque Turkey.

He seemed most concerned about the impact of these issues on his ability to finance his business. I pointed out that externalities like September 11 have all but destroyed the airline business. At the same time, lack of financing destroyed the growth in cellular telecom and state mandated deregulation forced California utilities into bankruptcy. We can never take our eye off these factors outside the immediate competitive environment as they can drastically affect market size and stability and opportunity.

Saturation shown in Box 7 of the Market Battlefield form is clearly 100 percent. There is no growth in the overall fast-food burger market in the U.S. and there is little or no growth in the per store revenue of the major competitors (except Wendy's). This means Tony will have to take customers away from the established competitors or market alternatives. He can't count on the lack of established customer preferences to get customers to come to Albuquerque Turkey Burger. They now have plenty of options to satisfy their needs with a fast-food burger outlet at most of the high traffic locations. We agreed this means that Tony's product must be more than just another offering; it has to address all of the customers' needs and have a significant competitive advantage that is effectively promoted to gain a position in this saturated market.

Box 8 in the Market Battlefield form is where we look at **Competitors, their strengths and weaknesses** and their **market share**. We usually start by listing the competitors in terms of size, with the largest competitor first. We always list our business at the bottom of the listing to compare our perceived strengths and weaknesses against the other competitors. I pointed out to Tony that the only strengths and weaknesses that matter are those that ultimately impact the customers' needs we described in Box 3. How we position Albuquerque Turkey in this playing field against these competitors is the essence of the strategy that Tony must develop to be successful. He must pick the competitors, where possible, to take advantage of their weaknesses and avoid their strengths given the resources at his disposal. He must look at who is gaining share and who is losing share relative to their strengths and weaknesses to pinpoint what is most important to the customers. We will spend considerable effort reviewing this information as part of developing Tony's strategy for Albuquerque Turkey after Tony has had time to digest this new information and develop his business concepts.

Box 9 shows that the overall **market size** for Albuquerque fast-food burgers is three times bigger than Tony estimated, but has peaked in the last few years and is starting to decline. This historical Albuquerque data is based on extrapolating national data into the local market and the forecasted data is based on continuation of current downward trends. The rate of future declines is a function of how fast the fast-food burger market is impacted by market alternative growth and the impact of externalities on a saturated market. Tony realizes that developing a strategy for a mature market requires substantially more effort to make it appealing for his investors than for a new or growth market.

Box 10 in the Market Battlefield form describes the **maturity of the market**; normally, this is evident from the market size data in Box 9. We categorize market maturity as New, Growth, Mature, Declining or Residual as a function of the growth characteristics in a market. It is a quick indicator of the type of opportunity in the market. Tony suggested that it is hard to tell at this point whether this market is just peaking (mature) or in decline (declining). We agreed to call it "mature" for the first draft of our strategic plan.

Tony left this meeting with a much more sober perspective on the market for Albuquerque Turkey Burger: a $124 million a year market in Albuquerque, fiercely competitive, with a wide variety of product offerings to a saturated market. Although we both knew the market battlefield description must be continuously updated and refined before a final perspective is established, he knew he would have a fight on his hands to launch and build this business. But at least he now knew with some reasonable degree of certainty what the market battlefield looked like and we could begin to develop a strategy against the known obstacles and for the known opportunities instead of just Tony's entrepreneurial hopes and desires.

His strategic objective was clear: demonstrate the viability of Albuquerque Turkey Burger as a national franchise opportunity by capturing a meaningful share of the Albuquerque fast-food burger market. Tony now must decide if he should proceed and, if so:

1. What competitors he would focus his offering against?
2. What competitive advantage would he try to exploit?
3. What competitor strengths would he avoid and how?
4. What customer needs would he emphasize in his offering?
5. Does he have a significant enough competitive advantage to sustain a market position, should he initially succeed in Albuquerque Turkey Burger?

Answers to these questions will lead to an effective strategy against which we can define tactics that will implement Tony's business plan. I offered to work with Tony to develop his strategy using the *Quick*Strategy planning format.

Developing the Strategic Plan for Albuquerque Turkey Burger

A few weeks later, Tony called and said he had tentative financial backing from his family and a local businessperson. He had at least $300,000, almost enough to open his pilot Albuquerque Turkey Burger fast-food restaurant. He also indicated that one of the major turkey producers would consider backing his test market but wanted to see a complete business plan before he made a financial commitment. Furthermore, he had refined his product offerings (menu) to be able to match the major fast-food beef burger competitors' menus with reduced calories and fat.

We met in my Albuquerque office where Tony, with his usual entrepreneurial enthusiasm, showed me a recent article from *USA Today* showing how extra weight and obesity causes an estimated 300,000 deaths each year. Furthermore, the article indicated that "31 percent of the U.S. population is obese (30+ pounds overweight) and an additional 33.5 percent of the population is overweight (10 to 30 pounds overweight), a total of 64.5 percent of the U.S. population." He would focus his product strategy on this market segment consistent with the growing customer need, identified in the market battlefield summary, for healthy choices in their fast-food restaurants. We also contemplated the contrary perspective: Could this data be an indication that 64.5 percent of the potential market does not care about healthy food?

Competitive Advantage: Healthy Menu Choices:

With great pride, Tony rolled out his initial menu, built around the Albuquerque Turkey Burger we tested at the beginning of our research and complemented by a variety of low-calorie low-fat offerings. We talked about the importance of having an overwhelming and sustainable competitive advantage to compete against such well-entrenched competitors as McDonald's in a mature market. He showed me how he could legitimately advertise "Fast Food at Half the Calories and Half the Fat." That certainly would be significant. His menu attempted to take advantage of the weakness of the three major competitors: their primary product offerings contain high levels of saturated fats and many calories.

Was this healthy burger competitive advantage adequate and sustainable? McDonald's recently added salad back to their menu and is testing a low-fat veggie-burger. Burger King has a BK Veggie Burger (290—330 calories and 7—10 fat grams) on their menu. What stops the major competitors from adding a turkey burger knock-off of Tony's product to their menu? Nothing, except the cost of making a nationwide menu change! However, they are unlikely to change or expand their entire menu to a low calorie, low fat menu. Tony pointed out that his entire menu provided low fat, low calorie alternatives to the big three fast-food burger competitors. He said when a customer comes into Albuquerque Turkey Burger, they will select from a menu that is designed to give them half the calories and half the fat of the combination of products offered by the major national competitors. He then showed me the following menu comparison to prove his point:

Menu Comparison: (Calories/Fat Grams)

Menu Item	Tony's	McDonald's	Burger King	Wendy's
¼ Pound Burger	262/11	430/21	490/21	410/19
Fish Sandwich	334/15	470/26	710/39	N/A
Medium Fries	270/10	450/22	360/18	390/17
Shake	250/10	570/16	720/21	440/11
Salad	100/8	160/16	N/A	345/29
Typical Combo Meal	530/22	1080/43	1050/39	1000/36

Tony's ¼ pound burger includes a roll, lettuce, sauce, Hatch green chile, and tomato. His fish sandwich is grilled salmon on a roll with special seasoning; his fries are baked, not deep fat fried. His shake is a fruit yogurt-based drink. Tony will only offer diet sodas, ice tea, coffee, and water. All calories and fat grams Tony calculated are based on "Food Counts" by Corinne T. Netzer.

From the above menu comparison, Tony can make the case for offering a much lower calorie menu. (However, we noted each of the competitors could reduce their combo meal 200 calories by switching to a diet drink or water.) Whether the lower calories and lower fat in Tony's menu are recognized by the consumer as a competitive advantage can only be determined with a market test. The market test will also reveal whether Tony is meeting the other customer needs at a level established by the three major competitors. If he does not at least match the competitors in meeting other customer needs, his market test could fail.

Meeting Other Customer Needs:
(Forget them and you disadvantage your business.)

Convenient location was also high on customers' lists of requirements for a fast-food outlet. Tony was confident he had found a location for his first fast-food restaurant. The local Burger King franchise shut down a number of outlets and he found one available near his home that was built just two years ago. It was also near the interstate highway that ran through Albuquerque. The question was why did Burger King shut down this outlet? I traveled to the location with Tony and found a perfect store, ready to go. There were, however, a few problems with the location. It was not on a highly traveled street; it was a block and a half away from old Rt. 66 (a highly traveled street), but behind a large grocery store parking area and a shopping mall. If you did not know it was there, you would never see it from the main roads. Furthermore, it was in the far eastern edge of the city and near very few competitors. Tony understands how important it was to have his first outlet near the major competitors, as he would have to take market share from their outlets. Tony will concentrate near-term effort on identifying another suitable location convenient to a large enough customer population to make the market test feasible and not have location be a competitive disadvantage.

We saw that each of the major competitors delivered **warm, fresh product in less than five minutes.** Tony would have to develop methods or copy methods used by the major competitors to meet these customer needs or be disadvantaged in the eyes of his customers.

Tony assured me he could match the competitor **prices** and still achieve adequate profit margins. However, one aspect of his initial market test was to explore the sensitivity to product pricing and start by offering his product at the high end of the competitive price range.

He had lined up suppliers for his product ingredients, many of them hoping to participate in a national chain of franchised restaurants should Tony be successful. He emphasized the need for **consistency** and **quality ingredients** in his offering as he knew the existing competitors were focused on these customer needs and meeting them in most outlets. As a chemical engineer, Tony researched product ingredients and has written specifications for each item purchased for his menu.

He had worked extensively on his menu offerings to make the product both **healthy** (lower fat and calories) and **tasty**. However, his taste tests to date were with friends, investors and family, and he recognized that the average consumer could be much more critical in their taste tests.

He recognized he would be disadvantaged relative to McDonald's and Burger King in child **entertainment**. He felt that a low-calorie low-fat alternative product menu would have little appeal to children and that this market disadvantage would not affect his test results as Wendy's had demonstrated an ability to achieve excellent results without offering child entertainment.

He had contacted several cleaning services in the Albuquerque area and would use their services to maintain the overall **cleanliness** of the facility and establish the standards for hourly cleaning by his employees. He recognized the importance of cleanliness as a customer need and would make sure it was not a competitive disadvantage.

Tony had also started a search for a store manager trained by one of the big three competitors in the fast-food burger market. He recognized much of the success of the major competitors is based on disciplined management to assure consistency in meeting customer needs. A store manager trained by one of the big three competitors would know the standards of his competition and be able to train Tony's staff to match the competitors' standards for service and cleanliness.

Targeting Competitors

Which competitors should he focus his strategy against? If he focused his strategy against the local or regional competitors, could he validate a nationwide franchise opportunity? If he focused his strategy on the large national chains, he would be more credible to investors. We assume, however, if he could beat them in the Albuquerque market, he had a much better chance of building a national franchise.

The biggest of these competitors is McDonald's with 43 percent U.S. market share. Next in market share is Burger King with 18 percent and Wendy's with 13 percent. That is 74 percent of the U.S. market for fast-food burgers held by the big three competitors.

What is a reasonable strategic objective to validate Tony's strategy?

As he will not have a breakfast menu in the initial test market, the best comparable competitor would be Wendy's, as it only recently added breakfast items to its menu. Its per store revenue was averaging $1.2 million per year before adding breakfast items. It also had the most profitable operations on a per store basis. If Tony's business measured up to the success characteristics of Wendy's, then it would turn investors' heads when he proposed a national franchise. This would mean the first Albuquerque Turkey Burger outlet would have to take about 1 percent of the Albuquerque fast-food burger market and operate at a rate of $100,000 per month in revenues with operating profit margins of 12—20 percent on sales to match Wendy's success without a breakfast menu. However, our research indicated that most fast-food burger buyers lived or worked within a 5 to 10-mile radius of the point of purchase. If there were two of each competitor within a 5 to 10-mile radius of Tony's first location, he would have to take 17% of their collective market to achieve the $100,000 per month revenue. A more realistic objective to demonstrate the viability of Albuquerque Turkey Burger would be to take 10% of the fast-food burger market within a 10-mile radius of his first location; the actual revenue target would depend on the location relative to the competitors.

I asked Tony if he recognized how the competitors, as they are positioned in the market battlefield, define his strategic opportunity? Their weaknesses reveal the opportunity for his business. Meanwhile, their strengths reveal the barriers to his market entry. In the mind of investors, competitors also define the standards of success in this market. Revenues per store, profit margins and start-up investment requirements are defined by investor comparison data on Tony's competitors. He must join in the market battle against these competitors and win market share in order to prove the validity of his business strategy: low-calorie low-fat alternatives to fast-food burger outlet products will capture significant market share.

Using the Strategic Plan

We can summarize Tony's strategy on the *Quick*Strategy Strategic Plan form 2.0 as follows:

STRATEGIC PLAN SUMMARY   *QUICKSTRATEGY*™   Form 2.0

11. Your STRENGTHS vs. Competitor or Market Alternative	12. Your WEAKNESSES vs. Competitor or Market Alternative
McDonald's: Healthy menu, lower fat and lower calorie products	McDonald's: Lack of market coverage in ABQ market, one outlet vs. 28 McDonald's outlets; lack of market recognition vs. McDonald's; lack of play area, lack of breakfast offering
Burger King: Healthy menu, lower fat and lower calorie products	Burger King: Lack of market coverage 1 vs. 22 in ABQ, lack of breakfast offering, lack of market recognition vs. Burger King
Wendy's: Healthy menu, lower fat and lower calorie products	Wendy's: Lack of market coverage 1 vs. 14 in ABQ, lack of market recognition vs. Wendy's

13. Strategic Objective:

Take 10% market share ($750,000 minimum revenue) from fast-food burger outlets within 10-mile radius of Albuquerque Turkey Burger outlet as a basis for financing a nationwide chain of fast-food burger outlets. Invest no more than $500,000 to verify profit potential with revenue in excess of $500,000 per outlet.

14. Type of Strategic Initiative: Probe—

15. Strategic Plan:

Probe fast-food market in the Albuquerque area to determine if a low-calorie, low-fat product alternative is an adequate and sustainable competitive advantage against McDonald's, Burger King and Wendy's to establish a viable performance position in the market.

16. Tactical Plan:

1. Recruit trained fast-food store manager by 5/10 (TR)
2. Research Albuquerque fast-food outlet locations and select location and site by 5/10 (hired realtor)
3. Complete facilities renovation and site improvements to house first Albuquerque Turkey Burger outlet by 7/10 (hired contractor)
4. Schedule outlet opening 7/10 (TR)
5. Select advertising agency and develop advertising and marketing program by 5/10 (TR)
6. Order and install all equipment, tables, etc. by 8/10 (store manager)
7. Obtain necessary permits to open food service business by 8/1 (store manager)
8. Recruit and train staff by 8/1 (store manager)
9. Finalize initial menu by 6/1 (TR and store manager)
10. Order initial food inventory and schedule deliveries. Order by 6/15; initial deliveries by 8/15 (store manager)
11. Initiate advertising program for grand opening by 8/15 (TR)
12. Open outlet, 9/1 tentative (TR/store manager)
13. Commence customer surveys to identify sensitivity to competitive position by 9/15 (TR)
14. Modify menu to react to initial customer input by 12/16 (TR/store manager)
15. Introduce modified menu by 1/15/04 (store manager)
16. Revise marketing and promotion around new menu and customer reactions by 1/15/04 (TR/store manager)
17. Conclude test marketing phase of plan 5/10/04 (TR)
18. Develop financial prospectus for national franchise or sell/close business 6/10/04 (TR)

17. History & Projections (performance measures)	Year-4 $(000)	Year-3 $(000)	Year-2 $(000)	Last Year $(000)	This Year $(000)	Next Year $(000)	Year 3 $(000)
Market size ($)					7,500,000	7,500,000	7,500,000
Market Share (%)					5%	10%	12%
Sales Revenue ($)					325,000	750,000	900,000
Operating Cost ($)					450,000	650,000	700,000
Operating Profit ($)					(175,000)	100,000	200,000
Investment ($)					300,000	200,000	0

Strategic Business Unit: ABQ Turkey Burger	Plan Manager: Tony Romero	Date Prepared: March 11, 2003
Company: ABQ Enterprises, Inc.	Strategy Advisor: Bruce Robinson	Date of Next Plan Review: June 10, 2003

I showed Tony how we could focus his strategy against specific competitors and establish tactics to accomplish measurable results using the above Strategic Planning Form 2.0, from *Quick*Strategy. It is easy to use in conjunction with the information documented in the Market Battlefield Form 1.0 to keep ahead of the continuously changing competitive market environment.

In Boxes 11 and 12, after we reviewed the Market Battlefield data, we identified the target competitors, the specific advantage we would use against them, and the weaknesses we had relative to their market position. Tony knew from the Market Battlefield summary that in a mature market he had to take market share from another competitor to build his business. To prove he had a viable national business opportunity, he had to go head-to-head with the big national competitors.

In Box 13, we summarized Tony's strategic objective: taking measurable market share from competitors to accomplish specific market position.

In Box 14, I suggested we define this type of strategy as a probe strategy and that I would explain in more detail later what other types of strategy we employ in our planning process. For now, he needed to know that we employ the Probe type of strategy to determine if a market opportunity exists by investing a specific amount of time and money against well-defined objectives to test our strategy.

In Box 15, we summarized the Strategy: It should state how Tony intends to position his business (or reposition his business) relative to competition to accomplish his strategic objective.

In Box 16, Tony listed the actions (tactics) he would take to accomplish the strategic objective. These should always be measurable in time (and, where possible, in expenditure levels) and have a responsible person identified (in initials) for each action.

In Box 17, we summarized the performance measures we would monitor to determine whether we are meeting our strategic objectives. We always start with market size, but what market? As we have seen, one fast-food outlet competes only within a 10-mile radius for most of its business. Few customers will travel further for a fast-food burger. The history of the market gives us an indication of the maturity of the market and the future market is forecast accordingly. The objective in all strategic plans should be measured in market share—that is the measure of your ability to compete. The rest of the measurements are consistent with Tony's objective to demonstrate that he has a national franchise business opportunity. These additional measures will vary from business to business depending on the critical variables associated with measuring its success.

Tony agreed to strictly adhere to the probe strategy outlined above and stay focused on his strategic objective, recognizing that we will continuously monitor changes in the market battlefield in order to let him react on a timely basis with adjustments to his strategy.

Summary of Albuquerque Turkey Burger

I told Tony my friends and I would consider an investment in his market probe (under terms and conditions to be negotiated), as long as we could verify the nationwide franchise opportunity. That means he has to prove his strategy is viable against the big three nationwide fast-food burger outlets.

Would you invest?

Albuquerque Turkey Burger Eat Healthy Menu
(ABQ TURKEY™)

ABQ Turkey™ Sandwiches

Menu Item	Price $	Menu Item	Price $
¼ lb. ABQ Turkey™ Burger	1.99	Stuffed Turkey Burger	2.45
½ lb. ABQ Turkey™ Burger	2.99	Cranberry Turkey Burger	2.78
¼ lb. Salmon Filet	3.34	¼ lb. Spicy Salmon Filet	3.99

Low Fat Cheese $0.40 extra

High Protein Menu (no bread)

Menu Item	Price $	Menu Item	Price $
¼ lb. ABQ Turkey™ Burger	1.79	¼ lb. Salmon Filet	3.14
½ lb. ABQ Turkey™ Burger	2.79	½ lb. Salmon Filet	4.59
¾ lb. ABQ Turkey™ Burger	3.79		

Sides

Menu Item	Price $	Menu Item	Price $
Baked Fries (small/med.)	.99/1.39	Turkey Chile	1.69
Broccoli & Cheese	1.99	Veggie Chile	1.69
Baked Onion Rings	1.39	Italian Veggie Soup	1.69

Salads and Lettuce Wraps

Menu Item	Price $	Menu Item	Price $
Turkey and Lettuce Salad	4.29	Turkey Wrap	4.29
Salmon and Lettuce Salad	4.29	Salmon Wrap	4.29
Green Salad	3.29		

Drinks

Menu Item	Price $	Menu Item	Price $
Diet Soda (sm/med)	0.99/1.29	Ice Tea (sm/med)	.99/1.29
Skim Milk	.75	Coffee	.75
Fruit Yogurt Shake (sm/med)	1.59/1.99	Hot Tea	.75
Bottled Water	1.29		

Desserts

Menu Item	Price $	Menu Item	Price $
Lite Fruit Yogurt	1.99	Fruit Cup	.99

Calories and Fat Grams printed on your receipt.

Open Issues:

As we mentioned in the introduction, strategic plans are not something you do once a year and set aside until the following year. They are living, working documents that should be used to track changes in markets and detail changes in strategy and tactics necessary to react to the changing market environment. As such, all strategic plans, when finished, have open questions associated with judgments made at the time they were formulated, such as:

1. Will $300,000 to $500,000 be adequate to perform an aggressive market test of the ABQ Turkey Burger business concept?
2. What's to stop one of the bigger fast-food burger outlets from multi-branding like Taco Bell, Pizza Hut and KFC and add a complete line of healthy alternative foods to their menu? They have the best locations.
3. Are there enough good retail outlet locations available to provide an entry opportunity for a new fast-food burger chain, or should Tony partner with Burger King or another existing chain to promote his idea?
4. Is the 61 percent of the overweight population the target market, or the remaining 39 percent that is not overweight?
5. Will the financial markets invest in a nationally franchised Albuquerque Turkey Burger when the performance of the publicly traded fast-food burger companies is in such turmoil?

Chapter 2

CASE #2:
Georgia Wireless Constructors
(February 2000)

In February 2000, an investment group interested in investing in the wireless telephone industry approached me to evaluate prospective companies using *Quick*Strategy™. They were particularly interested in the field of new cell site construction and maintenance for the wireless segment of the telecom market. Tim Murphy,[*] senior partner in the firm, invited me to New York to review their investment objectives.

I arrived at LaGuardia Airport on a cold, snowy February evening. I took a taxi to the Ritz Carlton on 59th Street between 6th and 7th where I had a beer with Tim and his young research associate, Bill Sullivan, at the Jockey Club while cajoling with Norman, the best bartender in the city. They told me how they had just raised a $500 million fund that was targeted for investment in the telecom market. They said the market was growing at a 20—30 percent annual rate in the wireless telecom segment and they had more investment and acquisition opportunities than they could evaluate. However, they were very worried about their ability to respond to this deal flow fast enough to make investments and were fighting the IPO market for deals at prices that seemed outlandish to all of us. Furthermore, their prospectus to their investors obligated them to put their $500 million fund to work in the telecom market so they had to find a way to compete for deals in this market.

I found, over dinner at the Manhattan Ocean Club, they had recently lost two telecom investments to other buyers, one a fund similar to theirs and another to WFII, which is a new publicly traded company with stock trading at a 100+ multiple of earnings. They needed to compete with the high market prices for these deals, but had to choose target companies with good strategic positions in order to assure growth adequate to support the anticipated high purchase price. They wanted me to look for strategic opportunities that would assure them growth in revenue and profit of at least 20 percent each year for the next five years and generate adequate return to their investors at the current high price the market placed on telecom deals.

---

[*] Note: Most names and locations in this case are fictitious and any resemblance to people or places is purely coincidental, except Norman.

The next morning, I walked to their offices on East 56th Street to review their investment objectives and learn more about their perception of the telecom market. I got off the elevator on the 46th floor and entered their office suite through large mahogany doors with their firm name emblazoned above the door in large gold letters. I was greeted by a stunning receptionist (they still have those in New York financial circles) and escorted to their conference room, complete with floor-to-ceiling windows and spectacular view of the city.

Tim and Bill joined me a few minutes later and introduced me to their junior partner, Sally Kempf, an accountant by training who is responsible for financial analysis of their investments. Tim hooked up his laptop computer to a projector and they began to show me the PowerPoint presentation they made to their investors when they raised the half billion-dollar fund: fifty-six slides showing investors why they should put millions of dollars of pension fund money or family trust money into their new telecom fund.

I summarized the several pages of notes on their presentation as follows:

- Since the Telecommunications Act of 1996, the telecom market has become one of the fastest growing markets in the U.S.
- It is driven by the public's insatiable desire to communicate more information by phone and computer and an influx of a large number of new businesses into the wire line and wireless market segments.
- The wireless segment of the telecom market is growing at 20—30 percent per year.
- The wireless (cellular) market build-out could be the largest investment in infrastructure in the U.S. since the original wire line telephone build-out early in the last century, with over $8 billion invested in 1999.
- Only 26 percent of the population currently has cell phones and only 50 percent of the country has good quality cellular coverage (cell sites).
- The transition from analog to digital cellular will require twice the number of cell towers as are in existence today and provide expanded services for the cellular communications carriers.
- Just to obtain FCC licenses for radio frequencies costs billions of dollars and only gives the buyer the right to invest in the radio cell sites and support infrastructure necessary to generate revenue. Once they have bought the license, the carriers must build out 1/3 of the licensed market area in five years and 2/3 of the licensed market area

in ten years or the FCC reclaims the uncovered areas and sells them to competitors.

- The investment in cellular telephone infrastructure will exceed $12 billion this year (2000) and grow at a 20 percent compound rate over the next three years.

- Wall Street has invested more than $9 billion into the cellular telephone market in the last year and does not expect to see cash flow break even on its investments until 2004 or 2005.

- The U.S. market is behind the Japanese and European markets in conversion to new digital cellular technology and in level of market penetration. These markets have more than 68 percent of their populations using cellular telephones compared with 26 percent of the U.S. population. Once cell phones' system coverage is adequate, they predict the wireless carrier services will bypass local wire-line carrier services.

- An investment in this market should grow at a 20—30 percent compound rate over the next five years with leverage up to 50 percent possible on each transaction given the current banking environment.

- There is a hot IPO market for anything wireless telecom related that could give them a good exit opportunity once they had combined several acquisitions into a single company.

Along with their presentation, they gave me a thick, leather-bound investment memorandum that ironically started with a succinct statement alluding to the speculative nature of investment in their telecom fund and the high-risk nature of the market. The above presentation insights were buried in the details of the leather-bound tome, but I took a copy of the memorandum along with copies of their slides to aid in my analysis of their business investment opportunities.

As I was riding back to LaGuardia, I reflected on the enthusiasm of the telecom fund managers and the challenge they faced to wisely invest the money they had raised. My job was to expedite the acquisition of companies in this market by using *Quick*Strategy techniques to evaluate the viability of target company strategies to meet their funds' stated investment objective. They would start feeding me individual company investment memoranda to evaluate within the next two weeks. As I had little prior experience in the telecom market, I was a bit panicked by the amount I had to learn in two weeks' time in order to support Tim and Bill in their investment decisions.

I knew I could rely on *Quick*Strategy methodology to organize my thoughts. The first step in *Quick*Strategy is to determine how each company is positioned in the market battlefield for its products and services. This meant I would have to get a clear definition of the **products and services** offered by companies in the market. As Tim and Bill wanted to focus on companies in the cell siting, construction, and maintenance market, I would start by looking at publicly available information on similar companies' products and services. Then I would look at the **customers** for these products and try to isolate and prioritize **customer needs** and price/performance orientation (**market shape**). I would then look at **market alternatives** affecting market size and shape and **externalities** to the market that could alter the market landscape. I would try to estimate market **saturation** as a key factor in future market growth potential and then look at **competitors**, particularly the market leaders, where public information may be available. Evaluating the strengths and weaknesses of the market competitors would let me determine if there was an opportunity to take market from a competitor and/or hold market position in the market battlefield. Finally, I would look at historic market growth to determine the level of **market maturity** as a basis for forecasting future market growth. I would use this summary of the market battlefield as the basis for evaluating each candidate's strategy and their ability to meet my client's investment criteria.

Products and Services

Two publicly traded companies stood out as direct competitors in wireless network implementation and the cell tower siting, construction, and maintenance market: Wireless Facilities, Inc. (WFII) and O2 Wireless Solutions, Inc. (O2 Wireless). I pulled all available information I could find from their web sites and pulled their 10K and 10Q reports from EDGAR Online (a great source of public company information) and Yahoo Finance online.

I found the type of service that formed their core business was called EF&I. This stands for **E**ngineer, **F**urnish and **I**nstall wireless networks and cellular towers. Typical jobs include stand-alone towers that are either monopoles, guyed towers or metal lattice towers, although some areas require towers to look like trees to blend into the natural surroundings. Each tower is engineered by radio frequency engineers to cover a maximum radius for transmission, comply with local and federal ordinances and regulations, and backhaul information to high-speed switches over local telephone connections. Once the engineering design and siting is completed and permits are obtained, the customer (usually a wireless carrier) either supplies the components or the EF&I company purchases (furnishes) them from customer-approved vendors. Installation of the tower requires special field personnel able to assemble the towers, connect the associated radio equipment, erect the tower, and test, trouble shoot and optimize performance of the equipment once on line. All of this is usually done on a fixed price basis with each completed tower costing between $150,000 and $450,000 with an average price of $250,000.

Customers and Customer Needs

The major customers are directly or indirectly the large wireless carriers: AT&T Wireless, Sprint PCS, Nextel, VoiceStream, Verizon, Cingular and Alltel. Relying on public information available in their 10K and 10Q filings, I was able to determine their capital expenditures for 1999 to be in excess of $8 billion. Their annual capital investment had grown by about 9 percent since 1998 and was forecasted to grow by 20—30 percent from 1999 to 2000. In addition to these primary customers, there are also regional telephone companies that have affiliated with the major wireless carriers that build out cellular towers in their local areas. Many of these regional affiliates have invested millions in building out wireless infrastructure. This market is further complicated by the position of four to five major cell tower real estate companies (American Tower and Crown Castle are the largest such companies) that build out or purchase cell towers for the carriers and lease the carriers antenna space on their towers. Additional small build-to-suit tower real estate investment groups also support the industry's needs on a site-by-site basis. My research revealed the most outstanding characteristic of these cell tower customers is their lack of adequate near-term return on invested capital to sustain their business. Growth would stop without a continuous infusion of new capital from the financial markets.

How long will investors continue to fund the build-out of cellular networks at below normal returns? If there is a shakeout, what customers will survive? Will the customers merge to survive and how will that impact the market for new site construction? Looking at each class of customer, major wireless carrier, affiliated local carriers and major wireless real estate companies may give us a clue about the customers' future.

Major wireless carriers like AT&T Wireless, Sprint PCS, Nextel, VoiceStream, Verizon, Cingular and Alltel dominate the industry and are in a bitter battle for market share with most U.S. customers able to choose among five or more wireless carriers in their market. They are offering services well below cost, averaging $45 to $50 each month per subscriber, as they scramble to implement new technology, add services, and complete coverage of their service areas. The reported strategy for these carriers is to be the biggest and best supplier of wireless services with the most customers. This will let them spread their high fixed costs for license fees and capital investment over more customers. With market dominance, they believe they will eventually become very profitable and, through their national market presence, create a formidable barrier to entry to incumbent suppliers. Once reliability and coverage objectives are met, they believe many wireless users will replace their local wired telephones with cell phones and wireless computer connections. However, to truly understand the customers' needs, we must look more carefully at the numbers that drive the wireless telecom market.

There are about 286 million people in the U.S., with the estimated maximum number of cell phone users at market saturation to be 200 million, or about 70% of the population. At $40 to $50 per month user fees, that translates into $8 to $10 billion per month or $96 to $120 billion per year of revenue potential.* These are numbers that will get Wall Street's attention, and they have attracted many investors. In February 2000, about 80 million wireless subscribers, or 28 percent of the population, had cell phones. That amounted to roughly 1,000 subscribers per cell site. As subscribers grow to the saturation level of 200 million, the number of cell cites should also grow from about 80,000 to about 200,000 to accommodate the increased usage.

Each cell site has to be located on a tower or similar structure. The average EF&I cost for each new tower is $250,000. But we can't just multiply the 120,000 new cell sites by $250,000 per cell site to determine the total amount EF&I customers will invest in new cell towers. That is where the tower real estate companies come into play in this market. They will reduce the number of cell sites by sharing antenna space. They may put antennas for several carriers at a single cell site. In fact, they need to have an average of 2.4 antennas per cell site at today's lease rate to provide adequate returns on their investments.

So we should divide the number of new towers to be constructed by at least 2, giving us a potential of at least 60,000 new cell sites. If these 60,000 new cell sites have an average cost of $250,000, we have a total market potential for EF&I services of $15 billion through the point of total market saturation. Given that about $8 billion has been invested in wireless build-out to date, the additional investment of $15 billion to go from 28 percent of the population using cell phones to 70 percent of the population using cell phones makes some sense, given the fact that the first cell phone build-out was in high density population areas and the last areas to build-out will be in lower population density areas. Does it make sense for Wall Street to continue

---

* Note: Contrary to the above analysis, Forrester Research International Data Corporation expects that by 2003, the U.S. wireless subscriber base will grow to over 185 million and generate revenues of $68 billion (per WFII 10K). That assumes a $37 average charge per subscriber.

investing into wireless infrastructure? Yes, if it believes the total market revenue potential will ultimately generate adequate returns to compensate them for the risk.

What will be the timing of the market build-out to the point of market saturation? Given the license requirements to build-out 1/3 of their market within five years of purchasing a radio license for each region and 2/3 build-out by ten years, it is probably going to be seven to ten years before the market coverage is complete. That still means there should be at least a $1 billion to $2 billion annual investment in new cell tower EF&I. This is a substantial market opportunity for EF&I companies, with the major wireless carrier customers driven by competition, high initial capital investment in licenses, and radio license time requirements to make their investment.

What about the **regional telephone company affiliates?** They are affiliated with the major wireless carriers to build out cell sites for the major carriers in their local service area, usually lower population density areas of the country. They affiliate with one of the major carriers like Sprint. They install and maintain the cell sites and towers to Sprint's specifications, then backhaul the traffic over their own high-speed T1 lines to their central switch and into Sprint's national telephone network. They get a large piece of the wireless traffic revenue that they otherwise could lose to another major wireless provider. Their investment is driven by the major wireless carriers' need to offer national market coverage in order to meet their customers' needs and to compete with the other wireless carriers. (A typical affiliate agreement with Sprint is structured with Sprint paying for the FCC license on the radio spectrum, the regional affiliate furnishing the capital to build and operate the wireless network, and Sprint supplying the national marketing, name recognition and national vendor purchasing. Sprint and the regional affiliate share the roaming charges in the region.)

The affiliate is also driven by the contractual commitments it makes to the major carrier they are affiliated with to build out their geographic area according to a predetermined schedule. These investments are independently financed by the affiliate and accounted for as part of the estimated $15 billion EF&I build-out described above. Many of the affiliates are heavily leveraging their local telephone company to cover the cost of this wireless build-out on behalf of the major carriers.

The **Tower Real Estate Companies** including American Tower Corp., Crown Castle International Corp., SpectraSite, SBA Communications, and Pinnacle Towers have introduced another set of customer requirements into the EF&I market for cellular towers. They have amassed capital to acquire towers from the wireless carriers and build towers for the wireless carriers, which they then lease back to each carrier to accommodate the carrier's cell site antenna. Their strategy is to lease each tower to multiple carriers in order to decrease each carrier's operating cost through sharing the capital cost of each tower site.

They currently are estimated to own 1/3 to 1/2 of all towers in the U.S., most of them purchased from the major wireless carriers in a bidding contest among the major tower real estate companies. This has provided capital for the wireless carriers to re-deploy in their business, but came at a high cost to the tower real estate companies as they paid prices well in excess of new tower construction cost. They also had to buy the towers in bulk covering large areas, with many of the acquired towers having little value due to poor construction, disrepair, low structural capacity or poor site location. Furthermore, the lease-back arrangement with the tower companies from which they made the acquisition will not cover the acquisition capital costs. They must get an average of 1.4 additional tenants on each tower (2.4 total) to break even on their tower investment at current market lease rates. Therefore, the real estate tower companies are all losing money. They are planning to recover from their financial dilemma by raising more capital to build more towers at a lower cost per tower and by leasing more cell sites on their existing towers. In the long run, after expiration of their current leases, they expect to be able to raise lease rates for each cell site.

Most of these tower real estate companies have in-house EF&I capability and subcontract only that EF&I activity that they cannot perform in-house. They, therefore, become both a customer and a competitor. As a competitor, they enjoy the advantage of a right of first refusal from most of the major carriers to build out new tower networks. For example, if they purchased a thousand towers from Nextel, they also may have received the right of first refusal to build-to-suit the next several thousand towers required by Nextel to complete their network. For independent EF&I companies such as WFII and O2 Wireless, this exclusive arrangement can represent a decrease in available direct tower build opportunities with the major wireless carriers.

The **small independent build-to-suit tower real estate companies** are scattered around the country and tend to build out 1 to 30 tower sites based on perceived future need for cellular coverage. They will target an area along a major highway, for example, which does not currently have wireless coverage. They negotiate real estate leases from property owners at key locations and negotiate local and federal permits for tower construction, subject to successful negotiation of cell site contracts with wireless carriers. If they get enough interest on the part of carriers to lease cell sites, they will raise money to build towers for each site. They then offer tower leases to the major carriers at market prices that let them recover their investment and generate returns for their investors. We found that they represent a small percentage of the market opportunity for EF&I companies at this time and there is little data available to identify their future requirements.

Shape of Market Battlefield

The customers determine the shape of the market battlefield, depending on their orientation toward price or performance in their purchase decision making. The overwhelming emphasis by the above customers as of February 2000 is on rapid deployment of service, being the first to offer reliable nationwide service with the latest technology. There is also a lack of EF&I tower suppliers to meet the current needs of the customers. This should indicate a performance oriented need on the part of most customers as meeting time deadlines should be more important than cost. As this build out is financed by external capital with all major carriers and tower real estate customers losing money on day-to-day operations, the market shape could turn to severe price orientation should the available outside financing slow down.

Market Alternatives:

We found few market alternatives to EF&I companies building towers to accommodate antennas for cellular communications carriers. One alternative is to locate antennas on the roof of existing buildings. Another alternative is to locate cellular antennas on existing power line towers or water towers. Both of these market alternatives are limited to availability of existing structures. The most serious market alternative threatening the independent EF&I companies' tower products is the in-house alternative posed by the tower real estate companies and wireless carriers.

Externalities:

External factors affecting future market growth include the following: availability of future radio licenses, implementation of high-speed digital networks (2.5G and 3G)[*], restrictive local zoning laws on tower construction, coverage requirements on existing radio licenses and availability of capital for new construction. These factors outside the control of the competitors in the

---

[*] 2.5G means slightly improved second generation technology, hence second and a half generation. 3G means third generation cellular technology.

EF&I market for wireless towers will have a major impact on the rate at which the market for their services grows and develops.

The radio licenses for wireless networks are auctioned by the U.S. Federal Communications Commission. They are acquired by the major carriers to provide wireless coverage for specific geographic areas. As noted earlier, these licenses require carriers to provide service to customers in the area on a five-year and ten-year timetable in order to keep their license. Recently, a carrier that acquired licenses to a large portion of the U.S. wireless market got into financial trouble and, therefore, may not meet its construction obligation under the licenses it purchased. This has also slowed construction of new cell sites in these license areas and decreased the rate of growth in the tower construction EF&I market.

Each of the major carriers has selected a high-speed digital wireless protocol that lets them digitize voice transmission and unscramble it into recognizable sounds at their receiver. Why go to digital wireless? Each wireless carrier can handle more calls on a digital network than on an analog network and provide high-speed digital information, increasing their revenue per dollar of capital invested. However, these same digital wireless networks may require more cell towers per area of operation. The latest digital wireless systems can also handle digital data directly into the customer's wireless hand-held or computer device to receive e-mail, digital messages, and video data. These systems are called 2.5G to 3G systems, meaning they are the second and a half to third generation technology. Most wireless systems will be converted to these updated systems by 2002, which will permit the wireless carriers to offer more services and, perhaps, charge a higher price for their services. Converting to these advanced technologies is also absorbing capital from the wireless carriers that is not being used to complete their system build-out, a negative for new tower suppliers.

The capital markets have been very patient with the wireless carriers and the tower real estate companies, with little hope of near-term return on their invested capital. However, as we have seen with the "dot com" investors, when and if capital markets lose patience with the companies or the market growth slows or fails to meet expectations, capital can dry up quickly. This could stop build-out of new tower sites and leave independent EF&I tower suppliers with little or no business.

Saturation:

As noted above, the market for cellular tower sites is directly tied to the number of cell phone subscribers. Saturation of the cell phone user market is estimated to occur when 70 percent of the population is using cell phones, substantiated by the market saturation figures seen in Japan and western Europe. With only 28 percent of the U.S. market currently using cell phones, we could estimate the market saturation for the EF&I of cell towers by dividing 28 by 70, or about 40 percent as of February 2000.

Competitors:

The competitors in the EF&I market for wireless towers used in the cellular communications industry are broken down into three categories. First, we looked at the large independent competitors such as WFII, O2 Wireless, Lexent, and LCC International. These are well-capitalized public companies focused on providing EF&I services to this market. Then we looked at the second set of competitors: large engineering/project management firms such as Bechtel Telecommunications, Black & Veatch, General Dynamics, and Parsons Corporation that have telecommunication services divisions that address the EF&I market for cell tower sites. Third, we examined a large number of private, independent construction companies that focus primarily on regional market opportunities.

As we mentioned above, the tower real estate companies also provide these services as a captive supplier to the large wireless carriers as part of their build-to-suit programs. Although we found little public information available on the large engineering firm practices and the private, independent construction companies, we were able to study WFII, O2 Wireless, Lexent, and LCC International in some detail. Our first view of the competitive landscape is heavily reliant on information obtained from these competitors and we recognize that substantial additional research must be done on the other competitors to complete our understanding of the market battlefield. This is not unusual; often, our first attempt at defining the market battlefield is only a starting point for the *Quick*Strategy process. We will gather and refine competitor information every day, once we initiate the *Quick*Strategy process, to better understand and position our business for success.

WFII (Wireless Facilities, Inc.) was founded in early 1995 in San Diego, California for the purpose of planning, designing, deploying and managing wireless communications networks. They provide EF&I services to the wireless cell tower market along with a variety of other network services, including network management and design optimization services. However, the majority of their revenue is derived from directly competitive EF&I services related to cell tower construction.

Their revenue and net income growth have been spectacular over the last four years and includes five acquisitions:

WFII Financial Information ($000)

	1996	1997	1998	1999	2000 (est.)
Revenue	15,400	22,700	51,900	92,700	250,000
Net Income	6,700	6,800	4,700	9,600	32,000
Margin	43%	30%	9%	10%	13%

The 1999 revenues from design and deployment (what we described above as EF&I tower construction) were $86.8 million, or 94 percent of the $92.7 million in revenue that generated 92 percent of their profit. The balance of their revenue and profit came from network management ($4.5 million of revenue) and business consulting ($2.3 million of revenue). Only $61 million of the $92.7 million of revenue was generated in the U.S. market.

Based on this outstanding financial performance, they were able to raise $62 million (net of costs) in a public offering effective November 4, 1999. Their stock has traded in the $40 to $65 per share range or a 148 to 240 times multiple of fully diluted 1999 earnings per share. This high price to earnings ratio stock is very useful as consideration in acquiring additional businesses and a clear part of their growth strategy.

They describe their business as providing outsource services to the telecom industry to include the following:

- Pre-Deployment Planning Services where they profile and forecast subscriber usage in a target market and provide business and financial modeling.
- GIS analysis to analyze traffic patterns, population densities, topography and radio propagation environments.
- Design and Deployment Services to include Radio Frequency (RF) Engineering and Design, Microwave Relocation, Fixed Network Engineering to connect wireline service to towers, Site Development including leasing and permitting sites, and installation and equipment optimization services.

- Project Management to coordinate and direct all outsource services, a proprietary process.

They have more than 800 employees and 250 engineers (35 percent of whom have advanced degrees). Their personnel are qualified and approved to provide design and installation support by most wireless equipment vendors. The company has also demonstrated its customer loyalty with more than half of their customer services to repeat customers, with three customers accounting for 35 percent of its business.

Their customer list includes the following:

Major Carriers:
- AT&T Wireless
- Sprint
- Nextel
- US West

Tower Real Estate Companies:
- American Tower
- Crown Castle

Their strengths are their strong financial capability, experience with the major wireless carriers and real estate companies, and proven project management experience that assures effective cost control and ability to deliver services against a specific schedule. Their disadvantages are their limited geographic focus and dilution of resources into foreign markets.

O2 Wireless (O2 Wireless Solutions, Inc.) was founded in 1991 as American Communications Construction and changed to Clear Communications Group, Inc. in 1997 with the merger of several suppliers of wireless communication services. It has grown from $24 million to $48 million in revenue during the last year, primarily through acquisitions. Recently, it has changed its name to O2 Wireless Solutions, Inc. and initiated a public offering to raise $60 to $70 million to fund future growth in operating capital, pay down debt, and finance additional acquisitions.

The company claims to be a leader in providing "comprehensive integrated network solutions to all sectors of the wireless communication industry." It offers services to plan, design, deploy and maintain wireless networks. Most of its revenue comes from the designing and deployment of wireless networks—another way of describing the EF&I services previously identified as the target market products and services.

O2 Wireless completed more than 11,000 communications facilities in 1999 for more than 125 customers, with over 30 percent of this business with two customers. Their customers include large wireless carriers like Nextel, Sprint PCS, Bell Atlantic Mobile and Bell South. It has also done work for three of the wireless real estate companies: American Tower, Crown Castle, and Spectrasite.

With more than 500 employees and business distributed throughout the U.S. and many foreign countries, they claim to offer the following comprehensive list of services:

- Planning: from pre-deployment analysis, business consulting, competitor analysis, technology selection, usage forecasting and regulatory planning.
- Design Services: including traffic pattern analysis, population density analysis, topography and radio propagation studies, RF engineering and network design.
- Deployment Services: including zoning studies and permitting, lease negotiations, civil and structural engineering, third party management of construction and procurement, and licensing.
- Maintenance Services: including post-deployment RF signal optimization services, network operation and maintenance.

It manages these services with on-line monitoring of network development and project management. This enables the company to maintain control over a variety of projects throughout the world and keep their customers informed on a real-time basis of their progress.

However, their financial performance over the last four years has been less than spectacular:

O2 Wireless Financial Information ($000)

	1996	1997	1998	1999
Revenue	2,208	6,003	24,485	48,631
Operating Income	(856)	(1,360)	(1,471)	1,075
Margin	Neg.	Neg.	Neg.	2.2%

A more rigorous analysis indicates their gross margin (revenues less cost of sales divided by revenues) to be 20 to 27 percent versus 36 to 50 percent for American Tower. Furthermore, only $7.1 million of 1999 growth came from

82

internal development, the rest came from acquisitions. The company has proven its ability to grow the top line through acquisitions, but has not proven it can manage the business profitably. Its low gross margin on sales indicates it is either inefficient in managing projects or aggressive in pricing its services. The industry perceives the company as a low-cost provider.

Its competitive advantage is its established relationship with many of the major customers in this market, particularly in the southeast and mid-Atlantic states. It appears to be aggressively pricing its services, making them a low price competitor. With the funds raised in their IPO, they have the near-term ability to sustain their aggressive pricing and to initiate acquisitions to give them broader geographic coverage for their services.

Its competitive disadvantages include their lack of national coverage, although they say it has done business in all fifty states. Its other weaknesses include the loss of domestic resources to international business ventures.

LCC International of McLean, Virginia was started in 1983 and says it is "one of the world's largest independent providers of wireless network services." It provides "end-to-end solutions" for the wireless voice and data communications networks including high level technical consulting, system design and deployment, and ongoing operations and network management services. Although the company is an early entrant into this market, it has not experienced much growth through 1999. In fact, revenue declined during this time period from $93 million in 1996 to $73 million in 1999. With 71 percent of its business in the U.S. with customers like AT&T Wireless, Nextel Communications, Sprint PCS, and Verizon and business in over fifty countries internationally, you would expect to see some growth in revenue during the last four years as we know the industry has grown dramatically during this time period.

The company says that it is qualified in every major wireless technology, owning and operating one of the industry's premier training institutes, the "Wireless Institute." It says it is qualified with "almost" every equipment supplier to the industry.

LCC International offers consulting services that include developing new technology implementation strategies, preparing regulatory strategies, and conducting field trials and audits. It also offers design and development services that include site acquisition, RF engineering, fixed network engineering and construction management. It uses a web-integrated Network Deployment System to manage all phases of design and construction of their customers' networks. It also offers Operations Management Services where they assume all or part of the operations responsibility for their customers' wireless networks. This sounds a lot like the offering of the above competitors.

LCC International Financials ($000)

	1996	1997	1998	1999
Revenue	93,156	91,298	86,328	73,289
Net Income	(20,476)	6,938	(11,519)	(8,889)
Margin	Neg.	7.6%	Neg.	Neg.

Not only has it had declining revenues, but it has also lost money in three of the last four years. In addition, its gross profit margin was 33 percent in 1996, only 23 percent in 1998, and 28 percent in 1999. It attributes this decline to a more competitive market for tower construction, which constitutes more than 70 percent of revenue. In spite of the above performance, the company's stock is traded at a price ranging from $5.50 to $15.81 per share that values the shareholder equity at $82 million to $237 million.

The company's competitive advantage includes its training facility, knowledge of a wide range of wireless technologies, and established customer base. However, it appears to have a reputation for not finishing work on schedule and over-running jobs. As most of the work is fixed price to the buyers, this results in substantial losses to the company.

Lexent, Inc. appears to be a well-managed provider of outsourced local telecommunications network services for established and emerging communications companies, including competitive local exchange carriers, Internet service providers and wireless carriers. It primarily focuses on providing resources to design, build-out, upgrade, and maintain these customers' communications networks. It started in the New York City area focused on competitive local exchange carriers that were given conditional access to local telephone networks as part of the Telecommunications Act of 1996. It now operates in 15 major U.S. markets and has grown from $49 million in revenue in 1996 to $151 million in 1999. They are planning on a public offering in 2000 to raise $90 to $100 million for future growth. Although its primary business is in local network construction, it is named as a competitor by some of the wireless carrier EF&I tower companies and should be watched carefully because of their market presence, cost effective management, and ability to raise capital for market expansion. We estimate it has only about 10 percent of its 1999 revenue related to the wireless market build-out.

Lexent Inc. Financials ($000)

	1996	**1997**	**1998**	**1999**
Revenue	48,989	53,718	70,959	150,862
Net Income	3,952	2,189	3,828	7,952
Margin	8.1%	4.1%	5.4%	5.3%

Although only about 10 percent of its revenue is estimated to be derived from the wireless industry, it appears to be able to manage with enough discipline to generate 5 percent profits on gross margins of 20—21 percent. In this highly competitive market, that indicates an ability to operate at a very low overhead.

Competitive advantages for Lexent in the wireless market include its existing relationship with a wide number of customers in some of the major U.S. markets and their ability to deliver cost-effective services. Its disadvantage in the wireless market is the lack of a broad range of experience with wireless technologies.

Bechtel Telecommunications is part of the multi-billion engineering firm, Bechtel Corporation. Although it is not possible to obtain as much detailed information about Bechtel as with the stand-alone public companies competing in this market, we know it is a major competitor.

With more than 11,000 cell sites and associated facilities worldwide, it can deliver services with all of the latest wireless technologies. In the U.S., Bechtel seems to be most closely associated with AT&T Wireless Services, Inc. and responsible for directing the build-out of their next generation wireless network in fifty U.S. cities. This will involve the upgrade of over 15,000 cell sites throughout the AT&T Wireless network from 2000 to 2003, a three-year effort valued at nearly $3 billion. This effort will include the addition of some 8000 new cell sites and upgrading the rest of the AT&T Wireless network to 3G technology.

Its competitive advantage is its long-term relationship with AT&T and an ability to finance major construction projects; it has the resources to ensure completion on a timely basis. Its disadvantage is reported to be its high cost of operations that drives up customer prices.

Black and Veatch is a mega-engineering firm based in Overland Park, Kansas (next to Sprint PCS), which has set up a separate division to handle the wireless telecommunications market. It says that it is "leading the development of wireless networks by self-performing network design, equipment selection, site acquisition, engineering and construction, putting them on top of the wireless world." It has experience in providing next-generation technology migration, network optimization, and license saving solutions using a large number of equipment configurations. As a private company, little additional information is available on its activity in this market, although its size and ability to manage large projects are its advantages. By the same token, it carries the disadvantages of many large firms with relatively big overhead and high prices.

Parsons Corporation is one of the largest engineering firms in the world with more than 10,000 employees. It recently formed a separate subsidiary to address the needs of the telecommunications market, "Parsons Communications Group Inc." or PARCOMM. Located in Charlotte, North Carolina, this group has been identified by *Engineering News—Record* as one of the top design firms in the telecommunications industry with 1999 revenue exceeding $124 million.

It specializes in "planning, designing and constructing fiber-optic, copper and wireless networks and their associated Critical Mission Facilities." It maintains that e-business approach and web-centric tools reduce capital deployment costs and schedules while alleviating system outage worries. It has strategic alliances with 3G suppliers like Ericson to provide transition to broadband wireless service and has experience with AT&T, Bell South and Verizon.

It provides a full spectrum of wireless system design and deployment services including: Program and Project Management, Network Planning and RF Engineering, Site Acquisition, Supply Chain and Asset Management, Radio Site Construction Installation and Testing, Switch Site Installation and Testing and Network Maintenance. Their wireless system experience includes 2G, 2.5G, 3G, microwave, satellite and two-way radio systems. Its disadvantage is the lack of presence in the U.S. market (focus on international market) and its relatively high cost/price.

Competitor Summary

The primary competitors as summarized above include the larger suppliers specializing in EF&I services for cell site construction and maintenance. They range from very profitable public companies (WFII) with good gross profit margins of 36 to 50 percent, to less profitable independent suppliers like O2 Wireless with 20—27 percent gross profit margins and consistent losses at their bottom line. They have all been able to raise capital in the public markets, assuring their near-term viability as a competitor in this market.

The larger engineering firms take a piece of this market and are formidable competitors by virtue of their depth of engineering resources, long-term relationships with the large carriers, and ability to finance large projects. It is difficult to determine their profitability in the telecom market but likely that they command 2.5 to 3+ multipliers on their direct labor cost of services and build in a healthy 20—25 percent margin on materials they supply to their customers.

This competitive market landscape can be summarized in the following Market Battlefield Summary:

MARKET BATTLEFIELD SUMMARY   *QUICK*STRATEGY™   Form 1.0

1. Product or Service: Engineer, furnish and install wireless cell site towers for use in the cellular telephone industry. Including cell site selection, permitting, RF engineering, materials purchasing, testing and construction of complete systems in the U.S. Typical cell site EF&I services are $150K to $400K, average $250,000/site.	**2. Customers:** Primary customers are large wireless carriers: AT&T Wireless, Sprint PCS, Nextel, VoiceStream, Alltel and their affiliated regional telephone companies. Secondary customers are large wireless real estate companies: American Tower, Crown Castle, Spectrasite, SBA Communications, and Pinnacle Towers and small build-to-suit real estate companies.

3. Customer Need: Cost effective and timely build-out of wireless cell sites to meet FCC license requirements to serve 1/3 licensed area in 5 years and 2/3 in 10 years. Conversion to high reliability next generation digital wireless technology to enhance revenue through additional product/service offerings and enhance revenue per dollar of capital invested. Provide adequate system reliability to minimize churn and attract wireline customers. Needs driven by regulations and need for cost effective and reliable national cellular coverage.	**4. Market Shape:** Performance: Now Price within 3-5 yrs.

5. Market Alternatives: 1. Direct market alternatives include attaching cell site antennas to existing structures, such as buildings, power line towers, water towers, silos and existing microwave or radio towers (-). **2.** In-house EF&I capability within major wireless carriers and wireless real estate companies (-).	**6. Saturation:** Based on industry estimates, only 28% of the U.S. population out of a possible 70% is using cell phones: **40% saturation**

7. Externalities: 1. Limited availability of FCC licenses (-). **2.** Technology upgrades to 2.5G and 3G require closer cell spacing (+) but take capital away from wireless cell sites (-). **3.** Availability of third party financing of wireless build-out (+/-). **4.** Merger of wireless carriers may reduce the number of antennas needed (-), but is limited by differences in communication technologies used by carriers (+).	This would indicate as much as $15 billion could be spent on new cell site construction in the next 5—7 years. However, this market build-out will end once national coverage is established.

8. Competitors	Strengths	Weaknesses	Sales $(000) Last Yr./This Yr.	Share (%)
Wireless Facilities, Inc. (WFII) San Diego, CA (BUILD)	1. Full planning to acceptance testing capability; 800 employees, 250 engineers. 2. Established track record, proven performance. 3. Strong positive cash position to finance job. 4. Customer and vendor qualified.	1. Limited geographic presence. 2. Loss of key resources to international market.	$61,000/150,000	3.9
O2 Wireless Solutions, Inc. Atlanta, GA (BUILD)	1. Total solution from planning to acceptance testing. 2. Customer and vendor qualified. 3. 500 plus employees. 4. Strong cash position to finance work, pending IPO. 5. Low price.	1. Poor financial history, lost money on fixed price jobs. 2. Some customers report slow delivery.	$48,000/80,000	3.1
LCC International, Inc. McLean, VA (BUILD)	1. Provides "end-to-end solutions" to wireless build out. 2. Customer and vendor qualified. 3. Leading wireless training institute.	1. Service quality problems, reducing repeat business. 2. Weak cash position from opening losses will limit growth.	$73,000/80,000	4.7
Bechtel Telecom. U.S. (HOLD)	1. Broad base of experience, completed over 11,000 cell sites, total service provider. 2. Principal contractor to AT&T Wireless with $3B contract. 3. Customer and vendor qualified. 4. Project financing.	1. Identified by industry as AT&T captive supplier. 2. High cost. 3. No interest in small jobs.	$500,000/1,000,000	32.3
1. Black & Veatch 2. Parsons Comm. 3. General Dynamics	1. Total service provider. 2. Broad established customer base. 3. Project financing available. 4. Customer and vendor qualified.	1. High cost. 2. Lack of interest in small jobs.	$560,000/1,000,000	36.1
Other Independent EF&I Suppliers	1. Focus on regional jobs, lower prices.	1. Lack of financial strength.	$250,000/500,000	16.2
Georgia Wireless Atlanta, Georgia (*added later*)	1. Good industry reputation (Sprint affiliates). 2. Customer and vendor qualified. 3. Low price.	1. Lack of financial strength.	$22,000/58,000	3.7

9. Market Size (Sales Revenue $000)						**Total $ Mil.**	1,514/2,870	100

Year-5	Year-4	Year-3	Year-2	Last Year	This Year	Year 2	Year 3	Year 4	Year 5
				1,514,000	2,868,000				

10. Market Maturity GROWTH Stage

Strategic Business Unit: Wireless Telecom, EF&I Services	Plan Manager: Rhett Diener	Date Prepared: March 5, 2003
Company: Georgia Wireless Constructors	Strategy Advisor: B. Robinson	Date of Next Plan Review:

In less than a week, I had a reasonably good perspective on the market battlefield for wireless cell site EF&I services and was able to summarize my findings in the above MARKET BATTLEFIELD SUMMARY. Although far from complete and subject to continuous change in characteristics, I could now look at acquisitions for my client in the context of the competitive market environment. This is a critical first step in determining if there is a strategic opportunity for acquisition candidates to grow or sustain their market position and profitability.

I no sooner finished the Market Battlefield Summary than Tim Murphy called me to visit him in New York for a look at several new acquisition proposals. I left the next day and headed directly to their midtown office for a briefing.

On arrival, I was led to their conference room where I met Tim and his staff. I handed each of them a copy of the Market Battlefield Summary for Wireless Telecom EF&I Services. They wanted to know what I thought after my brief analysis of the market. I started by showing them that the market for the services was well defined.

The customers are looking for turnkey providers of services that include cell site selection, permitting, RF engineering, materials management, testing and construction of complete cell sites. Each site was expected to cost on the average of $250,000, including all of the above services and the hardware and equipment. There were as many as 60,000 sites yet to be built in the United States.

The primary customers were the large wireless carriers formed to build out the wireless networks in the United States and included AT&T Wireless, Sprint PCS, Nextel, VoiceStream, Verizon, Cingular, Alltel and many regional telephone company affiliates. I told them that the carriers had decided to offload many of their cell sites to five wireless tower real estate companies in an auction process that left these buyers with overpriced inventory and the carriers with favorable lease arrangements. Few, if any, of the customers for new cell site construction were making any money and they were very dependent on continued financing from third parties to sustain the growth in this market.

The cell tower customers' needs were critical in the near term, as their FCC licenses required them to build out the areas covered by their licenses on a set schedule or lose rights under the license. Most of these customers were also losing a lot of money because of cell phone user dissatisfaction that created churn in the market when cell coverage was inadequate or intermittent because of a lack of cell site coverage. They were also driven to implement next-generation technologies to improve their competitive position and to improve their reliability, with national coverage thought to give the leaders overwhelming advantage over local carriers.

The suppliers of these services are faced with market alternatives to building new structures in the form of existing structures, but that is not the major market alternative to be concerned about in the growth opportunity for independent cell site services. The tower real estate companies were rapidly building their in-house competitive EF&I capabilities and they had locked up rights to build out major portions of the carriers' wireless networks at the time they acquired existing sites from the carriers. Unless the tower real estate companies did not have in-house capacity to build out carriers' new service areas, there would be less business spilling over to the independent cell site services companies. We should be looking for acquisition candidates that can deal with this eventuality.

The market is now impacted by a number of external factors affecting the size of the market and rate of growth. First is the freeze on new tower construction in many high-density population areas because the local populace feels they are unsightly and, in some cases, unsafe. The second is the limited availability of FCC radio licenses and failure of some licensees to be able to finance build-out of cell sites under their licenses. The lack of third party financing and a decline in the stock market could severely reduce market opportunity. A merger of wireless carriers, although limited by technology differences, could reduce opportunities as the merged companies would not need separate cell site antennas in many areas.

The market is only about 40 percent saturated. The industry will have to spend about $15 billion in additional cell sites to obtain complete coverage and meet the needs of the 200 million cell phone users forecasted to occur in the next five to seven years.

The competitors can be broken down into three categories:

1. Public independent wireless cell site EF&I suppliers like WFII, O2 Wireless, and LCC International;
2. Large engineering firms like Bechtel, Black and Veatch, and Parsons; and
3. Other independent suppliers that would be the hunting ground for acquisition candidates in this market.

The differences between the various competitors in terms of market strengths and weaknesses seem minimal, at best, but the difference in financial performance among the three leading public independent wireless cell site EF&I suppliers indicate there is real opportunity for those competitors who supply services on a timely basis against fixed price contract commitments and those who do not. I explained that WFII was consistently profitable and growing revenue in excess of 20 percent per year. While O2 Wireless was growing largely through acquisitions, it was, nevertheless, losing money most years; still, it will be well capitalized through a pending IPO. LCC International is the oldest competitor in this market, had declining sales for the past four years, and lost money in the last two years. This should make my client look very carefully at acquisition candidates' competitive advantages that can be leveraged into profitable growth.

The big engineering firms with revenue in excess of $1 billion and major positions in the market seemed to be tightly aligned with the major carriers and depend on their long-term relationships, financing capabilities, and depth of resources to lock down big long-term contracts with these customers. Bechtel, for example, just signed a $3 billion contract with AT&T Wireless for 3G build-out. They leave no room for a small independent supplier of these services to operate. Fortunately, these larger engineering firms seem to have a higher cost structure and avoid the smaller jobs, leaving a window of opportunity for smaller competitors.

The market is clearly in a growth phase of market maturity with growth in excess of 90 percent for the last few years and forecast to exceed 25 percent over the next four years. However, there are market alternatives, externalities and saturation issues that can change the forecasted growth very rapidly and should be monitored as part of our ongoing assessment of the market.

Acquisition Opportunities

Tim thanked me for the overview and the Market Battlefield Summary. In light of this analysis, we started a review of three prospective acquisition candidates.

The first of these candidates was a Houston-based company that specialized in site survey permitting services for cell sites in the southwest. It had $23 million in revenue last year but had grown from $7 million in the prior year and forecast $40 million in revenue this year. Its customers were largely small wireless real estate companies and I doubted its ability to continually grow this fast as most of their customers could obtain turnkey services from the larger service providers for all phases of their needs. It would most likely be acquired by one of the existing providers to expand its market share in the southwest.

The next candidate was a Minnesota-based supplier who specialized in building out microwave towers used to backhaul wireless data for some of the major carriers and was sure it could bid its way into the wireless cell site market as it had most of the technical expertise required to penetrate this market. We all agreed that the risk of a new market entrant was too high with the number of proven and qualified suppliers already competing in this market.

The last candidate we reviewed was Georgia Wireless Constructors, based in suburban Atlanta, Georgia and a well-known independent supplier of services into our target market. They had been in the market for six years, having been formed by engineers out of one of the major wireless carriers. It had a very good reputation in the industry and had grown profitably each year with a forecast of $48 million in revenue for 2000. This, we all agreed, should be the focus of our efforts to determine if there was a strategic opportunity to invest in the wireless telecom EF&I services market. I was to fly immediately to Atlanta to meet with the principal shareholder, Rhett Diener, the next morning.

First Visit to Georgia Wireless Constructors

I arrived in Atlanta late Tuesday night and took a taxi to the Ritz Carlton north of Atlanta in the Buckhead area about ten minutes from the offices of Georgia Wireless Constructors (GWC). In the morning, Rhett, the owner, met me in the hotel dining room for breakfast. He was about six foot four, in his late 30's, and obviously an athlete. Early in our discussions, I found he had played college football and graduated from Georgia Tech with a degree in civil engineering. A warm and friendly person, I could see how he would be effective in building relationships with his customers and employees; he was hard not to like.

He was quick to tell me how he was being pursued by O2 Wireless, a local public company with high-priced stock. It was only willing to do a pooling of interest transaction, an all-stock deal, but he was interested in cash. He also told me that his company was quoting more work than they could possibly perform, but he felt it necessary to bid aggressively to develop the market while it was growing. I asked if he had any particular customers that he thought presented the best business opportunity for his business.

He was quick to point out that his relationship with some of the southern wireless carriers was particularly close and they made sure he had a shot at each of their bid requests. He went on to tell me that he thought the Sprint affiliate companies were particularly good customers as they were not wrapped up with one of the big engineering firms with which he competes. It sounded to me like he had a sense for competitive positioning and had been successful in establishing his business based on meeting his commitments to smaller local customers and maintaining a preferred relationship with them through regular personal contacts.

I asked him why he wanted to sell. He told me he was being pursued by several competitors as mentioned previously and that he wanted to capitalize on the hard work he had put into his business over the last six years. He felt that the industry would consolidate into three or four large public companies providing EF&I services to the telecom industry and he wanted to be part of the consolidation process. He further stated that he was concerned about his ability to finance the rapid rate of growth that he saw happening in the current year.

We left for Rhett's office in a small office park a few minutes' drive from the hotel (in his M5 BMW) to begin serious discussions about the nature of his business. On the way to his office, I explained to him that I was hired to provide the New York investment group a quick evaluation of the strategic opportunity his business represented as part of a consolidation play they wanted to make in the telecom services market. He was interested in participating, but did not insist on leading the consolidation; he was perfectly willing to work for someone else who wanted to lead the consolidation activity.

GWC's office was a typical engineering and administrative office area of about 4,000 square feet with window offices for the officers and cubicles for the staff. The staff included sales, accounting, human resources, purchasing, quoting, engineering and project managing personnel with a PC on every desk tied to their central server. It also included a large conference room and a training facility. Outside at another facility, they housed their trucks and materials staged for transfer to job sites as required by their field construction sites.

I explained to Rhett that I was new to this market. When I studied communications technology in my engineering college days, we used vacuum tubes and relay switches; he should talk slowly and not overwhelm me with the latest technical acronyms. I also explained my attempt to describe the market to the investor group. I would like to see how his business would be positioned within the Market Battlefield framework I had developed to describe what we hoped would be a sustainable business strategy in this market. This strategic plan would form the basis for valuing his business.

First, I asked him to describe the nature of the services he provided to his customers. He said they were the best tower constructors in the cell phone marketplace. They could evaluate new cell sites with the help of a subcontractor RF engineering firm, select the best equipment, obtain the necessary local construction permits, design the tower platform and facilities, acquire the tower (he was close to several tower construction companies), subcontract the tower erection to an affiliated company, complete the installation of radios and antennas, fire up the equipment, and verify its operation to the customers' requirements. They could also perform upgrade services on existing towers to accommodate 2.5G and 3G technologies. I asked him why he did not have in-house RF engineering capability. He told me he could hire these services from firms specializing in this business, but if we were to acquire an RF engineering business it would help him compete with his larger competitors. I then asked him why he did not erect and climb the towers. He explained that the employee insurance costs for tower climbers made this part of the business marginally profitable and could pose financial risk in excess of insurance coverage.

GWC was able to quote competitive prices for new cell tower construction with the use of outside RF engineering and tower climbers while focusing on the aspects of the EF&I work that GWC could most effectively perform for their customers. Rhett told me that a good job for them was 10 to 30 towers in the range of $200,000 to $300,000 per tower. They were expected to quote fixed price on the $2 million to $9 million contracts and would typically mark up their direct labor by a factor of 1.8 to 2.1, then get 20—30 percent markup on subcontracted services or purchased materials. He had a special arrangement with a number of equipment suppliers, including tower and radio equipment suppliers that gave them good discounts from their list prices. These arrangements were critical to obtaining the equipment markups and let him underbid many of the smaller competitors.

I then asked Rhett about his customers. They were a variety of customers from small independent build-to-suit tower real estate companies to large tower real estate companies. They included several large Sprint affiliates but only the local wireless carriers like Bell South and Alltel. As he had started his career as a Bell South engineer, he explained that he had a lot of good connections with their wireless construction personnel and managers.

When I asked how they obtained sales leads, he told me it was by word of mouth and personal contacts. He and his two lead field sales managers knew most of the customers through years of personal affiliations and they were trusted to perform to the level of customer expectations. He digressed for a while to tell me how he had lost money on jobs that turned out to be more difficult to site than they projected in their estimates; however, he felt his personal commitment to his customers and reputation made it necessary to satisfy his customers' requirements as quoted. He explained that the wireless market is a small community and failure to perform will give you a bad reputation that will destroy future opportunities for your business. They attended the annual Tower Conference in Las Vegas and had a booth manned by his engineers and sales personnel where they met new customers and established their market presence. They also entertained their smaller customers whenever possible with dinner, Georgia hunting and fishing weekends, and occasional ski trips to his condo in Idaho. This was a business built on service and personal commitment to customers and he was a respected and trusted provider of these services.

When I asked him to break down last year's sales by customer, he studied his sales information for a few minutes and then gave me the following breakdown:

- Small independent tower real estate companies: 17 percent
- Large tower real estate companies: 22 percent
- Sprint affiliates: 36 percent
- Local large wireless and wireline carriers: 18 percent
- Others: 7 percent

His fastest growing business was with the Sprint affiliates and he expected they would exceed 50 percent of his business in the current year.

I then asked him whether he had concerns about his customers competing against him with in-house services, particularly the large tower real estate companies. He explained that one of his largest tower real estate customers had recently acquired an EF&I services company and was "hell bent" on keeping it busy and profitable. He expected he would lose business to their subsidiary in the next year. I told him this was a market alternative I was particularly concerned about as I knew the tower real estate companies were locking up future build-out sites from the major carriers as part of their cell site purchase and lease-back program.

We then talked about the things outside his market that could influence his growth opportunities (externalities). He mentioned the way the FCC managed the licensing process created delays in getting many areas of the country built out, as they would auction off licenses to companies without the financial capacity to immediately start building out their territories. He also mentioned the difficulty they were having getting local zoning boards to approve tower sites in some areas. This was a problem driven by both the "good taste" committees in densely populated areas and environmental groups in more rural areas.

I asked Rhett if he was concerned about the lack of profitability with any of his customers. He did not think a lot about this as many of them had recently raised enough cash to meet their near-term needs and the market for their stocks was at an all-time high. He did indicate that most of his customers were slow in paying for his services, taking 90 to 120 days from date of invoice to pay him. This delay increased his working capital requirement as he grew the business and was a factor in his decision to sell.

I asked him about market saturation for cell sites. He did not see that happening for seven to ten years; however, he was actively seeking opportunities to build maintenance and support service capability for existing cell sites to sustain his business after the current build-out cycle was completed. He thought we should purchase a group of small local service companies throughout the country to facilitate this activity. Furthermore, he thought changes in technology would occur every five years that would require continuous improvements to existing cell sites. When I asked him whether industry consolidation among the major wireless carriers would threaten his market, he stated that most of the wireless carriers were using different technology and that consolidation would be very difficult, if not totally impractical, to implement without advances in switching technology.

Rhett acknowledged that the competition was becoming aggressive. He said there were few jobs bid by fewer than three competitors. For his type of work, he was most effective close to his home base, as he did not have to pay field employees per diem in addition to their wages and benefits. He did have ongoing work in the Midwest that permitted him to hire local employees for the field work and build around their capabilities. His largest competitor was O2 Wireless, followed by LCC International and a wide variety of small regional providers. Often, the customers would only contract out a portion of the EF&I work such as tower siting, tower construction, or radio upgrades. This would permit smaller firms that specialize in these capabilities to be more cost effective than GWC. They preferred to take work that included the entire build-out activity for a number of cell sites or an entire wireless network. They seldom competed directly with the large engineering firms, but had bid subcontract work to these firms in their local market. He felt they always had to compete on price, but often the market was driven by a shortage of available personnel to perform the work against the customer's tight time frame. He pointed out that this was driven by the carrier's procrastination to award work until they were up against a tight regulatory time limit and then needed everything completed at once.

Rhett felt the market was in a very good growth mode and would continue to grow for the next 5 to 10 years at rates in excess of 20 percent. He felt his growth from $22 million in revenue last year to $58 million this year was "in the bag" and he would achieve at least 10 percent EBITDA (earnings before interest, taxes, depreciation and amortization). He further declared GWC could compete against any of the major EF&I companies based on their vendor and customer qualifications, industry reputation and low overhead operation.

I left my initial meeting with Rhett with the following questions:

- Was there a clear regional strategic opportunity as costs should be lower with local resources?
- Was there a strategic opportunity with the affiliates of the major carriers for medium-size EF&I suppliers that was below the radar of the large engineering firms?
- Which of his customers should we target for future growth?
- Which of his competitors should we target for future growth?
- Was it possible to build a support and maintenance operation in parallel with the EF&I activity that provided a more stable base of revenue?
- Which of his customers were least susceptible to a decline in third party financing and/or merger?

I would need to go back to the market and spend more time with Rhett to answer these questions, but I could see how Georgia Wireless Constructors could be strategically advantaged and a viable acquisition candidate as it may be able to meet the growth and profit objectives of the New York investment group. Furthermore, I felt they were worthy of additional time to develop a strategic plan and forecast to be used by the New York investment group in valuing the business.

Developing the GWC Strategic Plan

A few days later, Rhett called and said he was planning to ski Taos in northern New Mexico and asked if I wanted to join his group. I told him I was an intermediate skier, at best, and that Taos was oriented toward advanced skiers and athletes like him. However, I suggested he visit me for a day in Albuquerque on his way to Taos and we could complete a *Quick*Strategy Strategic Plan Summary for the New York investment group to use as part of their investment analysis. He agreed to meet and give me a full day to complete the Strategic Plan.

I met him at Albuquerque's "SunPort" air terminal on a Thursday afternoon in February and took him to dinner at Geronimo's in Santa Fe, as he loved good southwestern food. He told me he read my book <u>Strategic Acquisitions</u>◆ that contains instructions on developing a strategic plan and thought about the material we would need to develop a strategic plan for his business that would support a financial forecast. We talked about which competitors he took business from and which competitors he never encountered. We talked about his strategic objective to be the lowest cost competitor in the eastern half of the U.S. in the EF&I market and capture over half the available market. We also talked about his longer-term objective of building a strong aftermarket support team that would service and maintain cell cites for his customers. He described his strategy as a "build" strategy in a growing market and was confident he had five years of market growth opportunity. We agreed to meet at my office early the next morning to summarize his strategy and to work on the detailed tactics he would employ to accomplish his strategic objectives.

The next morning at 8:30 A.M., I met Rhett in my Albuquerque office. I had copied the one-page *Quick*Strategy Strategic Plan Summary Form 2.0 and we used it as a guide to document his business strategy for GWC. I found Rhett had a clear strategic vision for his company and we should be able to complete our plan in time for him to drive to Taos by Friday afternoon to begin his skiing weekend.

We first reviewed the Market Battlefield Summary (*Quick*Strategy™ Form 1.0) I had prepared for the investment group and he made a few minor changes based on his first-hand knowledge of the market. He agreed on the

---

◆ <u>Strategic Acquisitions, A Guide to Growing and Enhancing the Value of Your Business</u>. Irwin, 1995, Bruce R. Robinson/Walter Peterson.

product and service description, but thought the regional telephone companies that affiliated with the major wireless carriers should be a separate set of customers as they had somewhat different requirements than the large carriers. He also pointed out that he only competed in the U.S. market and we should limit our customer definition accordingly. He thought that the market shape was more price driven and would be more so in the near future.

He expressed a real concern about the in-house EF&I capability at the tower real estate companies as he said they were in desperate need to cover their losses on cell tower rentals. He agreed on the way we estimated market saturation, but felt our estimate of annual spending on new cell towers was too low. The externalities we identified also concerned him, particularly the lack of profits in most of the industry.

He said that the major carriers could not stop the build-out or conversion to next-generation technology or they would lose market share to their competitors. We then focused on his competitors to establish the basis for understanding his market driven strategy.

Target Competitors

Rhett was quick to point out that he could never compete with the big A&E firms like Bechtel, Black & Veatch, and Parsons. They would always take the large contracts from the major carriers as they had the financial capacity to build out and finance billion dollar networks that smaller suppliers like GWC could never be able to match. He focused his competitive strategy on O2 Wireless, LCC International and several smaller regional suppliers of EF&I services.

Starting with O2 Wireless, he felt he had a more disciplined approach to project management and job costing that gave him the ability to underbid O2 Wireless and still make a good profit margin. However, he also said he had lost business to O2 Wireless when they underestimated job costs. After their IPO, he felt they could not continue to bid jobs at a loss or even low margins and this would give him a consistent price advantage. He also felt he had a better reputation for meeting delivery deadlines than O2 Wireless; however, he acknowledged their ability to provide a comprehensive solution, including RF engineering and tower erection, that some customers may feel gives them more control over contract management. They also had a larger number of employees and could deploy large field teams to take on larger contracts than GWC.

LCC International was his next target competitor. Rhett pointed out that it had declining market share, mostly because of its reputation in the industry for missing deadlines. Moreover, it seemed as if LCC International lost money on most jobs. Although it was qualified by many customers in the area and most vendors, it was perceived as a company that had trouble executing jobs. Rhett was confident that had been a factor in the company's declining revenue and profits and he would continue to focus on their weakness in project and cost management. He recognized it had an ability to train people to work in the industry and contacts with all of the major customers, and he could never ignore their attempts to "low ball" business to keep their doors open.

Rhett was also confident he could continue to share work with small independent EF&I suppliers who worked with regional telephone company affiliates. He was respected by them as a trusted larger supplier who could bring powerful project management and field support capabilities to their business on joint ventures. He felt neither O2 Wireless or LCC International was able to instill the same level of trust and respect in these smaller local suppliers, who often had the low-cost local resources and relationships necessary to win contracts with the regional telephone companies' affiliates. Owners of many of these small EF&I companies enjoyed Rhett's hospitality at his fishing and hunting lodge and ski condo. Rhett felt he could roll many of these smaller EF&I companies into his business with the right financial backing.

Strategic Objective

Rhett felt he could increase his current market share in the east of the Mississippi market from five percent to ten percent within the next two years and twenty percent with acquisitions of smaller regional EF&I suppliers, accomplished while maintaining his current ten percent EBITDA margin on revenue and spending no more than five times EBITDA for each acquisition. A BUILD strategy is the type of strategy to be implemented, as the objective is to build market share.

Strategic Plan

His strategic plan had two components: he would build market share against O2 Wireless and LCC International by continuously improving his superior project management capabilities and reduce costs, enabling him to bid below them in their markets. He would overcome his shortfall in personnel by subcontracting to smaller suppliers in the near term and build his staff as new work permitted. He would build his presence in the rest of the market by acquiring those smaller EF&I companies that would give him a stronger presence with regional telephone companies affiliated with the major carriers.

Tactical Plan

How he would implement his strategy was the essence of his tactical plan. I asked Rhett to identify the actions he would take during the next year to implement his strategic plan:

1. Upgrade his project management system by adding an online project management center for each customer. That would cost $125,000 and would take four months to complete. This will reduce project costs and let him maintain tighter management control over contracts while giving customers continuous status reports. Responsible manager: B.B.
2. Reduce overhead by setting minimum billability requirements on all direct employees. Time to complete: two months; responsible manager: R.D.
3. Eliminate internal overhead function by contracting out administrative services: payroll, benefits management, and insurance to Administaff; accounting to local accounting firm. This would allow costs to be variable with fluctuations in business. Costs: $42,000 severance and transfer costs. Time to complete: three months; responsible manager: R.D.
4. Initiate acquisition program of selected regional EF&I suppliers to build additional $100 million revenue base. Estimated cost: $50 million over two years; responsible manager: R.D.

Given the appetite for acquisitions by the New York investors, his plan should put more emphasis on an acquisition program. He should also identify in the near future the specific acquisition targets, their size, and market position in order to add credibility to this approach to building market share.

History and Projections

We talked about the historical market size in his target market (east of the Mississippi) as about 65 percent of the U.S. market and growing at the same rate as the overall market. I questioned whether the large eastern metropolitan areas were ahead of the more rural areas of the market in percent build-out of cell sites. He said he would get some market data on this subject, but noted that most of the future market build-out would be outside the major metropolitan areas, based on population density, so we could easily verify this assumption. He felt comfortable targeting a 20 percent market share of his target market, assuming he could complete the acquisitions on a timely basis. He would maintain his ten percent EBITDA numbers throughout the forecast period and estimated his required capital investment (trucks, trailers, and tower installation and maintenance equipment) over the forecast period based on historical costs.

We filled in the Strategic Plan Summary as shown below and Rhett was able to leave by 2:00 P.M. for his drive to Taos.

STRATEGIC PLAN SUMMARY   *QUICK*STRATEGY™   Form 2.0

11. Your STRENGTHS vs. Competitor or Market Alternative	12. Your WEAKNESSES vs. Competitor or Market Alternative
O2 Wireless: 1. Lower cost/price on services 2. Better on-time delivery/project management	**O2 Wireless:** 1. Lack of total in-house EF&I services 2. Unable to finance or staff large jobs
LCC International: 1. Better on-time delivery/project management 2. Better reputation for product quality/delivery	**LCC International:** 1. No established mid-Atlantic work force 2. No technical training school 3. Not qualified by as many suppliers

13. Strategic Objective:

    Increase market share for EF&I cellular tower services in east of Mississippi U.S. market from 5% to 10% through internal growth over next two years while maintaining at least 10% EBITDA on operations. Increase market share to 20% over next two years with acquisition of small regional EF&I suppliers with strong regional telephone company presence, paying a maximum of 5 times EBITDA.

14. Type of Strategic Initiative: Build—

15. Strategic Plan:

    Take advantage of lower costs and better project management skills that permit lower pricing and better on-time delivery to take market share from major east coast competitors, O2 Wireless and LCC International. Build and defend strategic advantages through continuous reduction in costs and improvements in project management systems. Partner with or acquire small regional suppliers to establish local presence, lower cost support for regional telephone companies in affiliate programs with major wireless carriers.

16. Tactical Plan:

1. Upgrade project management system, adding field accessible on-line project management center for each customer to reduce cost, provide real time customer support, and status information by 06/30/00. Cost: $125,000, Responsible manager: B.B.
2. Reduce overhead by reducing unbilled hours on direct labor. Improve employee scheduling, bill for contract delays, and set minimum billability requirements on all direct labor by 06/06/00. Cost: $10,000, Responsible manager: R.D.
3. Reduce costs by eliminating internal administrative overhead, contracting out payroll, benefits management, and insurance to Administaff Services, and accounting to local independent accounting firm by 09/30/00. Cost: $40,000, Responsible manager: R.D.
4. Initiate acquisition program (after securing financing) targeting selected regional EF&I suppliers to build additional $100 million in revenue over 2 years. Estimated financing required: $50 million, Responsible manager: R.D.

17. History & Projections (performance measures)	Year-4 $(000)	Year-3 $(000)	Year-2 $(000)	Last Year $(000)	This Year $(000)	Next Year $(000)	Year 3 $(000)
Eastern U.S. Market	520,000	650,000	780,000	960,000	1,300,000	1,600,000	1,950,000
Market Share	1.15%	1.8%	2.0%	2.3%	4.5%	10%	22%
Revenue	6,000	12,000	16,000	22,000	58,000	160,000	195,000
EBITDA	350	1,050	(100)	2,060	5,800	16,000	19,500
EBITDA margin	5.8%	8.75%	0%	9.4%	10%	10%	10%

Strategic Business Unit: Wireless Telecom EF&I Services	Plan Manager: Rhett Diener	Date Prepared: March 16, 2000
Company: Georgia Wireless Constructors	Strategy Advisor: Bruce Robinson	Date of Next Plan Review: May 15, 2000

Summary

I modified the Market Battlefield plan to reflect Rhett's input and sent it along with his Strategic Plan Summary to my client with the following summary thoughts:

There are significant market risks that can impact this investment. Rhett and the investors should detail how they can minimize those risks with shifts in strategy should they occur. For example:

1. In a stock market decline, for reasons outside the cellular market, the investors may run from further investment in cellular carriers and tower companies that may not be profitable for another three to five years. In a down stock market, investors move to shorter terms and more secure returns. Lack of new investment will bring build-out of new cell towers to a screeching halt.
2. Technology upgrades to next-generation technologies may go on from 3G to 4G to 5G, taking money from new tower build-out to fund new technology deployment on old towers. New technology can even reduce the number of required towers by permitting more traffic per antenna or greater range.
3. Resistance to new cell towers by local zoning agencies and environmentalists may slow down tower deployment.
4. Continued growth of in-house EF&I capability by carriers and tower real estate companies could significantly reduce GWC's market opportunity.

We need to continuously monitor these externalities along with the shifts in competitor positions as they react to GWC's strategic initiatives in order to make changes in strategy and tactics to respond appropriately.

On the upside, we need to stay aware of the positive characteristics of this opportunity:

1. The expansion of local affiliate programs to regional telephone companies can represent a good niche opportunity for GWC if they partner or acquire a local EF&I support capability.
2. The rate of growth in cell phone usage, churn, and new users has to be monitored for any change in trend. A more rapid rate of growth in users will drive new site construction.

3. GWC is focused on reducing costs and competing on price. As the market matures, this will be critical to sustain their market position. The investor group must do a careful financial review of GWC to determine if these cost reductions can be achieved.

Rhett has based much of his success on his personal relationships with customers and suppliers. He can charm customers, vendors and, given the opportunity, New York investors. Keeping him involved and motivated is critical to implementing the above strategy. The investors must decide if he can sustain his personal influence and commitment to implementing his strategic plan as the business doubles or triples in size.

The Strategic Plan and Market Battlefield Plan must be looked at as a starting point for understanding this business opportunity. Only as the underlying data is verified by contact with customers, suppliers and industry analysts will it gain credibility. These plans will be in continuous flux as the cellular market is changing rapidly. Daily changes in market alternatives, externalities, and competitors must be monitored and reflected against the underlying plan assumptions to determine the viability of forecasted performance of Georgia Wireless Constructors.

This leads to the inevitable list of open issues to be contemplated in the ongoing analysis of GWC's market and strategic plan.

Open Issues:

1. Will Rhett stay with the business once it is sold and he has put millions of dollars in his pocket?
2. Will the tower real estate companies squeeze out the independent tower EF&I suppliers?
3. Will 2.5G and 3G increase the number of users per antenna at each cell site and/or reduce the number of towers required in the future?
4. Will the FCC force release of cell site licenses that are tied up in bankruptcy court, causing a very rapid increase in EF&I demand?
5. Can GWC really build a service and maintenance business or do they look at a market that dies in four to seven years when all cell sites are built-out?

6. Should GWC look to emerging third world opportunities instead of limiting their market to east of the Mississippi in the U.S.?
7. Is GWC developing and training adequately skilled labor to support growth in revenue?

Bruce R. Robinson

108

Chapter 3

CASE #3:
Eclipse 500♦, Personal Jet

In the late 1990's, Vern Raburn, founder of Eclipse Aviation and ex-Microsoft employee, had a vision that he could make a quantum leap forward in air transportation by using aggressive engineering, manufacturing, and marketing techniques from the computer industry. He envisioned a next-generation small jet aircraft—the Eclipse 500—that would carry five to six people at speeds in excess of 400 miles per hour at an operating cost of 50 cents per mile and be easy and safe enough for private general aviation pilots to operate. He would use state-of-the-art manufacturing techniques and modern electronics and plan to sell more than 1,000 units per year by pricing each aircraft below $1,000,000. As a private pilot, I recognized the revolutionary impact this could have on air charter/taxi operations, general aviation and business aviation. If successful, the Eclipse 500 could revolutionize the way we travel. As an Albuquerque-based business, this could also have a major effect on our local economy. With great enthusiasm, I visited the factory and watched the product take shape through its maiden voyage in mid 2002. Could this revolutionary new product from a start-up company succeed? Who would buy this new aircraft? What market alternatives would be the source of air taxi passengers and buyers? Will there be adequate air traffic infrastructure to manage a large number of small jet-powered aircraft? Will there be enough pilots that are qualified to fly these sophisticated aircraft? Is there a well-defined market battlefield and a clear strategic opportunity? First, I decided to look at the current aviation market in order to understand the basis for the Eclipse Aviation strategy.

♦ Eclipse and Eclipse 500 are registered trademarks of Eclipse Aviation.

Aviation Market Background

The market for commercial aircraft can be divided into four categories based on the aircraft size, speed and customer application: Commercial Airline Aircraft, Charter Aircraft, Business/Corporate Aircraft and General Aviation Aircraft[*].

The current aviation market is dominated by *large commercial airline operations* like American, United, Delta, Continental, Northwest and Southwest Airlines. In the U.S., they fly more than 1.3 million people each day in large and medium-size multi-engine aircraft. In 2002, they operated 5,156 passenger jet aircraft, with new aircraft added primarily in the two-engine large wide-body aircraft (16) and medium-size regional jets (194). Typically, passengers pay an average of 12 cents per passenger flight mile with actual prices depending on their ability to outwit the complex airline pricing system. (If I try to book one day in advance from Albuquerque to Denver on United Airlines, I may pay up to three times the average price per passenger mile.) With Internet booking, the passengers must be winning this battle of wits as only Southwest Airlines was profitable in the last year and the average price per mile has dropped nearly 20 percent in the last two years.

The next category in the aviation market is *charter aircraft* (air taxis). Most charter or air taxi aircraft are smaller aircraft than the commercial airline aircraft and are flown under special (Part 135) FAA rules. They are often referred to as Part 135 operations. (Note, however, that you can charter any size aircraft up to a four-engine jet.) These FAA rules place a number of strict rules on the aircraft used as well as their operation and maintenance to assure adequate passenger safety. They include a requirement for at least two engines (at night or in bad weather) and at least one professional pilot meeting minimum training and experience requirements for the aircraft used in Part 135 operations. There are hundreds of charter aircraft operations in the U.S. market operating more than 6,400 aircraft. They fly thousands of people per day, charging passengers from $1—$2 per flight mile for 150 to 200 mph twin-piston engine aircraft to $3 per flight mile for a 250 mph twin turboprop aircraft and up to $5 per flight mile for a 500 mph Lear Jet. Most of these smaller aircraft carry from two to six passengers and are flown on demand by professional pilots according to the schedule needs of the passengers.

---

[*] Market categories may differ from FAA categories.

There are more than 9,400 **business/corporate aviation aircraft** flown by more than 6,500 businesses using their own pilots and flown according to the needs of the business. Their costs per passenger flight mile on each aircraft are essentially the same as the above charter aircraft. These aircraft are owned by the individual businesses and flown by either professional crews or owner pilots. They are available for immediate use by company employees and management for business-related transportation, providing speed and convenience often not available from commercial operations. There were 531 U.S.-manufactured business and corporate jets and 187 turboprop business aircraft sold during 2002. That was 40 percent fewer turboprops than sold in 2001.

There are over 170,000 piston engine **general aviation aircraft** in the U.S. These are aircraft primarily flown by private pilots for pleasure and business, have operating costs in the range of 20 cents per mile, and typically fly from 100 to 250 miles per hour. There were 1,496 new piston engine aircraft sold in 2002 at a typical price of $250,000 with prices ranging from $150,000 to $1.2 million. (Note: see www.generalaviation.org for more information. Also note that the FAA defines general aviation aircraft to include aircraft flown by professional pilots.)

Where does the Eclipse 500 jet fit into these markets? The Eclipse 500 is not designed to be used by airlines, as it is too small to meet their passenger load requirements. However, the Eclipse may take away airline passengers as a market alternative to passengers currently flying commercial airlines, if operated by an air charter company as an air taxi at passenger costs per mile approaching high-end airline prices.

The Eclipse 500 will fit nicely into the existing air charter and business aviation fleets as a lower cost alternative to much of the existing fleet of jet or turboprop aircraft. By cutting the cost of travel in half, there could be greater demand for these services from existing users. However, there were only 719 turboprop and jet aircraft sold into this market in 2002 and many of these aircraft had to be larger and/or faster than the Eclipse to fulfill their flight mission requirements.

The Eclipse 500 will be admired and sought after by the general aviation market as its performance and costs are within reach of many general aviation pilots. However, qualifying to fly a high performance aircraft like the Eclipse 500 at high altitudes will require significant additional pilot training.

Pilot Requirements for Flying the Eclipse 500

The Federal Aviation Administration (FAA) of the U.S. Department of Transportation licenses pilots to fly aircraft in the United States. In general terms, a pilot is licensed by the FAA in private, commercial, or air transport grades and for flight in either visual or instrument conditions. Further license requirements must be obtained to fly simple, complex, turbine and large (over 12,000 pounds) aircraft. A pilot who is licensed to fly a typical single-engine aircraft with fixed gear (wheels cannot be retracted) in clear weather is not qualified to fly a more advanced aircraft (retractable gear, 200hp+ engines or multiple engines) without additional training and licensing. In addition, to fly in low visibility conditions or above 18,000 feet, the pilot must complete Instrument Flight Rule (IFR) training and pass rigorous FAA tests. In fact, two or more pilots are required on all airline aircraft and many charter or business aircraft. In most jet aircraft, pilots may also be required to be certified for the specific type of aircraft. A pilot who is certified to fly an airline Boeing 747 jumbo jet is not authorized to fly an Eclipse 500 without additional type-specific training and certification.

In addition to limitations imposed on pilots regarding the aircraft they are qualified to fly and their weather and altitude restrictions, pilots must pass special FAA tests to be rated to fly for hire or work for an airline. There are about 593,000 licensed pilots in the U.S. today. Of these, 120,000 pilots are rated to fly for hire as commercial pilots and 144,000 are rated for hire as Airline Transport Pilots (ATP). The remaining number represents 243,000 general aviation pilots and 86,000 student pilots. Based on this information, only 53 percent of pilots are instrument (IFR) qualified to fly aircraft that operate over 18,000 feet as required to operate the Eclipse 500.

Most commercial or airline transport grade pilots with an instrument rating could easily be trained to fly the Eclipse 500. However, considerable training may be required for the 50,000 IFR-rated general aviation private pilots to pass FAA requirements for flying the Eclipse. Even so, meeting the FAA requirement may not qualify the general aviation pilot to operate the aircraft to the satisfaction of the aircraft insurance industry.

Each aircraft flown in the U.S. needs to have liability insurance to cover any damage it may cause to passengers and ground-based material and personnel in the event of a crash. The industry statistics show that the general aviation pilot is forty times more likely to have a fatal crash per flight hour flown than a pilot operating a regularly scheduled airline. The insurance industry will price the cost of insurance for marginally qualified general aviation pilots at levels that may prevent them from operating the Eclipse 500, even if they pass all of the FAA test requirements. For example, my insurance cost for a piston single-engine 200 mph complex aircraft is $2,200 per year. A similar twin-engine piston aircraft will cost $6,000 to $8,000 per year to insure until I have actually flown the twin-engine aircraft over 200 hours (about 40,000 miles). The insurance companies work from actual statistics and their data must tell them that I am three to four times more likely to have an accident in the twin-engine aircraft until I have accumulated 200 hours of experience in that aircraft. I was told by my insurance company to not even consider flying a pressurized high altitude (over 18,000 feet) twin-piston engine aircraft until I had accumulated hundreds of additional hours of flight time in a less complex twin-piston engine aircraft. To fly an Eclipse 500, most insurers would require at least 1000 hours of flying time with much of that in a complex pressurized twin aircraft.

Eclipse Aviation must address this issue of pilot qualification by the insurance companies as well as the FAA in order to open up sales to the general aviation pilot. Furthermore, many believe the safety record of the Eclipse will be more a function of the qualification and training of the pilots who fly it than the aircraft design (see table on next page). As you can see, corporate professional pilots flying business aircraft have about one tenth the accident rate of business owner pilots flying their own aircraft.[♦]

[♦] Note: The company plans to train pilots in their factory to meet the insurance and FAA requirements with training an integral part of each aircraft purchase.

FATAL AIRCRAFT ACCIDENT RATE ANALYSIS

Fatalities Per 100,000 Hours of Flight

Year	General Aviation	Air Taxi	Commuter Airlines	Major Airlines	Corporate Prof. Pilot	Business Owner Pilot
2000	1.18	0.62	0.27	0.02	0.06	0.37
2001	1.17	0.57	0.66	0.03	0.03	0.23
2002 (est.)	1.37	0.56	0.45	0.02	0.045	0.36

Estimated Miles Traveled in 100,000 Hours

	General Aviation	Air Taxi	Commuter Airlines	Major Airlines	Corporate Prof. Pilot	Business Owner Pilot
	13,000,000	20,000,000	20,000,000	40,000,000	30,000,000	20,000,000
	@ 130 mph	@ 200 mph	@ 200 mph	@ 400 mph	@ 300 mph	@ 200 mph

Fatalities Per 100 Million Miles Based on the Above

Year	General Aviation	Air Taxi	Commuter Airlines	Major Airlines	Corporate Prof. Pilot	Business Owner Pilot
2000	9.08	3.10	1.35	0.05	0.20	1.85
2001	9.00	2.85	3.30	0.08	0.10	1.15
2002 (est.)	10.53	2.80	2.25	0.05	0.15	1.80

FATAL AUTOMOBILE ACCIDENT RATE
Fatalities Per 100 Million Vehicle Miles

1999	1.6
2000	1.6
2001	1.5

However, the above table also points out that a properly trained business owner pilot can fly with about the same safety rate as driving an automobile (1.8 fatalities/100 million miles compared with 1.6 fatalities/100 million miles for automobile driving).

Advantages and Disadvantages of Eclipse 500 Jet Over Market Alternatives

Currently, no well-defined market for small personal jets exists. Eclipse Aviation must take market share away from the market alternatives to achieve their 1,000 units per year sales objective. Eclipse Aviation must take share from the airline passenger market, the medium-size turbine charter market, the business aviation market, and the general aviation market to meet its cost objective derived, in part, from the 1,000 unit per year manufacturing volume.

Comparison of the Eclipse 500 to Commercial Airlines

What are the passenger advantages and disadvantages of an Eclipse 500 charter flight over a commercial airline flight?

ADVANTAGES:

1. Long delays in commercial airline screening and ticketing add one to two hours to each airline flight. Eclipse 500's passengers would have immediate access to the aircraft.
2. Overcrowded seating in commercial airlines is uncomfortable. The Eclipse 500 jets would seat four passengers and a pilot.
3. Exposure to airborne viruses and bacteria on commercial airlines is hazardous. The recent epidemic of the SARS virus highlights the exposure airline passengers can receive to new and deadly diseases. The limited number of passengers on the Eclipse 500 would reduce this exposure.
4. Hub-and-spoke airline systems often require a stopover between many destinations, causing one to two hour delays on each flight. The Eclipse 500 jet has a range of 1,472 miles and can fly non-stop to any destination within that range.
5. Airline flights are often limited to larger airports, requiring commuter aircraft connections or long automobile drives to final destinations. The Eclipse 500 jet can be flown directly into most small airports.

6. Schedule flexibility allows passengers the ability to select the timing of departure/arrival to suit their personal needs.

DISADVANTAGES:

1. On extended flights of more than three hours, there is no room on the Eclipse to get up and walk around or conveniently use a restroom.
2. There is a higher accident rate on single pilot air taxi or charter operations than on regularly scheduled commercial airlines.
3. Passengers must be willing to pay 70 cents per mile operating cost for the Eclipse 500 jet, plus the cost of a pilot (13 to 15 cents per mile), amortization (30 to 50 cents per mile), and operator overhead and profit. With only four passengers, this could cost each passenger two to three times the cost of an average airline ticket.

Comparison of the Eclipse 500 to Existing Air Charter Aircraft

What are the advantages and disadvantages the Eclipse 500 jet offers the charter or business aviation passenger over the existing medium-size charter and business aviation aircraft?

ADVANTAGES:

1. Eclipse 500 jets have a lower cost of operation by a factor of two over turboprop aircraft and by a factor of four over most existing jet-powered aircraft.
2. Eclipse 500 jets are 30—50 percent faster than most turboprop charter and business aircraft.
3. Eclipse 500 jets can operate at higher altitudes than most turboprop charter and business aircraft.
4. Eclipse 500 acquisition costs are substantially lower than most new charter and business aircraft. A new small twin-turboprop aircraft costs in excess of $2.3 million and a new medium-size jet

aircraft typically sells for more than $4 million vs. the $1 million target price for the Eclipse.

DISADVANTAGES:

1. The Eclipse 500 is smaller than most charter and business aircraft with less convenient restroom facilities and food storage or preparation facilities. There is no room to stand up during a flight.
2. The Eclipse 500 is 20—30 percent slower than some of the faster medium-size jets, such as the Lear Jet.
3. Many of the medium-size jet aircraft have 50—100 percent greater range than the Eclipse 500, letting them travel much greater distances without stopping.

Comparison of the Eclipse 500 to Fractional Ownership Service

Same as above air charter advantages and disadvantages except aircraft may be available at more locations and, for frequent flyers, there may be lower costs per hour of operation. However, there is usually a requirement to purchase part of the aircraft ($300 to $500 thousand) and there is a monthly management charge even if the aircraft is not used by the customer.

Comparison of the Eclipse 500 to Piston General Aviation Aircraft

What are the advantages and disadvantages the Eclipse 500 has for the general aviation pilot over most piston-powered general aviation aircraft?

ADVANTAGES:

1. High-speed performance (430 mph) gets passengers to their destination in less than half the time of most of today's general aviation piston aircraft.
2. The Eclipse 500 has a smoother and safer ride above the weather with a pressurized cabin and high altitude capability. Most piston aircraft are only capable of flying at altitudes up to 15,000 feet and

require supplemental oxygen above 12,500 feet. However, if the piston aircraft have turbochargers, found only in the most advanced aircraft, they can fly in the 23,000 to 28,000 foot range and may be pressurized. The Eclipse is designed to fly in pressurized comfort above the weather to 41,000 feet. With the exception of thunderstorms, you can get above most bad weather by flying above 30,000 feet.

3. The Eclipse 500 has more reliable operation with jet turbine engines. Jet turbine engines are inherently more reliable than piston engines and have fewer moving parts. They can go almost twice as long between overhauls as high performance piston engines.

4. Eclipse 500 jets offer ease of engine operation. With the use of automatic computerized controls, the Eclipse 500 will be easier to fly than many piston-powered aircraft. When I fly a multi-engine piston aircraft, I must manage three primary engine controls for each engine: the fuel mixture, the propeller pitch, and the engine manifold pressure. The Eclipse 500 has one power control for each engine; push it forward to add power and pull it back to slow the engines.

5. The Eclipse 500 jets have easier cockpit resource management with integrated computerized displays and controls. With my older generation piston twin aircraft, I have separate switches and controls for every function in the aircraft located to my left, on the panel ahead of me, on the floor, and to my right. The Eclipse has all controls and information gauges integrated into large color video displays and a keyboard directly ahead of the pilot. The Eclipse also includes much more automatic control functionality and displayed data than my older aircraft.

DISADVANTAGES:

1. Pilots must obtain additional FAA certifications and training to qualify for turbine engine aircraft like the Eclipse.

2. The Eclipse 500 has a higher initial cost of aircraft compared to the piston aircraft. A typical used twin-engine piston aircraft can be purchased for $200,000 to $500,000 compared to $1,000,000 plus for the Eclipse.

3. Eclipse 500 jets have potentially higher maintenance costs.
4. Insurance costs will be greater for the higher performance Eclipse 500 aircraft, if insurance becomes available.

From the above analysis, it is clear the Eclipse 500 is defining the new personal jet market and must attract buyers from all of the market alternatives to achieve its sales objectives. Can it achieve this objective? According to its most recent press releases, it has an order backlog in excess of 2,000 aircraft, so there clearly is interest on the part of individuals currently using alternative forms of air transportation.

I interviewed Michael McConnell, VP of Sales and Product Support, and Andrew Broom, a PR specialist at Eclipse, and they agree that their market will evolve primarily from market alternatives. Mike believes more than half of their market will come from emerging air taxi operations, taking business from existing charter companies and airlines. In fact, Mike says this market was targeted as part of the aircraft design and its order book strongly supports their success in penetrating this market. About 20 percent will come from general aviation pilots stepping up to jet-powered aircraft, with the balance coming from pilot training and an assortment of unique commercial operations such as airfreight or emergency medical applications. He believes this will be supported by the retirement of many of the 30+ year-old aircraft currently used in this market.

However, the Eclipse 500 faces many obstacles outside its control and the competing marketplace that impinge on the size and shape of its market. Most of these market externalities are regulatory in nature, although some are technical in nature.

Externalities Affecting the Size and Shape of the Small Personal Jet Market

The regulating federal authorities (FAA) must approve the design airworthiness of all new aircraft as well as approve the pilot training program, the maintenance program, and the number of pilots required to fly the aircraft. They have little incentive to make these approvals on a timely basis. If they overlook something in an approval or certification, they are severely reprimanded or may lose their jobs if the result is crashed aircraft. If they take too long, it can be justified by their concern for the safety of the passengers with minimal consequence to the government employee.

The Eclipse 500 uses new technology to achieve its performance characteristics at a lower cost than existing technologies. The Eclipse 500 uses lower-cost friction-stir welding instead of rivets to fasten together the aluminum parts of the aircraft. The Eclipse 500 will use a new low-weight high-thrust turbofan engine manufactured by Pratt & Whitney Canada, never before used in a production aircraft. The Eclipse 500 will use the most advanced electronic and computerized aircraft system the general aviation market has ever seen, similar to that used in high performance military aircraft. All of this innovative technology will look more like risk to certifying government regulators than an opportunity. The current schedule is to deliver the first production aircraft by the first quarter of 2006. Will the regulators approve the aircraft for sale by that date? Every effort, such as pre-approval of the friction-stir welding process and early flight testing using temporary military jet engines, has been made to get the regulators to approve new processes and equipment before the final aircraft acceptance testing begins.

If the aircraft fails for any reason once deliveries commence on the certificated aircraft, the FAA regulators can ground the aircraft until a complete understanding of the problem is established. A correction is then put in place through what they call an FAA Airworthiness Directive prescribing necessary modifications to all existing aircraft.

Unlike Microsoft that can ship software before all of the bugs are out of the system, Vern Raburn must be sure that the Eclipse 500 is bug free before the first aircraft is shipped or face months of delays in shipping additional aircraft. As an engineer, I know that all the bugs are not out of any design until substantial field testing has been performed. The FAA and the engineers at Eclipse are keenly aware of this reality and are implementing an exhaustive evaluation of eight test aircraft over the next few years to make sure they meet the regulatory requirements and have corrected any design problems before shipping the first production aircraft. Their test program will include 3,000 flight hours, as rigorous as the Boeing 777 test program.

Insurance companies are getting tougher on high performance aircraft pilot requirements. Recently, USAIG, a large player in the aircraft insurance business, began informing its customers of turboprop aircraft (jet engine-driven propeller aircraft) that they would have to engage a co-pilot, even on their single-engine turboprop aircraft like Pilatus PC12 and Socata TBM 700, to obtain insurance. This is a direct result of the recent accident history of these aircraft that has led to higher costs to the insurance companies, which in turn pass these costs along to the owner of the aircraft. The cost of insuring a single-pilot operated $1.6 million dollar turboprop, according to a recent aviation consumer article, has risen to $31,000 a year for a 2,600-hour private pilot. Adding a co-pilot may be less expensive than paying higher insurance costs.

Terrorist attacks on commercial airlines and the discovery of new communicable diseases like SARS could dramatically increase the demand for personal jet transportation. Airline travel is now considered inconvenient and unsafe by most travelers. The unfortunate reality of the September 11 attacks was a dramatic drop in commercial airline traffic (20—30 percent) and many additional inspection delays at the terminal. We all know many people who will not fly commercial airlines for fear of terrorist attacks. The Eclipse 500 is likely to be of little political value to terrorists and can fly out of airports that will not require the level of passenger screening required by commercial airlines. Furthermore, you can choose your four to five fellow passengers on an Eclipse 500 ride and not expose yourself to communicable diseases from the 165 to 400 passengers crammed into a commercial jet. In a typical flight in an Eclipse 500, you would arrive at a small FBO (Fixed Base Operator) at either a small or major airport and be escorted to your waiting aircraft. You would fly directly to your destination, in most cases non-stop, at speeds in excess of 400 miles per hour above most of the weather. You would depart the plane at another FBO and proceed immediately to your local transportation. A trip from New York to Chicago would take about two hours at a cost as low as $200—$300 per passenger. No airport screening, no lines, no tickets, no exposure to hundreds of other passengers, inquiring grandmothers, screaming kids, or terrorists and you travel on your schedule.

Bankruptcy and reorganization of the major air carriers in the United States is all but inevitable and could dramatically impact demand for air taxi/air charter. The major air carriers have lost money for the last two years and need to reduce costs to survive. This means a direct reduction in quality and speed of service for airline passengers. Southwest Airlines is making money and gives us a clue as to the future of commercial air travel: no first class, no seat selection, no warm food, minimal service, "cattle car" loading lines, frequent stops to pick up passengers, keeping the aircraft crowded at all times. This inevitable degradation of service should drive business and wealthier passengers to air taxi and charter operations, a primary market opportunity for Eclipse.

Hub-based routing of commercial air traffic has dramatically increased en route delays with major air carriers. In the last three years, from 300,000 to 450,000 commercial airline flights were delayed in excess of 15 minutes. Economic factors drive the major air carriers to operate out of large hub airports like Chicago, Dallas, Denver, Atlanta, New York, Los Angeles and San Francisco. Chicago's O'Hare International Airport alone had over 923,000 arrivals and departures last year. When operating with such a high volume of air traffic, the smallest weather or air traffic control problem results in substantial delays to arriving and departing aircraft. With small aircraft like the Eclipse 500, passengers can arrive and depart at less busy regional airports and reduce the likelihood of en route delays by flying directly to their destination.

NASA's Small Aircraft Transportation System, (SATS) was funded in the late 1990's to study the feasibility of opening up an additional 3000 runways in the United States to safe and affordable direct point-to-point air service. The Eclipse 500 is ideally suited for this application and is an active participant in this feasibility study. NASA believes that industry must develop four new operating capabilities to make SATS feasible: on-board computing, advanced flight controls, Highway in the Sky display, and automatic air traffic separation and sequencing.

In a March, 2003 speech by Dr. Bruce J. Holmes, Director of the SATS program at the NASA Langley Research Center, he provided information indicating the need for 7,000 to 52,000 new small aircraft to satisfy the air taxi demands that SATS will create. His analysis indicated that the maximum number of aircraft (52,000) would be required if provided at a cost of $1.72 per mile. His study indicated demand for these services would be highest in communities most remote from commercial air service and will require significant advances in both aircraft technology and air traffic control technology to implement the SATS program. Continued government funding to develop the requisite technologies will play a significant role in the growth and size of the Eclipse 500 market.

Market Saturation

The Eclipse 500 is defining the new market for personal jet aircraft much like Xerox defined the copier market or Apple defined the personal computer market. Competitors are emerging as they see Eclipse orders build. In this new market, it is up to Eclipse to define and control their current leadership position or they will wind up like Xerox and Apple, yielding market leadership to competitors who take advantage of their errors.

Competitors

There are no competitors delivering directly competitive new aircraft into the personal jet market defined by the Eclipse 500 jet. (Only Eclipse Aviation has actually flown a prototype aircraft at the time of this writing.) However, there are four viable companies that have announced competitive aircraft in development: Cessna Aircraft Mustang Jet, Safire Aircraft S-26 Jet, Adam Aircraft A700 Jet, and Diamond Aircraft D-Jet. The following table of preliminary specifications highlights the differences in the product offerings:

PRELIMINARY AIRCRAFT SPECIFICATIONS

	Eclipse	Mustang	Safire S-26	Adam A700	Diamond D-Jet
Price	$1,175,000	$2,295,000	$1,395,000	$1,995,000	$850,000
Specifications:					
Wingspan (ft)	36	42	39.4	44	39
Length (ft)	33	39	36	41	35
Height (ft)	11	13.75	15	9.6	10
# Seats	6	6	6	6	5
Pressure Differential (psi)	TBD	TBD	8	8.33	5.2
Useful Load (lb)	2250	TBD	2254	3000	2162
Payload (lb)	710	800	1400	725	881
Engines	PWC PW610F	PWC PW615	WIFJ33	WIFJ33	TBD
Thrust (lb) ea.	900X2	1350X2	1,100X2	1200X2	1400 (1 eng.)
Max. Cruise Speed, (MPH)	431	391	437	391	362
Range (miles)	1,472	1,495	1,167	1,265	1,518
Ceiling (ft)	41,000	41,000	41,000	41,000	25,000
Takeoff Distance(ft)	2,060	3,120	2,500	2,950	2,372
Construction	Aluminum	Aluminum	Aluminum	Carb./Graphite	Composite
1st Delivery	Mar/2006	Dec/2005	n/a	4Q/2004	2006
Operating Cost/Mile	$0.69	n/a	n/a	n/a	n/a

Notes:
1. Eclipse price increased, after delivery of first 1553 aircraft, to $1,175,000.
2. Only FAA certified, factory-built aircraft are considered direct competitors.
3. Safire data from *www.safireaircraft.com.*
4. According to a recent Adam Aircraft A700 press release, customer deliveries will start in late 2004. However, many in the industry expect this delivery will slip into 2005.

5. Pressure differential is a measure of cabin altitude vs. outside (ambient) altitude. A large differential permits a comfortable cabin pressure at higher altitudes.
6. n/a means information not available at time of writing; TBD means to be determined at a later date.

Of the above competitors, only Cessna, the builder of the Mustang, is currently a manufacturer of jet-powered aircraft. Schedules, prices and performance specifications on all of the above aircraft are, therefore, expected to change between now and the actual delivery of the first aircraft. Operation cost per mile includes fuel, maintenance labor and materials. It does not include estimated costs for pilot ($55/hour), hanger ($8,000/year), insurance ($10,000 to $30,000/year) and pilot training ($6,000/year). For the private pilot qualified to operate the aircraft (typically 200—400 hours per year), these additional costs per mile could be $0.15 to $0.28. For the air taxi operator with a hired pilot at 1000 hours per year, it could cost an additional $0.20 to $0.26 per mile of operation.

How do we interpret the above specifications relative to the perceived market needs? Will the aircraft be FAA certifiable for air taxi operation or air charter operation? Is it designed to operate above most weather systems? Does it have carrying capacity for all seats? Does metal construction vs. composite construction make a difference? Is it using proven technology or developing new technology? What is the likelihood of meeting the first delivery date? Each manufacturer has a different perspective on customer needs in this new emerging market. The winning strategy is the one that most closely matches their product to customers' needs in defining the new market and has the financial and marketing strength to get their product to market in time to meet customer demand. Let's look at how each company positions themselves on the market battlefield.

Cessna Mustang:

Cessna is part of the Textron Company, a $10+ billion conglomerate with more than $4.9 billion in revenue from its aircraft-related businesses in 2002. They are the largest U.S. producer of small and medium-size jet aircraft, manufacturing 305 jet aircraft in 2002. After watching the order book for Eclipse grow to over 2000 aircraft, Cessna decided to enter the personal jet market in September of 2002 with the Mustang as their entry-level competitor.

With a history of making economical small jet aircraft dating back thirty years, it is a competitor to be reckoned with and the only "800-pound gorilla" to enter the market.

Cessna believes there is still an unmet market for pilots ready to step up from pressurized twin-piston aircraft and turboprops to small jets. Its offering is to be an aluminum constructed aircraft, slightly larger and heavier than the Eclipse 500 and costing twice as much as the Eclipse. It will seat six and have the full glass cockpit instrumentation with a maximum cruise speed of 391 miles per hour. It will be able to carry a 600-pound payload with full fuel and one 200-pound pilot to obtain the 1,437-mile range. That means the average passenger with baggage must weigh 120 pounds or that the jet could only carry three passengers who weighed 200 pounds. The alternative is to reduce the range of the aircraft by carrying less fuel. With fuel weighing about 6.7 pounds per gallon and two 1,350-pound thrust engines burning about 550 pounds of fuel per hour, taking 391 miles off the aircraft range (leaving you with only 1,046 miles between fuel stops) gives you an ability to carry a full load of passengers and more luggage.

With a takeoff distance of 3,120 feet on a standard day (not too high an elevation and not too hot), the aircraft will be able to get out of most commercial airports and many small airports. Its target maximum ceiling of 41,000 feet puts it on top of most weather and as good as any competitor.

Cessna plans to use construction techniques, aluminum riveted airframe, and controls similar to those on existing more expensive aircraft. This should give Cessna minimal technical risk and FAA certification risk as they are sticking to proven technology. However, it also affords minimal opportunity to reduce costs.

From a customer perspective, Cessna offers the advantage of proven technology and is known to produce safe, reliable aircraft. It is offering a slightly bigger aircraft than the Eclipse and will have correspondingly higher operating costs; based on engine size, such costs would be about 35 percent higher. The customer must put twice the initial investment into the Mustang as in an Eclipse or Safire S-26. With no flight testing to date, the risk of missing a December 2005 shipment date is high, but Cessna is not new to this type of aircraft development and historically has met their delivery commitments. Will prices escalate? If past Cessna prices are an indicator, the answer is yes. Cessna's single-pilot Citation Jet was introduced in 1993 for $2.6 million and now sells for $4+ million. The question is whether Cessna will price itself out of the market by the time it delivers its first Mustang. In fact, if you tried to purchase a Mustang today, they would quote you a price of $2.8 million and a delivery position in the year 2009.

Safire S-26:

The Safire Aircraft Company is a start-up company with limited funding to produce the Safire S-26 jet. The company seems to be following behind Eclipse in pursuit of the personal jet market but does not appear to have the same level of capitalization. Although the S-26 has passed wind tunnel tests, Safire Aircraft failed to meet a 2002 deadline to fly their first aircraft. It recently selected the Williams FJ33 engine and will use a combination of aluminum and composite material to minimize construction costs. Its engines will each develop over 1200 pounds of thrust and propel the aircraft to a maximum cruise speed of 391 miles per hour up to a ceiling altitude of 37,000 feet. This should put it well on top of most weather and allow airline-quality comfort with an on-board lavatory to make long-distance travel tolerable for us more mature (older) travelers. Its target is mid-range trips from 150 to 1,000 miles with a maximum range (to meet IFR minimum requirements) of 1,173 miles. Safire says that it is able to take off from 2,500-foot runways, a clear advantage over many larger jets. It also says it can carry a 1,400-pound payload. Safire engineers may have sacrificed range to allow the S-26 to carry the higher payload. With a target price of $1,395,000, the issue with the S-26 is not whether it meets the needs of the personal jet market as much as whether it can obtain adequate funding to take the concept into reality.

From a customer perspective, the Safire S-26 jet seems to offer all of the things a customer could ask for in a personal jet, such as low price, low operating cost, good payload capacity, and an all-glass cockpit. They offer 25 percent less range than Eclipse and many question their selection of construction materials. Safire also has not established credibility in their ability to meet delivery commitments as it has repeatedly missed its target dates to test fly a prototype aircraft.

Adam A700 Business Jet:

Adam Aircraft is another start-up aircraft company. It was started in 1998 and located in Pueblo, Colorado to produce a pressurized in-line piston twin-engine aircraft, the A500. This piston-engine powered A500 aircraft will be delivered in 2003. Using the basic airframe design of the A500 aircraft, Adam Aircraft announced the development of the A700 business jet in October of 2002. It will use the Williams FJ33 turbine engine and is specified to achieve 391 mile per hour speeds up to an altitude of 41,000 feet. It is designed using carbon graphite materials and all modern glass cockpit displays. It will have a range of 1265 miles and carry four passengers and two pilots with a payload of 725 pounds. It will require a 2950-foot runway, adequate for all commercial airport operations and many small airports. However, their targeted delivery date of June 2004 seems highly optimistic to nearly impossible given all of the engineering and manufacturing required to convert the A500 design into a jet-powered aircraft and obtain FAA certification.

From a customer perspective, Adam Aircraft is a start-up company that has done a good job designing a pressurized twin-piston aircraft and getting it ready for delivery in 2003. However, a lot of design and testing will have to go into converting their first aircraft into a full performance jet, and many believe it will be two to three years in the making. All-carbon graphite aircraft bodies still scare away some customers, as they are concerned about the effect of lightning strikes and aging on the aircraft materials. However, it is less expensive to construct than conventional aluminum riveted-skin aircraft and has proven itself in the past on aircraft manufactured by larger aircraft companies. Their performance specifications fall right in line with most of the other personal jet aircraft, although their price is on the high end of the spectrum at $1,995,000.

Diamond Aircraft D-Jet:

Diamond Aircraft is a Canadian and Austrian aircraft manufacturer of general aviation aircraft. It is known for its innovative designs using composite construction techniques to produce high-performance piston aircraft at affordable prices. For example, it recently announced a twin diesel-powered piston aircraft, the first of its type in the North American market. The D-Jet is an even more innovative entry into the personal jet market; it is powered by a single 1400-pound thrust jet engine (manufacturer to be determined at a later time) to speeds of 362 miles per hour and up to 25,000 feet. It will seat five people (pilot and four passengers) and carry a payload of 881 pounds plus fuel for 1,518 miles. It will be able to take off in less than 2,400 feet, giving it access to most paved airports in North America.

The customer's perspective on the D-Jet will be tempered by the perception of higher structural risk with composite material construction and single-engine propulsion. There will be no backup power if you lose your only engine; although its low stall speed, 63 knots, should permit controlled forced landings in many locations, pilots and passengers generally like the added security of two engines. The limitation of 25,000 feet in maximum altitude is similar to many pressurized piston-powered aircraft and may leave many trips stuck in low altitude bad weather while other jets go over the top. The purchase price of $850,000 seems very competitive and, given that it only has one jet engine, likely to be achievable.

As a successful small aircraft manufacturer with possible financial support from the Canadian government, it is likely to succeed in bringing this plane to market. With a scheduled delivery of 2006, it will come into the market about the same time as the other competitors and should achieve Canadian/European (JAA) certification on schedule although FAA approval may take longer.

Eclipse 500

The Eclipse 500, which started and defined the personal jet market, has attracted the most buyer deposits and raised the most capital of any competitor in the market. It seems poised to realize its founder's dream of a small twin-jet engine aircraft that will revolutionize air travel. To accomplish this revolution, Vern Raburn put together over $320 million in capital and created one of the most motivated and dedicated teams in the industry. He flew the first Eclipse 500 on schedule in the summer of 2002 only to find the Williams manufactured jet engines failed to meet their performance objectives. The company recently selected Pratt & Whitney's model PW610F engine (downsized from an existing family of Pratt & Whitney designs), which will be ready to fly in 2005. Until then, Eclipse will continue flight tests with temporary, short-range 1,000 pound thrust Teledyne manufactured military jet engines.

Many believe the Eclipse 500 performance specifications are aggressive. However, with assurance that the Pratt & Whitney engines will meet specifications, Eclipse is relying on its highly experienced team of aircraft designers and manufacturers to deliver promised performance. The three key technical factors for their success are: 1) low cost construction afforded by friction-stir welding, 2) comprehensive unified avionics and aircraft systems management electronics, and 3) next-generation small, efficient jet engines.

The friction-stir welding process was approved by the FAA one year ahead of schedule, the avionics and systems management electronics development and testing is on schedule, and Pratt & Whitney, a proven supplier of turbine engines, has committed to engine delivery. Given Vern Raburn's proven ability to raise capital for this project and the competence and enthusiasm of his team, the aircraft will likely become a reality in early 2006.

The 2,000 plus customers are expecting to receive a small five to six-passenger jet that has an operating cost of $0.69 per mile and flies up to 41,000 feet at speeds in excess of 400 miles per hour. The integrated computer electronics will make this one of the safest small jets with continuous monitoring of all onboard systems and automatic engine control to simplify engine operation. The glass cockpit will display terrain, weather, engine parameters, integrated radio communications information, and IFR routing charts. The autopilot and auto-throttles will perform at a level achieved only by aircraft costing forty times the cost of Eclipse. With redundant critical systems, the aircraft will automatically identify system faults and alert the pilot to the required corrective measures. The aircraft will carry 710 pounds of payload with IFR reserves up to 1,472 miles. That is enough for one pilot and three normal-size passengers. Each additional pound of load will reduce the aircraft range by about one statute mile; i.e., to carry another 200-pound passenger, the range will be reduced to 1,272 miles. This should be more than adequate for most air taxi, business and general aviation applications. The ability to take off from short runways, requiring only 2,060 feet plus required safety reserves, gives the Eclipse 500 the ability to operate from almost all paved airports in the U.S.

The all-aluminum construction is considered by most pilots as the safest form of construction as it is resistant to lightning strikes and used in most commercial aircraft sold today. The exhaustive testing and certification process under way at Eclipse Aviation has given the customers assurance that Eclipse will deliver against its revised schedule a safe and affordable aircraft at a price below $1.2 million. The only concern we have heard customers voice about the Eclipse 500 is its small size and lack of some comfort features. They expect it will be difficult to accommodate more than a pilot and four passengers. However, few of the 2000+ customers have withdrawn orders and the industry is waiting for Eclipse to lead the revolution in small jet aircraft with its first aircraft delivery in early 2006.

Eclipse 500 Market Battlefield Summary

After studying the market, the competitors and their market positions, I developed the following summary of the market battlefield as it exists in May of 2003. Several market characteristics jump out of the Market Battlefield Summary consistent with the above analysis:

- The Eclipse 500 jet currently defines the market with most competitors building around their product definition.
- The market will be very dependent on travelers migrating from scheduled air carriers and higher priced charter flights or fractional ownership to air taxi service made possible by Eclipse 500 jet-type aircraft.
- Market alternative characteristics are changing daily with terrorists, airborne viruses, and airline bankruptcy likely to have a near-term impact on the size and growth of the Eclipse 500 market.
- Externalities affecting Eclipse 500's market can have a major impact on the speed of deployment of product into this market.
- The competition, with the exception of Cessna, is relatively new companies and very dependent on availability of financing.
- As with all NEW markets, the Eclipse 500 market will evolve over the next few years and be shaped by changes in market alternatives and externalities.

How Eclipse 500 positions itself in the rapidly changing market landscape outlined in the Market Battlefield Summary will be critical to developing a winning strategy.

MARKET BATTLEFIELD SUMMARY   *QUICKSTRATEGY*™   Form 1.0

1. Product or Service: Small 5—6 passenger jet turbine powered aircraft with pressurized cabins, 1000 mile + range, speed in excess of 375 mph, selling for less than $2.3 million, direct operating cost less than $0.75/mile.	**2. Customers:** Air Taxi and Air Charter Services 50%, Medical Air 5%, Business Aircraft Operations 20%, Emergency Freight 5%, Personal General Aviation 20%

3. Customer Need: 1. Customers need a safe, high-speed, cost-effective air transportation alternative to crowded hub-connected commercial airline travel, high cost charter aircraft, and slow propeller-driven personal aircraft. It is driven by safety risks, time delays and costs of market alternatives.	**4. Market Shape:** Value

5. Market Alternatives: 1. Commercial airline travel (-). 2. High price air charter services (-). 3. Fractional aircraft ownership/operation (+). 4. Piston-powered slower aircraft (-).	**6. Saturation:** 0% As a new market, no market saturation has occurred

7. Externalities: 1. Speed of FAA approval of new aircraft and operations (+/-). 2. Insurability of pilots (+/-). 3. Cost of product liability insurance (-). 4. Terrorist attacks on commercial airlines (+). 5. Spread of airborne disease, like SARS (+). 6. Failure and bankruptcy of major U.S. air carriers (+/-). 7. Availability of safe alternative small airports (+/-). 8. SATS program funding for improved flight data and air traffic control (+).

8. **Competitors**	Strengths	Weaknesses	Sales $(000) Last Yr./This Yr.	Share (%)
Eclipse Aviation ECLIPSE 500	Low operating cost (<$0.69/mile) Low acquisition cost (<$1.2 million) Aluminum construction (safety), flight tested, ease of operation, short field capable, adequate capital	Small cabin size and lack of passenger facilities, first aircraft product	0/0	
CESSNA Aircraft Mustang Jet	Aluminum construction (safety) Proven technology, reputation (largest small jet manufacturer), adequate capital	High acquisition cost ($2.3 million), poor short field capability, no flight test data	0/0	
Safire Aircraft S26	Low acquisition cost ($1,395,000) Good payload capacity (1400 lb.)	First aircraft product, no flight test data, questionable financial strength, Al/Composite construction safety risk	0/0	
Adams Aircraft A700	Proven hull design from A500 aircraft Promised delivery 2004??	High acquisition cost ($1,995,000), carbon graphite construction safety risk, first jet aircraft product	0/0	
Diamond Aircraft D-Jet	Low acquisition cost ($850,000) Low operating cost from one engine	Single engine safety risk All-composite construction safety risk Low maximum ceiling (25,000 ft)	0/0	

9. Market Size (Sales Bookings $000,000)   **Total**

Year -5	Year-4	Year-3	Year-2	Last Year	This Year	Year 2	Year 3	Year 4	Year 5
			500	600	1,300	1,000	1,000	1,000	1,000

10. Market Maturity GROWTH Stage

Strategic Business Unit: Eclipse 500	Plan Manager: TBD	Date Prepared: April 22, 2003
Company: Eclipse Aviation	Strategy Advisor: Bruce Robinson	Date of Next Plan Review:

Developing the Eclipse 500 Strategic Plan

What competitors will Eclipse 500 target to build its business? What are its competitive advantages and disadvantages against those competitors? What are its strategic objectives? What advantages will it leverage or disadvantages will it make the most of to accomplish its strategic objective, i.e., carry out its strategic plan? What specific actions (tactics) will it employ to affect its strategic plan? How will it measure its success against its objectives? These, as you have seen in prior cases, are the essential questions that must be answered to establish the Eclipse 500 strategic plan.

However, in a NEW market like the Eclipse 500 is defining, it is not taking business away from its direct competitors (Cessna, Safire, Adam, and Diamond Aircraft) as much as it is taking business from the major air carriers, the existing charter operations, the larger business jet manufacturers, and the high-performance propeller aircraft manufacturers selling to business and general aviation pilots.

GET IN THE WAY OF THE MONEY is the first rule of successful business strategy development. Does Cessna, Safire, Adam or Diamond Aircraft have significant orders they are taking from Eclipse at this time? No, they are just getting started. Where is the money that Eclipse must get in front of to be successful in selling 1,000+ jets per year?

Let's look for the money:

- Major air carriers are flying 1.3 million people each day in the U.S. If the average price per passenger was $350, the total annual cash flow would be $166 billion. How do you get some of this cash flow?
- Existing U.S. charter aircraft operations and air taxi operations are operating over 6400 aircraft. If each year they fly an average of 500 hours per aircraft at an average speed of 350 mph charging $1 to $5 per mile ($3 average), that represents $3.36 billion in revenue per year. How do you get some of this cash flow?
- There were several billion dollars spent on business jets and turboprop aircraft last year (718 aircraft). How do you get in front of some of this cash flow?
- There were hundreds of millions of dollars spent on high performance high priced general aviation aircraft. How do you get at this money?

There are billions of dollars to get in front of with the Eclipse 500 and related services. As the market matures, the direct competitors become the primary target of the Eclipse strategy. They must watch for any loss of orders to these direct competitors, modifying their strategy to focus more keenly on the dollars going to direct competition as the market matures. Many successful start-up businesses have been extremely successful in taking business from market alternatives in a new market but never became successful competitors against direct competition as their market matured—think about Apple Computers, Xerox Copiers, and Fairchild Semiconductor Memories.

How does Eclipse attack the commercial airline business and take away some of the estimated $160+ billion spent per year on air travel? We know that the commercial airline passengers who are spending all of this money pay an average of $0.12 per passenger mile. We also know that emergency airline travel booked at the last minute can cost $0.40 per mile. The Eclipse 500 operating cost (including maintenance) should be about $0.70 per mile, plus the cost of a pilot and amortization of investment, for a total cost of $1.13 to $1.35. But someone has to manage the operation of the aircraft, an air taxi operation. The managing business will also have advertising, insurance, training, administrative, and facilities costs. This could put the total cost per mile in the $1.60 to $1.90 range. With four passengers, this is a breakeven deal for the last minute traveler and, at worst, a reasonable premium to pay to fly directly to your destination, thereby saving considerable time and money on rental cars, hotels and employee compensation.

Most of these airline passengers are not going to purchase Eclipse 500's. Some percentage of the airline passenger revenue can be redirected to amortize the cost of an Eclipse 500, but the buyer must be an air taxi or air charter operation. Does Eclipse Aircraft start its own air taxi operation or partner with existing air taxi operations? How does it make sure that the air taxi operations are properly capitalized? Selling Eclipse 500's to air taxi operations that fail could create a glut of used Eclipse aircraft in the market and take away new aircraft sales.

Cessna Aircraft, as part of Textron, has its own financing organization. Should Eclipse provide lease or other equipment financing options to its air taxi customers? A better strategic alternative may be to team with existing aircraft financing operations and offer their services to prospective buyers. Should Eclipse set up and arrange financing for a new national air taxi operation? These are all options to be considered in pursuing the commercial airline passenger revenue, but the airline passenger is still likely to pay some additional amount to fly in an air taxi, just like many people are willing to pay more for a limousine or taxicab instead of riding a bus. What are the advantages to the passenger that would drive them toward an Eclipse 500 air taxi?

- Faster travel: port to port, no hub connections, small airport access
- No lines and exposure to many other passengers
- Ability to travel at passengers' time schedule
  The disadvantages to an airline passenger with Eclipse 500 travel are:
- Discomfort on longer trips: no room to walk around and no lavatory facilities
- Higher perceived accident rate than commercial air carriers
- Higher cost unless aircraft has four passengers
- 40—50 cents per mile compared to 12—40 cents per mile for airlines

These negative issues must be minimized in order to attract airline passengers to air taxi operations using the Eclipse 500.

How does Eclipse 500 attack the existing charter aircraft operations and capture market now going to larger turboprop and jet aircraft? How do they get in front of the $3.6 billion spent annually by this industry to purchase these market alternative aircraft? There will be resistance on the part of many existing charter aircraft operations to the Eclipse 500:

1. They have existing aircraft lease or finance costs that must be covered by passenger fees.
2. They have older depreciated aircraft that will generate better profit margins than a new Eclipse 500.
3. They have passengers who prefer larger, faster aircraft and need more range.
4. They must maintain high overall revenue (charge more per aircraft hour) in order to cover overhead. A lower cost per mile alternative could reduce their total revenue by giving existing passengers a lower cost alternative.

How does Eclipse 500 overcome this resistance by the charter aircraft operator?

1. Eclipse 500 will reduce operating costs and aircraft acquisition costs by a factor of two to four over existing larger turbine-powered

aircraft. If prices are lowered accordingly, this may attract customers that were heretofore unwilling to charter aircraft.

2. Eclipse 500 will let them offer higher speed and higher altitude ceilings than most market alternative piston or turboprop charter aircraft to arrive faster over the top of most weather.

Will these advantages attract additional customers to air charter operations or just take existing business away at lower revenue per passenger mile? If it attracts new customers at a profit to the air charter operator, there will be little resistance to Eclipse 500 and some portion of the air charter aircraft purchases will be directed to purchase Eclipse 500's.

The business/corporate aviation aircraft market has been declining recently as business overheads have been reduced to compensate for falling revenue and profits. The lower cost Eclipse 500 jet should capture some share of this market given its lower acquisition cost and lower operating cost compared to most of the business aircraft sold today. The advantages and disadvantages in this market are similar to the charter market. Today, a low-cost business jet costs in excess of $4 million, compared to $1—$1.2 million for an Eclipse 500, and a new low-cost turboprop costs $2.3 million. Although these aircraft are bigger and carry more payload than the Eclipse 500, many business trips do not require the additional size and payload capability. Of the 187 business turboprop aircraft sold in 2002, the Eclipse 500 will outperform all models in speed and comfort for short (under 1000 mile) trips. Of the 531 jet-powered aircrafts sold in 2002, the Eclipse 500 will perform as well as half of these aircraft in speed and operate at a quarter to half the cost. The hope is that some significant portion of the 719 business turbine aircraft sold each year will be redirected to Eclipse-type aircraft.

There were 1,496 new general aviation aircraft sold in the U.S. in 2002. Many of these were acquired at prices in excess of $1 million and none of them had the speed and ceiling capability of the Eclipse 500 jet. As a general aviation pilot, I know most of us dream of flying above the weather at jet aircraft speed. If we could afford it and meet the regulatory and insurance requirements to fly an Eclipse 500 jet, we would buy one. How can Eclipse Aviation capture a large share of this market?

- Hold the price point near $1 million and make financing available
- Keep the operating and maintenance costs low

- Institute a training program that would qualify general aviation pilots to act as Pilot in Command for this type of aircraft under FAA regulations
- Provide insurance coverage for FAA qualified pilots
- Make fractional ownership or aircraft leasing possible to general aviation pilots

Many of the general aviation pilots will never be able to afford even a fraction of the cost of an Eclipse 500 or be able to rent/lease such an aircraft. Of the 593,000 pilots in the U.S., only about 360,000 are qualified to begin training in such a high performance aircraft. However, there are still many thousands of pilots who will qualify for training and have the money to move up to an Eclipse 500 jet with the appropriate support from the company.

The strategic objective of Eclipse Aviation is clearly stated by its founder, Vern Raburn: to revolutionize the air transportation industry with a low-cost jet-powered aircraft that will capture sales in excess of 1,000 aircraft per year in the market.

The strategic plan is to capitalize on their acquisition and operating cost advantages over market alternative aircraft to sell over 1,000 aircraft per year into the air taxi/charter market, the business aviation market, and the general aviation market.

Based on available public information, the Eclipse 500 tactical plan to overcome known obstacles and accomplish their strategic objectives seems to be made up of eleven components, (dates not available as public information):

1. Continue the assembly of the next six test aircraft.
2. Continue flight-testing airframe with temporary (Teledyne) engines to verify performance and meet FAA testing requirements.
3. Continue testing and qualification of flight controls on test aircraft.
4. Continue development and testing of Pratt & Whitney jet engines to meet the flight test date of _____:
5. Complete and obtain process certification on the friction-stir welding equipment and manufacturing facility in Albuquerque.
6. Continue developing and obtain certification on flight instrumentation and displays by_____:
7. Finish development of simulators and flight training program and obtain insurance and FAA approval.
8. Build new manufacturing and test facility at Double Eagle Airport.
9. Initiate production of 1000 aircraft for first delivery early in 2006.

10. Continue to work with aircraft insurance companies to assure availability of insurance for the target market.
11. Team with innovative new air taxi operations and fractional ownership companies to develop a market alternative to commercial airline and air charter operations.

The above tactics are clearly not inclusive of all of the actions under way at Eclipse Aviation to help them achieve their strategic objectives, as they are keeping most tactical information confidential. They are tactics based on my observations and from reading public statements by the management. Their specific backlog and production information is also held confidential with public statements alluding to a 2000+ aircraft backlog. However, I think we have enough information to develop a first draft strategic plan summary that gives some indication as to the viability of their strategy.

STRATEGIC PLAN SUMMARY   *QUICKSTRATEGY*™   Form 2.0

11. Your STRENGTHS vs. Competitor or Market Alternative	12. Your WEAKNESSES vs. Competitor or Market Alternative
Commercial Airlines: 1. Faster point-to-point air transportation with no stop in hub airports. 2. No airport delays in screening and ticketing lines. 3. Passenger scheduled service.	**Commercial Airlines:** 1. Less passenger comfort with no standing room or toilets. 2. No proven safety record. 3. 20% slower speed.
Jet Air Charter/Fractional/Business/Operations: 1. Lower operating cost per mile vs. larger existing jet aircraft. 2. Single pilot certification lowers cost. 3. Lower acquisition cost.	**Jet Air Charter/Fractional/Business/Operations:** 1. Less passenger comfort vs. larger jets. 2. Unproven safety and reliability of existing jets. 3. Slower as many existing jets are faster (10%—20%), reducing travel time.
Turboprop Air Charter/Fractional/Business/Operations: 1. Faster speeds reduce travel time. 2. Lower operating costs than twin-engine turboprops. 3. Ability to fly above most weather. 4. Lower acquisition cost.	**Turboprop Air Charter/Fractional/Business/Operations:** 1. Less room and passenger comfort, no toilets. 2. Unproven reliability and safety record.
Piston Twins and Singles: 1. Higher engine reliability with turbine engines. 2. Faster, reducing travel time. 3. Ability to fly above most weather.	**Piston Twins and Singles:** 1. Requires significantly more pilot training and experience. 2. Higher cost of operation. 3. Higher acquisition cost.

13. Strategic Objective:
Build a market leadership position in the manufacture and marketing of small personal jet aircraft, investing $400—$500 million in the development, production set-up and marketing of the Eclipse 500 Jet at a rate of 1000 units per year.

14. Type of Strategic Initiative: BUILD

15. Strategic Plan:
Capitalize on the lower acquisition and operating costs of the small Eclipse 500 Jet to support air taxi, fractional ownership, and air charter operations' efforts to take passengers away from airlines. Focusing on short (under 1000 mile) direct trips where airline delays are most significant.

Capitalize on lower acquisition and operating costs to take a share of the charter/fractional ownership and business jet aircraft market.

Capitalize on higher speed and lower operating costs to take a share of the turboprop aircraft market.

Capitalize on higher speed, better weather avoidance, and higher engine reliability to take share from the piston aircraft market.

16. Tactical Plan:
1. Complete assembly and testing of six prototype aircraft. Use with temporary Teledyne engines to facilitate airworthiness and performance testing: two by --/--/03, two by --/--/03, and two by --/--/04.
2. Continue to test, evaluate and certify advanced flight controls and avionics, complete by --/--/03.
3. Continue to develop improved jet engines with Pratt & Whitney/Canada for delivery by ---- 2004, complete aircraft certification with these engines by ---- 2005.
4. Continue to build marketing relationships with air taxi operators, charter freight carriers, and charter medical emergency carriers to build order backlog to 3000 aircraft by --/--/05.
5. Continue to develop training simulators and a training program that will help pilots meet insurance and FAA requirements while ensuring high level of flight safety. Complete training simulators by --/--/04.
6. Complete friction-stir welding facility in Albuquerque and production facility at Double Eagle Airport (west of Albuquerque) by --/--/03.
7. Continue to work with insurance companies to assure availability of insurance by --/--/04.
8. Initiate production of 2000+ aircraft by --/--/06.

17. History & Projections (performance measures)

	Year-2	Last Year	This Year	Next Year	Year 3	Year 4	Year 5
Market Size ($000)	500,000	600,000	1,300,000	1,000,000	1,000,000	1,000,000	1,500,000
Market Share (%)	100%			50%	50%	50%	66%
Bookings ($000)	500,000	500,000	1,000,000	500,000	500,000	500,000	1,000,000
Backlog ($000)	500,000	1,000,000	2,000,000	2,500,000	3,000,000	3,000,000	3,000,000
Revenue ($000)						500,000	1,000,000
Operating Profit ($000)						N/A	10,000

Strategic Business Unit: Eclipse 500 Jet	**Plan Manager:** TBD	**Date Prepared:** June 2003
Company: Eclipse Aviation	**Strategy Advisor:** Bruce Robinson	**Date of Next Plan Review:** 12/15/03

Eclipse Business Strategy Summary

Eclipse Aviation has a focused strategy in a new emerging market for passenger air transportation. New emerging markets are, by definition, not structured with competitors, defining the market battlefield with customers established to define their strengths and weaknesses. As the market leader, Eclipse will define the market battlefield by taking customers from market alternative forms of air transportation, airlines, higher cost charter/fractional ownership operations, higher-cost bigger jets and turboprops, and slower piston propeller aircraft. Is their strategy viable in today's market?

Donald Burr, founder of Peoples Express that started the revolution in low-cost airlines like Jet Blue and Southwest Airlines, believes, according to a recent Wall Street Journal article, that the "real next-generation innovation will be in private transportation, not mass transportation." According to the article, Mr. Burr is in the process of raising money for a new air transportation venture and working with Eclipse Aviation as an aircraft supplier. Will he start a new air taxi operation? As a respected industry innovator, he believes in the viability of personal air taxi operations as an alternative to airline transport.

However, the backlog of more than 2000 Eclipse 500 orders (about $1.8 billion) speaks most effectively to the viability of the Eclipse Aviation strategy. If Vern Raburn can deliver on his product promises and meet the above tactical objectives, he should redefine the market for personal jet air transportation the way Henry Ford redefined automobile transportation with the Model T.

Open Issues:

As with all strategic plans, there are a number of open issues to be reviewed continuously in order to predict the success of the Eclipse 500 jet:

1. Will the new Pratt & Whitney engines be delivered on schedule and perform to expectations?
2. Will the price continue to escalate as true production costs are established?
3. Will the training program offered by Eclipse qualify an adequate number of pilots to pilot the Eclipse 500?
4. Will those pilots be able to obtain insurance?
5. Will the FAA and insurance companies permit single pilot operation?

6. Will the SATS program receive adequate funding to open up the 3000 additional airports to commercial IFR traffic?
7. Will a major market externality, like terrorist attacks or SARS virus, drive immediate demand for air taxi service to levels beyond those anticipated in this plan?
8. Will safety and reliability issues associated with early operating performance create a favorable or unfavorable reputation for the Eclipse 500?

Just how these open issues are resolved, not only by Eclipse but also by market externalities, will be the keys to the success of the Eclipse 500.

Chapter 4

Strategic Planning—Basic Concepts
Defining the Market Battlefield

We define Business Strategy as: "the art and science of meeting your competitors in the market battlefield under advantageous conditions."

When General Electric CEO Jack Welch says to his managers that his company will either be first or second in the market or it will exit it altogether, he mandates a winning strategic position relative to GE's competitors. He knows if you have either the largest or second-largest market share, you should be competitively advantaged. He also knows the market leaders historically have higher profit margins and the resources to react to market change. But are there strategies that lead to other viable market positions?

What is the staying power of the niche competitor—one who has a small market share relative to their competitors? Are there strategies that let small competitors survive and prosper in the market battlefield? Before we can identify winning strategies and positions on the market battlefield, we must first establish a better conceptual understanding of the market battlefield.

What is a market battlefield? What is its shape? How do we identify our competitors? What are the most important competitive strengths and weaknesses? What are winning positions on the market battlefield? How can we avoid a losing position? How does the size and shape of a market battlefield change over time? What are the impacts of market alternatives, externalities and saturation on the size and shape of the market battlefield? The *Quick*Strategy Model gives you a way to look at market battlefields to answer these questions.

Visualizing the Market Battlefield, the First Step in a Strategic Plan

In the last three chapters, you were thrown into the application of *Quick*Strategy without any explanation of the underlying theory. We hope these chapters gave you a feeling for the utility of our approach to strategic planning.

It is based on our own first-hand experience over the last thirty years in battles for the survival and prosperity of our businesses. Did we win all of the battles? No, but we now look at each market in a way that lets us visualize the opportunity or run from imminent failure. Here is how *Quick*Strategy visualizes markets.

The simplest Market Battlefield model shows your business against a single competitor fighting for two uncommitted or transient customers.

FIGURE 4-1
Market Battlefield

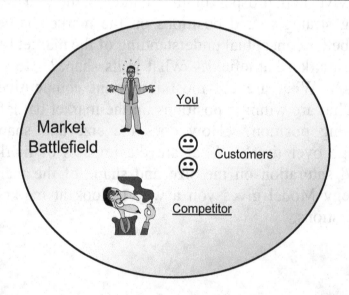

This model shows you that the essence of the battlefield is you and your competitor and your struggle to take customers. Winning customers is what business is all about. If you win a customer on a long-term basis, we call them a loyal customer. We all know they are better customers as they recognize your competitive advantages and are more difficult for competitors to capture.

<u>Customer Loyalty and the Market Battlefield</u>

We can visualize customer loyalty by showing the loyal customers behind the market competitor to whom they are loyal:

FIGURE 4-2
Loyal & Transient Customers

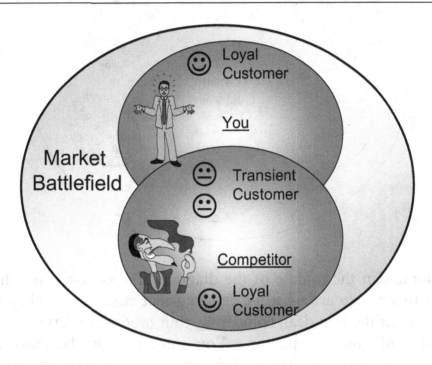

This model can be expanded to include many customers and competitors as shown in Figure 4-3.

FIGURE 4-3
Multiple Competitors Market Battlefield

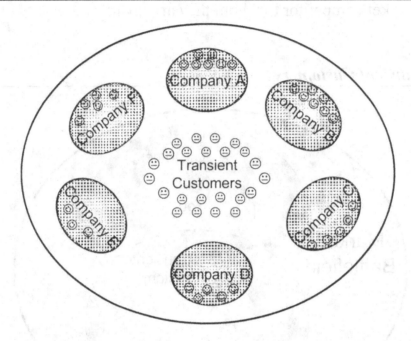

Customers in the middle of the diagram are not loyal to either you or your competitors; they are what we call transient customers. They shop with each purchase for the best deal, comparing your product or service features and prices to that of your competitor. You can't change the make-up of the customers in your market; some markets tend to be full of transient customers and some tend to have mostly loyal customers. However, you can position your business to focus on those customers who will generate the highest return on investment.

Markets that tend toward loyal customers are markets that have developed strong brand identity, require long-term product support, require continuous customer interaction, or require trust. For example:

- A business associate of mine always buys his tools at Sears. Why? To him, Craftsman tools are the best and his dad bought his tools at Sears. Brand Loyalty!

- My father always bought Plymouths. Why? Because the local Plymouth dealer always gave him the best service. Product Support!

- One of my companies manufactures complex electro-optical test equipment for military aircraft. Although we work to a contract specification, the customer and our engineers know that continual interaction is necessary to make sure the product fits ever-changing customer needs. Continuous Customer Interaction!

- When I buy jewelry, I go to a local jeweler. Do I pay more than an on-line supplier? A little, but I trust them to provide quality in a product that I can't evaluate on-line. Trust!

Loyal customers often let you charge them more for your product or service as they recognize your competitive advantages. They will tolerate minor disadvantages in your product without switching suppliers. They are hard to take from a competitor. In most cases, you can't take a loyal customer away from a competitor without an overwhelming competitive advantage.

Transient customers tend to dominate commodity markets. Unfortunately, many of our markets are becoming commodity markets. These customers are easier to attract to your products, but they are one-time buyers; you have to invest in a selling effort with each order. They will quickly move to the competitor offering the slightest advantage in price.

- When we purchase gravel, do we look at quality or just call around for the best price?
- When we purchase gasoline, how quickly do we move to a lower-cost supplier?
- When we purchase soda or beer, do we go to the outlet advertising the lowest price?
- When we purchase generic drugs on-line, do we care which supplier we use?

We are all transient customers with many of our purchases when we show little or no customer loyalty to a particular brand or supplier, only shopping for the best price.

Transient customers also tend to dominate new markets as the competitive advantages and disadvantages change so rapidly and there is no experiential basis for loyalty. Think about the early personal computer market. Except for Apple, there was little brand loyalty as each competitor offered a different operating system, making comparisons difficult for the beginning user; each successive purchase was a process of re-evaluating all product offerings. As a transient customer in a new market, we are looking for the latest innovation and are easily swayed to a new supplier with the latest gimmick.

Loyal and Transient Customers in the Case Studies:

In Case 1, the Albuquerque Turkey Burger, what type of customers does the owner of the new fast-food burger business encounter? The big four competitors in the fast-food burger market spend billions on advertising and promotion to attract loyal customers. In spite of the highly publicized dissatisfaction with their high fat and high calorie menus, customer loyalty in the fast-food burger business is higher than many other businesses. Most buyers are not going after the 99-cent product, a commodity product that attracts the transient. Most buyers have the taste of their preferred product in mind before they place their order; they know what a Big Mac or Whopper tastes like and they want it. The market segment Tony wants to attract will come from this loyal customer base, as he is offering no discount items on his menu. He will only get one chance to convert them from their McDonald's or Burger King habit that is the basis for their loyalty.

In Case 2, Georgia Wireless Constructors, customers are purchasing complex systems requiring investments of large sums of money and considerable technical interface with each supplier. GWC has a good reputation in the industry with its existing base of customers, but as the market matures and the transient customers become happy with their suppliers, they will become a harder sell for GWC. In some cases, GWC has discounted to the point of taking a loss to get in the door of target customers. This lets it prove its capability and build customer confidence, but could lead it into a price-driven market position. However, its strategy of teaming with local telecom suppliers having existing relationships with regional telephone companies in the wireless carrier affiliate programs is a good approach to overcoming supplier loyalty issues in this portion of its market.

The fact that several of its competitors are losing money and operating at extremely low margins may indicate the strong price orientation of many customers and should caution GWC to stay away from transient customers who chase price over performance with every purchase order.

> In Case 3, Eclipse Aviation, in a new emerging market with competitor products only as real as their paper designs and promised performance specifications, faces a market full of transient customers. If its new engines fail, if it encounters further delivery delays, or if a test flight crashes while a competitor delivers equivalent or better performance at an equivalent price, its customers will jump to the competitive products. Customer loyalty will only be established in this market as Eclipse and their competitors deliver quality products that meet their customers' expectations. (Cessna, with an established brand and customer loyalty in larger jet market alternative aircraft, may be the exception.) Customers loyal to their higher priced products may transfer their loyalty to products they introduce in direct competition to Eclipse in the personal jet market.)

As you envision your market battlefields, think about where the customers are positioned. Are they mostly the loyal customers who are hard to attract but easier to keep? Or are they mostly transient customers who move quickly to the supplier with the lowest price or latest gimmick? How you develop your strategy will depend on recognizing the level of customer loyalty in your market battlefield.

One CEO friend of mine says: "You can never make money selling to transient customers; customer loyalty is the basis for profit." Are you positioning your business to attract loyal customers?

Customer Needs and Their Effect on the Shape of Market Battlefields

What motivates a customer to purchase your products or services? We call these customer needs. Do you know your customers' needs and how they will change tomorrow?

Abraham H. Maslow postulated the generally accepted theory of customer motivation based on the following premises:[*]

1. A person will have many needs.
2. These needs will vary in importance and, therefore, can be ranked in hierarchy.
3. The person will seek to satisfy the most important need first.

---

[*] Abraham Maslow, 1908—1970.

4. When the person succeeds in satisfying an important need, it ceases being a motivator for the time being.

5. The person will then turn his or her attention to the next most important need.

Maslow is telling us that a customer's needs change continuously and so will your markets as they are no more than a collection of customer needs.

Case Studies and Changing Customer Needs

If I have $1,000 in my pocket, do I care whether McDonald's has a $1 burger sale if it does not meet my taste needs or gives slow service? If my company has two personal jets at my disposal, do I take a Southwest airlines flight because it costs less? If my investors refuse to invest in additional cell towers until I show better financial returns, will I be a price-driven buyer of new cell towers?

Although we work hard to identify market needs, we should recognize they are people driven and, like people, change fast and often. Seldom do any two people rank their needs identically and they change them at different rates. Therefore, our market battlefield diagram is only a snapshot of our perception of today's customer needs in the market we serve and our vision is only a one-time macro perspective.

When you envision your market battlefield, are customer needs driven primarily by price or performance? Why do you care? A winning strategy in a market dominated by performance-driven customers may not work effectively in a market dominated by price-driven customers and vice versa.

All markets have some customers driven primarily by price and some customers driven primarily by performance. We envision the shape of the market battlefield as a function of the ratio of price-driven to performance-driven customers. As shown in Figure 4-4, we group the price-driven customers on the left and the performance-driven customers on the right of the market battlefield. When the majority of the customers are grouped on the price (left) side of the battlefield, we call this a PRICE MARKET as they make their purchase decision based primarily on low price.

FIGURE 4-4
Price Market

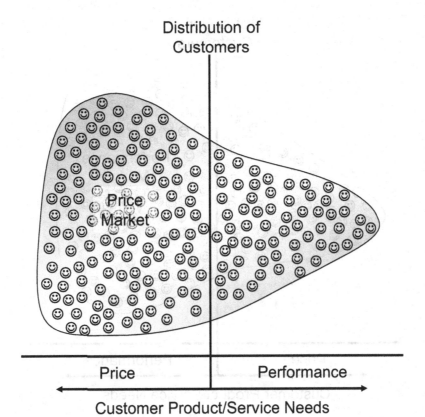

Typically, commodity products such as salt, copy paper, sand, grains and manufacturing feedstock are price markets with most of the customers shopping for the lowest price on each purchase. Can you compete in these markets with a performance position—with a unique salt, better quality copy paper or premium grains? Yes, but you cannot become market leader, only a niche competitor with continuous price pressure on your products.

When the majority of the customers are primarily driven by performance needs, we envision them as grouped on the right side of the market as shown in the following diagram. We call this a PERFORMANCE MARKET.

FIGURE 4-5
Performance Market

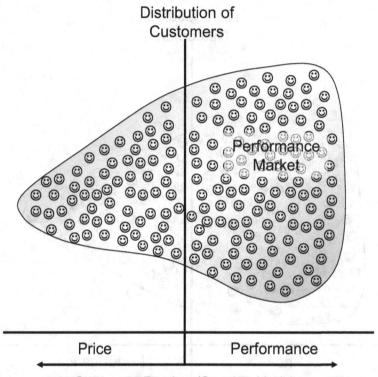

Most of these customers are making their purchase decision based on the performance characteristics of the product or service they are purchasing. Typical performance products are premium priced, recognizing the unique attributes of the product or service. For example, most perfume, premium wines, surgical services (for me, anyway), architect services and jewelry would be considered by many to be performance markets. Are there people who shop for a compromise in performance on premium wines to get the best prices or purchase discount jewelry or low-cost surgery? Yes, but price considerations are not the dominant driving force behind their purchase decision. To have a winning strategy in a performance-driven market, you will be more successful with a superior product offering than a discount price.

Often, we look at markets and it is not clear that the market is driven mostly by either price or performance needs of the customers. We call this a VALUE MARKET and show the customers equally divided between price and performance requirements as shown in the following diagram.

FIGURE 4-6
Value Market

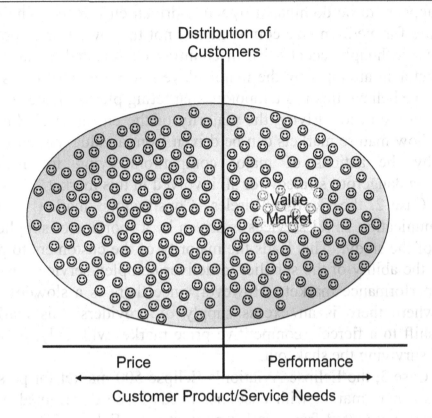

Although we often find *Quick*Strategy users defining their market as a value market based on a lack of careful research into customer needs, there are some good examples of markets where many customer purchases are driven by price and just as many driven by performance. The new midsize automobile market is an example of a value market. We all know people who shop for the lowest-cost vehicle and an equal number who always look for the latest product features. The midsize auto market is dominated by customers who look for a good compromise in price and performance from cars like Ford Taurus and Toyota Camry. Value market leaders offer the right compromise between price and performance in their product offerings. The rest of the competitors usually occupy niche positions either on the price or performance ends of the market.

Market Shapes of the Case Study Competitors:

In Case 1, the Albuquerque Turkey Burger market for fast-food burgers appears to be dominated by value-driven customers. The majority of sales are for medium-size combo meals, not the lowest-price options on the menu. Although recent price discounting on selected menu items has been a factor in attempts by the major players to move customers to their products, we believe this is a temporary marketing ploy and does not reflect a change in the needs driving the majority of the customers. However, it indicates how mature markets can be driven from a value market to a price market by the actions of major competitors vying for incremental business—a dangerous strategy for all involved in this market.

In Case 2, the Georgia Wireless Constructors' market for wireless telecommunication EF&I services is driven by a shortage of suppliers as of the date of the study. This leads the majority of the customers to purchase based on the ability of the supplier to deliver complex services on a timely basis, a performance market. However, once there is a slowdown in the market where there is an excess supply of providers, this market will quickly shift to a fiercely competitive price market with only the low-cost suppliers surviving the shakeout.

In Case 3, the Eclipse Aviation's Eclipse 500 market for personal jet aircraft is a new market with customer needs to be determined when the customers are attracted from market alternatives. Eclipse 500 has defined its market by providing a personal jet aircraft at half the purchase price and operating cost of any existing competitor. The market, therefore, has attracted many customers with a strong price-driven need versus the market alternatives.

However, it also offers exceptional performance features in its aircraft. If it fails to meet the performance requirements, it will not be able to grow the market as projected. Eclipse is defining the market and will be the market leader, but offering the right compromise in price and performance will be required to hold that leadership position. We call its market a value market at this time, as customer needs are not just price driven or performance driven but an indeterminate combination of both needs. As the market matures, we will have a clearer understanding of customer needs.

What is the shape of your market battlefield? How has it changed over the last few years and why? Many markets start as performance markets, transition to value-driven markets, then wind up as price-driven mature commodity markets. If you don't shift your strategy as the shape of your market shifts, you may fail to meet the changing needs of your customers.

What happens to customer loyalty as the shape of your market changes? As you can see in Figure 4-7, Market Battlefields and Customer Loyalty, transient customers tend to be clustered on the "price" end of the market battlefield diagrams and loyal customers on the "performance" end of the market battlefield.

FIGURE 4-7
Market Battlefields and Customer Loyalty

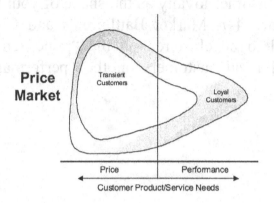

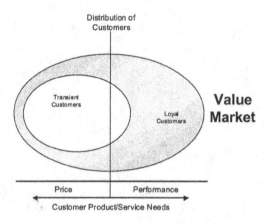

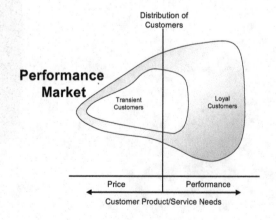

What are the implications of these market battlefield perspectives to your strategic decision process? Remember, "Strategy is the art and science of meeting your competitors in the market battlefield under advantageous conditions." It's all about positioning relative to your competitors in the eyes of the customers that make up the market. You must not only know your competitors, but also how they are positioned on the market battlefield. Further, you must also know the shape of the battlefield in terms of customer needs and how they change in order to develop a winning strategy. For example:

1. Is it easier to enter or change market share in a price market or a performance market by undercutting competitor prices? How can you hold market share with transient customers always shopping for the next lower price?

2. Would you expect to spend more money to attract loyal customers in a performance market? Would the investment be justified if they were more likely to be a repeat customer? What happens when performance markets shift to value or price markets? Would you be better off positioning as a price competitor in a performance market about to shift to a value or price-driven market?

3. Are you just unable to rank changing customer needs in your market, so you envision you are in a value market? Maybe it should be segmented into two markets, one a price market and another a performance market? Maybe you only see one section of the market because your customers are clustered in that end?

Envision the market battlefield as shown in Figure 4-8, Market Battlefield Competitor Positions. Look at who has the largest market share and why. That will give you a clue as to how customers' needs are ranked and the shape of the market.

FIGURE 4-8
Market Battlefield Competitor Positions

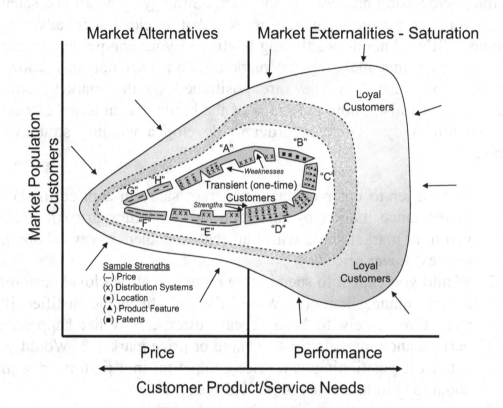

As you can see, customers define the terrain of the battlefield, its size and shape. They also fight for positions as shown in the diagram. Competitors (A through H) are arranged around transient customers who constantly move from one competitor to another. The battle for transient customers is continuous as they define the "no man's land" portion of the battlefield. They are of little strategic value and often cost more than the returns they provide to the winner. The valuable customers in the market battlefield lie behind each competitor; they are well-defended loyal customers. Weapons used on the market battlefield are shown as competitive strengths (X, O,-, etc.); competitive weaknesses are shown as gaps between competitors and the absence of strengths in competitors' positions.

These competitive strengths may be price, as shown on the far left side of the battlefield, a combination of price and performance as shown in the middle of the battlefield, or as specific performance advantages as shown in the competitors clustered on the far right side of the battlefield.

Competitors should be envisioned as arranged on the battlefield according to their market share and the market needs they serve. Market share in this market battlefield model is defined as those loyal customers directly behind each competitor, as shown in Figure 4-8. Note: some would suggest transient buyers not be considered as part of market share. We envision market leaders as holding the largest share of customers by offering a range of products and services, and they define the middle of the market battlefield model. Specialized performance competitors are usually smaller and hold the far right side of the battlefield. Competitors offering low-price products and services hold positions on the far left side of the battlefield relative to the market leaders.

The Market Battlefield Competitor Positions model (Figure 4-8) is intended to help you visualize your position relative to your competitors and communicate to your employees and coworkers your struggle for market share. Ask them the following questions:

1. Where is our business positioned in our market battlefield?
2. Are we a market leader trying to defend a broad range of customers with products and services covering the range of offerings from low price to high performance?
3. Are we a specialized supplier of high performance products?
4. Are we a specialized low price supplier?
5. Where do we have strengths and weaknesses?
6. Where do our competitors have strengths and weaknesses?
7. Are we ready for the next change in market size and shape?

Answers to these questions will help you decide your strategic objective, gaining or holding customers. It will help establish your strategy; positioning yourself in the market battlefield to accomplish your strategic objective. But what customers do you include in your market battlefield?

Segmenting Your Market Into Well-defined Market Battlefields

Your company may be fighting in more than one battlefield. I have made more profit by properly segmenting businesses into those battlefields with strategic opportunity and those with no opportunity than in any business endeavor. My partners and I once acquired a company with $40 million in revenue. Our analysis revealed they were fighting in over 61 market battlefields. They were losing the battle in most of their market segments, resulting in substantial financial losses. We eliminated all the business segments that were fighting losing battles and combined the remaining good segments. We then had a $30 million profitable company fighting in 11 market battlefields. How did we initially determine they were fighting in 61 market battlefields?

First, we made a list of all of the products and services they were offering. Next, we had the business managers describe the customer they served with each set of products and services. Then we asked them to describe the customer needs they were satisfying with each set of products and services for the customers they served (the first three boxes on the Market Battlefield Summary). With these three variables identified, they described 61 different market segments (battlefields). A market battlefield is defined by a unique product or service selling to a defined set of customers satisfying a specific set of customer needs.

When we found they were supplying similar products to the same set of customers satisfying the same customer needs, we asked whether these markets should be combined. We asked whether one similar segment was a market alternative to the other. If one product or service is a replacement product for another, then it is likely to be a market alternative. If you are the market leader in the new product, then we ask if it is profitable to still supply the older market alternative; often it is not.

When we found different products sold to the same set of customers satisfying the same set of needs, we combined market battlefield summaries unless the competitors were different between the two markets. Where we found the same products sold to different sets of customers with different needs, we further segmented the markets creating new market battlefield summaries.

After we redefined the market battlefields by virtue of similar products, customers and customer needs, we could take the next step with the company management and look at those segments where they had significant competitive advantages vs. their competitors. Where they could not clearly and quickly identify a significant competitive advantage, we eliminated the market segment. We then reconstructed the business description and forecast the business with only the remaining advantaged segments. The company we acquired has been a profitable operation every year since we eliminated the underperforming market segments and focused management on the remaining strategic opportunities.

How do you segment your business? Start with a description of your product or service, identify the customers to whom you sell, and try to summarize their needs.

If you find that certain sets of customers have different needs or priorities, segment your market battlefield into two separate segments to address the unique needs of those two sets of customers. If you describe the market alternatives, externalities, and saturation factors affecting your market and you find some factors apply to some of your products or services and some factors to others, segment your markets again. If your competitor analysis reveals many competitors that do not compete with all of your products or services, you may want to segment your markets again.

Through the process of identifying your products/services, customers, and customer needs, you identify market segments. Each market segment is a market battlefield. When you look at factors affecting the size and shape of your market and competitors as they impact your segment, you can decide if further segmentation should take place to define your market battlefield. The Market Battlefield Summary will help you make each iteration until you have adequately defined your competitive position in the market you serve.

With this description of your market battlefields on the one-page Market Battlefield Summary, *Quick*Strategy Form 1.0, you have a snapshot at a single point in time of your market battlefield. However, it must be updated regularly as customer needs and competitors change continuously.

Anticipating Changes in the Size and Shape of Market Battlefields

What makes the size and shape of your market battlefield change? Changing customer needs? But how do we anticipate those changes? If you develop your strategic plan around a static market battlefield model, you will never anticipate changes and adjust your strategy accordingly. To anticipate changes to the size and shape of your market battlefield, watch three forces:

1. *Market Alternatives*: Those alternative products or services that fill the same customer need. An automobile, for example, is a market alternative to a horse and buggy. When customers move to automobiles, the horse and buggy market declines. A customer who decides to build a product in his own factory represents a market alternative to purchasing the product in the competitive market.
2. *Market Externalities*: These are factors external to the market and beyond competitive activity that can change the size and shape of the market, such as government regulation, natural catastrophes, financial market shifts, wars, etc.
3. *Market Saturation*: Customer needs that are satisfied and will not require additional products or services within the forecast period. For example, once a customer has acquired a set of fine silverware, their needs are satisfied.

Although these forces may act randomly to change your market battlefield, they normally act in a predictable manner we call "market maturation." Knowing the maturity of your market and how these forces are acting to change the size and shape of your market gives you more insight into the strategic opportunity. For example, an investment in a new market with few competitors represents a significantly different strategic opportunity than an investment in a mature market with old well-established competitors.

Market Maturation—Its Effect on Market Size and Shape

As we saw with Case 3, Eclipse Aviation, new markets are poorly defined while in Case 1, Albuquerque Turkey Burger, mature markets are well defined. A winning strategy in a new market probably won't work in a mature market. In addition, both markets are changing and a strategy that will succeed today in either market may not work tomorrow. How do we know how our markets will change and when?

As we said above, to predict changes in market size and shape you must know the three forces that impact the size and shape of your market: Market Alternatives, Market Externalities, and Market Saturation. How they impact each stage in the maturity of your markets is demonstrated in Figure 4-9, Market Maturity, as a curve showing how total market size (sales revenue) changes over time. To help understand how these forces impact the market differently over time, we have divided the market maturity curve as a function of time into 5 segments: New, Growth, Mature, Decline and Residual. We will show how market saturation, market alternatives and market externalities uniquely impact every stage of market maturity and will help you see how each stage can be identified and anticipated by paying close attention to market history and the three market forces. First, let's define each stage of market maturity.

FIGURE 4-9
Market Maturity

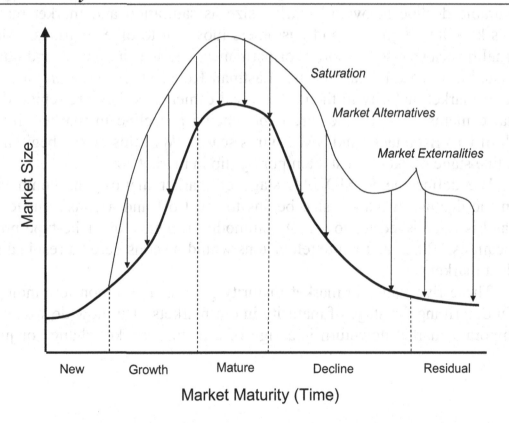

We define the NEW stage of market maturity as the time from product concept to the time consistent sales are established in a competitive environment. The Eclipse 500 Jet is in this phase of market maturity. All sales are taken from market alternative products and the market is in the process of defining and prioritizing customer needs.

We define the GROWTH stage of market maturity as commencing when well-defined customer needs and competitors are present in the market and market growth is coming from market alternatives and competitors. The market for wireless telecom EF&I services in Case 2 is an example of a growth stage market (as of early 2000).

We define the MATURE stage of market maturity as commencing when the rate of growth in market size begins to slow and sales start to level off. It is the impact of market saturation and the shift to other market alternatives on customer decisions that characterizes this phase of market maturity. In Case 1, we see the fast-food burger market maturing, as there is a fast-food burger outlet available within easy driving distance of all customers in the market (saturation) and the market alternative products (tacos and subs) are taking customers from the fast-food burger market.

We define the DECLINE stage of market maturity as commencing with measurable decline in overall market size as saturation and market maturity factors kick into high gear and customers move on to other markets. Market externalities can cause temporary or permanent declines in market and must be evaluated on a case-by-case basis. Eastman Kodak is experiencing a decline stage of market maturity in their film-based cameras as they are replaced with digital cameras. The airlines are experiencing a decline in market size as a result of terrorist attacks and SARS virus scares. Will this be the beginning of a decline stage market or just a temporary dip in market size?

We define the RESIDUAL stage of market maturity as commencing when the decline in market size begins to level off and a consistent level of demand is established for low-cost commodity products or niche-type product applications. Black-and-white televisions would be considered a residual stage product market.

These five stages in market maturity give us a common terminology to use in describing the stage of maturity in our markets. But how do we know if a temporary market downturn is a sign of a mature market change or just an anomaly?

Recognizing Market Battlefield Maturity

When we look at the entire Market Maturity curve in Figure 4-9, it is easy to identify the various phases of market maturity. In real market battlefields, you have only a few data points to work with and must predict your market's maturity and how fast it will move on to the next stage in order to properly adjust your strategy. During the growth stage of a market, all you see is rising sales and rising market size and many think it will continue indefinitely. How do you know when this market will stop growing? In the mature phase, how do you know how long the market will stay at its peak before it declines? As we have said, there are only two ways to identify the current state of market maturity in your markets and project the future:

1. Carefully analyze the historic growth in your market. This means you have to know your competitors' growth over time to get accurate market size data.
2. Analyze trends in market forces that shape your market: market saturation, market alternatives and market externalities.

Usually, historic market data is the best indicator of the current stage of market maturity and trends in market forces are the best guide to forecasting market changes.

There are many ways of analyzing market size. You can look at the total units sold, total sales revenue, or total number of customers and come up with three different answers in many markets. I have ongoing arguments over the proper selection of a measure for total market size. We use total sales revenue in almost all of our analyses as this number is easily obtained for most competitors without violating their privacy. (In new markets, we sometimes use total booked orders.) It can be obtained most readily through industry associations, market research reports, independent research, and talkative salesmen at trade shows.

When using sales revenue as an indicator of total market size and market share, some of our associates recommend normalizing the sales revenue numbers to reflect the effects of inflation where inflation rates are significant relative to market growth rates. For example, in some Latin American countries where inflation is 20% + each year, you must adjust the market revenue numbers in most markets or you could think your markets were in a growth stage well after they had saturated and entered a more mature stage.

Another way total revenue can be distorted as an indicator of total market size is by shifts in product mix to higher or lower-cost products. For Example, in Case 1 describing the fast-food burger market, has super-sizing products and shifting the customer to larger, higher-priced menu items represented a real growth in the fast-food burger market? Has the shift to higher-priced four-wheel drive automobiles indicated growth in the automobile market? These factors can distort your market size analysis unless you are aware of the magnitude of their impact on your analysis.

We typically recommend an evaluation of the last three to five years of market revenue to establish data points on the market maturity curve that will indicate the current level of market maturity. However, in some markets, you need to look at monthly trends as market life cycles may be only two years. Historic data for a new or growth stage market will show significant increases in total revenue (adjusted for inflation and other distortions) over time. Historic data for a mature stage market will show a significant slowing of revenue growth and maybe some decline. Historic data in a decline stage market will show consistently decreasing overall sales revenue. Level market sales revenue after a period of decline may indicate a residual stage market. Looking backwards at the market size data, properly adjusted, may tell you where you are in market maturity; but market force trends are what we analyze to forecast imminent changes in market growth.

The following chart summarizes how trends in market externalities, market externalities, and market saturation help predict changes in market growth.

Market Stage (Market Size)	Market Alternatives Trend	Market Externalities Trend	Market Saturation Trend
NEW (Small Growing)	No Growth Begin Decline	No Major Barriers to Growth	None
GROWTH (Rapid Growth)	Rapid Decline	Few Barriers to Growth	None
MATURE (Slowing Growth)	New Alternatives Emerging	May Have Negative Barriers Emerging	Starting
DECLINE (Shrinking)	Alternatives Taking Large Market Share	Negative Externalities May Drive Decline	Started
RESIDUAL (Flat to Slow Decline)	Alternatives Take Over Customers	May be Keeping a Lid on Market Size	May be Dominant Factor in Market

Let's see how market alternatives help us predict change in market size.

In a NEW market like Eclipse Aviation faces with its Eclipse 500 Jet, it is beginning to take market share from the market alternatives: airline transportation with sales to air taxi operations, higher priced corporate jet and turboprop aircraft products, air charter and freight operations that need lower-cost high-speed transport, and general aviation as pilots move up to higher performance aircraft. It has to focus its strategy on these declining market alternatives. As the competitors line up against them, customer needs will become more defined and market growth will become more predictable. They will then transition to the growth stage of the market.

In a GROWTH market like the wireless telecom EF&I services offered by GWC in Case 2, it has to look at market alternatives like in-house customer capability and externalities like available growth capital for customers to determine when a market growth will slow and drive them into a mature market.

In a MATURE market like the one Albuquerque Turkey faces in the fast-food burger market of Case 1, the market alternative growth such as tacos and sub sandwiches must be watched to forecast transition to a decline market. It also must watch externalities, such as foodborne illnesses and lawsuits against industry leaders, as they will drive customers away from this market segment. It must watch saturation. An excess number of outlets in its market, for example, will drive competition to more aggressively compete for a limited number of customers and further impact market growth with price cuts.

In a DECLINE stage market, such as large mainframe computers, suppliers like IBM have to watch the market alternative of networked smaller computers to estimate the impact they will have on taking market share from the mainframe business. They will also see market saturation as a major factor in slowed market growth as most companies have adequate computer power for their applications and are years away from replacement.

In a RESIDUAL stage market, like the black-and-white television market, the color television market alternative has taken all but the low-cost and niche applications away. Market saturation is complete and the small residual market is stable at a very small percentage of the overall television market in the U.S.

In these dynamic market battlefields, you can see how history combined with an understanding of the market forces that impact the size and shape help predict market changes. You can do little to impact these changes. You can only reposition your business relative to your competitors in the market battlefield to capitalize on change. In a growth market, where your sales depend on your unique product features, will you be ready for market maturity (it is inevitable in today's changing markets) when customers migrate to the low-cost supplier? Look what Dell did to upset the maturing PC market and what Southwest Airlines did to the air passenger market. The alternative is to reduce operating costs and prepare for a smaller niche performance position in a mature market.

Positioning in a Changing Market Battlefield, the Basis for Winning Strategies

The first step in positioning your business in a changing market battlefield is to know where you are relative to your competitors. Your position is determined by your market share relative to your competitors. It is also determined by your strengths and weaknesses relative to your competitors, *as perceived by your customers. Strengths and weaknesses are relevant only to the extent they address the needs of the customers.*

What good is a competitive strength if few customers care about it? Is a competitor's weakness that is not translated into customer dissatisfaction something you can capitalize on in your strategy? Unfortunately, I have seen too many revolutionary products that were overwhelmingly advantaged only in the mind of the inventor. I have sat in too many meetings where managers talked about the weaknesses of the market leader they will take advantage of in their strategy only to find that the market leader has created the weakness by dropping a money-losing product.

Many years ago, I patented the first practical home soda machine. It is about the size of a coffee maker. It makes 200 one-liter bottles of soda for about five cents a bottle. No more lugging bottles of soda from the store and you save five or ten times the cost of bottled soda. On top of that, there is no need to dispose of bottles as they can be reused in my machine. Overwhelming competitive advantage? Only in my mind! Customers wanted convenience, not the hassle of charging a bottle of water with CO_2 and adding syrup. One customer said the kids would make a mess of the kitchen with the syrup and occasionally, in early models, the one-liter plastic bottles would explode when they were being charged with CO_2.

Lesson: If the customer does not perceive an overwhelming need for your product, it is not a competitive strength.

Cost: About $300,000 invested in development and marketing expense—a cost I recovered by selling the invention a year later.

I co-own a weather instrument company. It is 138 years old and a trusted name in the industry; the Wright brothers used our weather instruments. We make high-end weather instruments tested and approved by the National Weather Service, the military and the FAA for use in reporting critical weather parameters at major airports. As a pilot, I realized that the windsock was the only weather instrument at thousands of smaller private airports and I had the solution. I invented a small weather station that cost about one-tenth the price of an official government-approved weather station. My new product reported weather data in a digital format to the pilots within a ten-mile radius of the small private airport.

The pilots' reaction: they have been flying over the airport, rolling to one side and looking at the windsock for years and they have had no problem. The ones that did are probably no longer flying. The airport owners' reaction: we get funding for our airport from the federal and state government; it must be approved by them to get the funding.

Two years later, we are completing the process of getting federal approval on the system so that it qualifies for federal funding. Where we have met federal and state funding requirements, we are selling units—at a higher price than the original design to cover the costs of mandated product changes. Even though I was in the industry as a supplier and a pilot, I did not properly understand customer needs and the influence external market factors had on those needs.

McDonald's is the clear market leader in the fast-food burger market. Case 1 in this book is built around a perceived weakness in McDonald's and the suppliers to offer a low-calorie, low-fat product. They are even being sued for making customers obese. However, do you remember the McLean burger, a veggie burger dropped from McDonald's menu when it did not sell? Last year Burger King, number two in the market, introduced a BK Veggie sandwich to its menu. We understand the market response has been less than enthusiastic. The high-fat, high-calorie menu of the fast-food burger chains is a weakness in the minds of what percentage of the consumers? If it is a weakness, can the market leaders fix this weakness with one or two additional items added to their menu? Can Albuquerque Turkey Burger capitalize on this weakness to build a new low-fat, low-calorie fast-food burger business?

When you identify competitor strengths and weaknesses—if they are not verified by customers' behavior and address specific customer needs—they may be of little value in positioning your business on the market battlefield. Winning strategies must address real strengths and weaknesses as perceived by your customers relative to your competitors. If the competitor can easily correct a market weakness, is it a weakness that leads to a strategic opportunity? If they can easily add market strength, do they neutralize your strength?

Identifying and Ranking Market Competitors

Competitors should be easy to identify. They are the entities your business faces when you vie for a customer order. However, I have often seen businesses competing against imaginary competitors or surprised by competitors they did not recognize in their markets. For example:

1. When Albuquerque Turkey Burger first looked at competitors in the fast-food burger market, it thought on a national level. However, its Albuquerque-based business only attracted customers in the Albuquerque area. In fact, its customers will live, work or shop within a ten-mile radius of its outlet. The competitors are those that vie for the business of this local customer. A national fast-food burger chain not located in their local market is not a competitor.
2. A friend of mine operates an industrial hardware distribution business in California. He identifies his competitors as the traditional competitors with similar operations in California. Can he omit the on-line distributors of the same products to his customers from his competitive analysis?
3. Can local pharmacies leave mail order competitors out of their competitor analysis? We have all seen the mail order houses, especially foreign-based operations, significantly under-price local drug stores.
4. Why do we not view a customer-owned supplier as a direct competitor? We think of it as a market alternative because, in most cases, we don't even get a chance to compete for this business.

How do you identify your competitors? They are any supplier of the same or essentially the same product or service to the set of customers you define as your target market to satisfy customer needs you have identified as characteristic of those customers.

To validate a competitor, ask the following questions:

- If that competitor disappeared, could I get more business?
- Does that competitor try to take business from me on a competitive basis?
- Does that competitor have brand recognition with my customers?
- Is that competitor qualified to do business in my markets?

If the answer to any of the above questions is yes, they are a competitor.

We rank these competitors by market share, not company size, as it is their presence in our market that we compete against. I have often seen very large companies enter our markets only to be beaten back by much smaller companies in a market leadership position.

Once, a multibillion-dollar conglomerate called me and told me it wanted to buy one of our product lines. I talked to the operating manager of our product line and we decided to visit the person making the inquiry. The buyers were quick to tell us they intended to enter our market and would overwhelm our market position (we were market leader in this 20 million dollar market). However, they would pay us a fair price for our business if we wanted to sell. We said we would think about their offer.

At our next customer meeting, we discreetly asked our key customers what they would do if this large conglomerate entered the market. Most said they did not trust the large conglomerate, as they had bad experiences with them as a supplier of related products. We did not sell. They entered the market a year later and failed to attract any of our customers. Their company size was a negative to our customers and certainly not a basis for comparing their market position. We focus on market share in the specific market segment identified by our battle plan to determine our competitive position.

Case Studies and Size of Competitors:

In Case 1, we only look at the size of the fast-food burger competitors in our regional market. McDonald's national share is less important than their local market share.

In Case 2, we only look at the revenue the multibillion-dollar A&E firms have received from the wireless telecom market. We were not able to accurately determine in our first draft plan how much of this revenue was specific to the customers in our target market area.

> In Case 3, we did not look at the overall size of Cessna Aircraft, a multibillion-dollar operation, only the portion of their business that focused on the personal jet aircraft market.

A famous old Massachusetts politician once offered the following advice to a new politician: "All Politics is Local." Although you may not agree with his politics, he knew it was the hearts and minds of his constituents that he had to win to win elections. He understood the needs of his local constituents and he understood his local political rivals (competitors). That is how he won elections—not by competing on the national political level.

In developing your market battlefield summaries, think of how you win the hearts and minds of customers you understand. Don't chase large imagined groups of customers with your business strategy or compete with amorphous conglomerate organizations. Focus on those customers where you know, through first-hand experience, their needs and the competitors you compete against for their business. Know that every day, your competitors are trying to take away your loyal customers and you have no choice but to fight for their business in the market battlefield.

The Market Battlefield Summary

How can we summarize the market battlefield for each market segment of your business that translates the above concepts into a working document for the management of your business? The essence of *Quick*Strategy is its ability to aid you in rapidly identifying your market battlefield situation as a basis for your strategic plan. The Market Battlefield Summary, *Quick*Strategy Form 1.0 on the following page, is designed to accomplish this objective.

MARKET BATTLEFIELD SUMMARY *QUICK*STRATEGY™ Form 1.0

1. Product or Service:	**2. Customers:**
3. Customer Need:	**4. Market Shape:**
5. Market Alternatives:	**6. Saturation:**
7. Externalities:	

8. Competitors	Strengths	Weaknesses	Sales $(000) Last Yr./This Yr.	Share (%)

9. Market Size (Sales Revenue $000)   Total

Year-5	Year-4	Year-3	Year-2	Last Year	This Year	Year 2	Year 3	Year 4	Year 5

10. Market Maturity _____Stage

Strategic Business Unit:	Plan Manager:	Date Prepared:
Company:	Strategy Advisor:	Date of Next Plan Review:

The first four boxes in the form, (1) Product or Service, (2) Customers, (3) Customer Need, and (4) Market Shape help you define your market battlefield by segmenting it from other related markets offering market alternative products or services. The next three boxes (5) Market Alternatives, (6) Saturation, and (7) Externalities are where you identify the forces affecting future market growth. Box 8 is where you identify your competitors and their market share as well as their market strengths and weaknesses to establish your position relative to the competition in your market. In Box 9, you identify the historic market size and trends and forecast future market growth based on analysis of the above information. In Box 10, you identify the stage of market maturity.

A detailed set of instructions for completing the form is found in Appendix A.

By putting all of your market segments into a common one-page *Quick*Strategy format, you can quickly observe the key variables impacting your market and readily share information with other members of your organization. It is intentionally concise and meant to force you to choose your words carefully and precisely to describe each variable. You are then prepared to develop a strategic plan to advantageously position your business in each market battlefield.

Chapter 5

Strategic Planning—Basic Concepts
Developing the Strategic Plan

The Market Battlefield Summary gives you a perspective on the size and shape of your market, your product or service offering, customers, customer needs, competitors and their relative strengths and weaknesses. Again, business strategy is "the art and science of meeting your competitors in the market battlefield under advantageous conditions." There are no cookbook methods to define when you have an advantageous condition. How advantaged must you be to win market share? Just enough to accomplish your strategic market share objective.

Why not just focus your efforts on building your "core competence," as many strategic planning advisors would suggest? Because the market may not care about your core competence and, if it cares about your core competence today, it may not care about it tomorrow. A strategic plan must be dynamic, changing to meet the ever-changing needs of the customer and challenges of competitors.

The starting point for all dynamic strategic plans is to carefully analyze your business strengths and weaknesses relative to your competitors. If you have a "core competence" that leads to an advantageous condition, so much the better to execute your strategy. If you don't, you can retreat from the market or acquire the requisite advantage against your target competitor or market alternative competitor. Whatever is required to take business and achieve your strategic objective is what your strategic plan should reflect.

Most business is a zero sum game—you must either take customers from your competitors or from market alternative competitors or they will take them from you. (If you believe customers come from some free space, stop right now. We have never found that magical place.) Once your market battlefield is defined, your strategic plan starts by selecting those competitors against which you are going to compete. Why select specific competitors? Why not compete against all competitors? Targeting selected competitors focuses your strategy on those competitors most susceptible to your market initiatives and limits the required resources. Whether your company's strategic initiative is to build market share, hold market share, harvest or retreat from the market, your strategic plan should reflect how you will maximize your gains or minimize your losses against your target competitors. (As you will see, probe strategies must also be focused on specific competitors to see if they have exploitable weaknesses or you have superior strengths.)

This chapter will help you understand our perspective on strategic plans and how to position your business to meet competitors under advantageous conditions in order to grow or sustain market position. If this is not possible given your business's resources, it will help you position your business to harvest cash or retreat from the market battlefield with minimum losses. If you can't decide whether you have a sustainable competitive advantage or can exploit a competitor's weakness, it will show you how to probe a market to test the viability of a strategic initiative.

SELECTING THE APPROPRIATE STRATEGIC INITIATIVE

When you look at your market battlefield, do you have a significant competitive advantage? Do you have a weakness you can fix? Are competitors willing to defend their market position with resources far in excess of those available to you? Is the market growing and providing high potential returns on investment or declining into a price-driven battlefield? Based on your overview of the market, what type of strategic initiative should you pursue?

To help you with this decision, we have identified five different types of viable strategic initiatives: BUILD, HOLD, HARVEST, RETREAT, and PROBE. You can probably think of other descriptions for your strategy like Duck for Cover, Take No Prisoners, or Run Away Fast. However, we think our five types of strategic initiatives give you an adequate conceptual basis for identifying winning strategies.

How can Harvest or Retreat be a winning strategy? The best-managed businesses know when to exit a market battlefield keeping a maximum number of resources to redeploy to another market opportunity. The fool fights to the last nickel when the competition is overwhelming their market position.

How can Probe be a winning strategy? Often, you cannot determine if your competitive advantage is adequate or you don't fully understand the extent of your competitors' strengths and weaknesses. With a Probe strategy you apply limited resources to test the market conditions, applying the bulk of your resources only after a Probe strategy indicates a clear strategic opportunity.

In order to make sure we have a common understanding of each type of strategic initiative, we define them as follows:

- **BUILD**: To invest in a strategic initiative to increase market share.
- **HOLD**: To invest only in strategic initiatives that help hold and defend market position (share).
- **HARVEST**: To withdraw from a market battlefield making no additional investment or reducing investments as required, maximizing cash extracted from the business.
- **RETREAT**: To exit a market battlefield as fast as possible while attempting to minimize losses.
- **PROBE**: To make a small investment to explore market battlefield opportunities. This investment is limited in amount and terminated at a specific date.

Most business managers measure success by growth and will select the BUILD strategy whenever possible. This leads to the risk of trying to justify your competitive position to suit the selected strategy. When faced with no competitive advantage and overwhelming competition, selecting a BUILD strategy is like the "Charge of the Light Brigade." It will be exciting and filled with the sort of short-term bravado that great stories are made of, but result in unacceptable losses.

The appropriate strategy does not mean being the market leader. In business, it means you have selected the type of strategy consistent with the market opportunity and resources at your disposal.

Steps to Selecting the Appropriate Type of Strategy

One way to think through the selection process for a strategy appropriate to your business situation is by use of a decision model like the one shown in Figure 5-1.

Figure 5-1
Strategic Initiative Decision Model

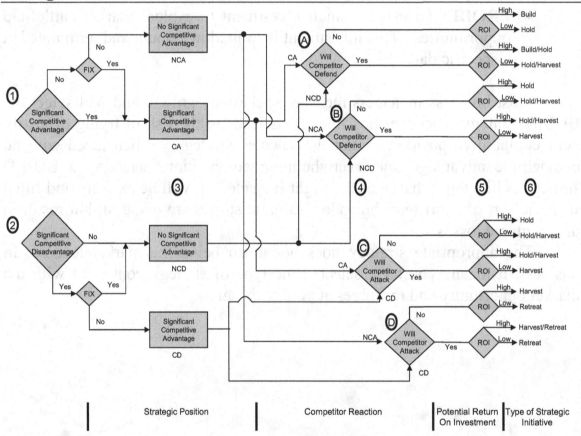

This model is built around selecting your strategy based on having a significant competitive advantage over your target competitor. (You can develop similar models based on targeting a competitor's weakness.) By "significant," we mean a competitive advantage that passes the following test:

1. It is recognized by the targeted customers as a significant factor in their purchase decision—meeting specific customer needs.
2. It is meaningful enough to attract loyal customers from the targeted competitor, not just transient customers.

3. It is unique to your product or service offering.

If you do not have a significant competitive advantage, the decision model asks whether it is worthwhile to develop or acquire the necessary advantage.

The next step in the decision model is to evaluate your competitive disadvantages against your target competitor or competitors. By "significant" competitive disadvantages, we mean:

1. They are currently resulting in some loss of your loyal customers.
2. They are recognized by your customers in their purchase decision.

If you have a significant competitive disadvantage, you have to decide if it is worthwhile to fix it or acquire the necessary resources to fix it.

The third step in the decision model of Figure 5-1 is to establish which of four competitive positions you occupy on the market battlefield:

(A) Competitively advantaged (CA) with no competitive disadvantage (NCD).

(B) No competitive advantages (NCA) with no competitive disadvantages (NCD).

(C) Competitively advantaged (CA) with competitive disadvantages (CD).

(D) No competitive advantages (NCA) with competitive disadvantages (CD). Ugh!

Knowing what position you occupy on the market battlefield relative to your competitors enables you to evaluate possible competitor reactions to your competitive position in step 4 of the model. It is generally true (though not always) that competitors will defend against your strategic advances and attack where they see a competitive disadvantage. (In today's information age, it is more likely that your competitors will recognize your strategic advances or competitive weaknesses and react accordingly.)

For example, if you are competitively advantaged with no competitive disadvantages, a competitor may or may not be able to defend against a strategic initiative. If you have no competitive advantage and are competitively disadvantaged, a competitor will very likely attack your market position. Your estimate of competitor reactions should not only be based on your competitive position but on the history of competition in your markets. In some market battlefields, like commodity products, competitors will react very swiftly to weakened competition to take market share. In other market battlefields, like nuclear power plants, competitors take many years to react to competitive disadvantages. Your market battlefield analysis will help you assess how your competitors will react to your strategic initiative.

The fifth step in the decision model is to assess the potential return on investment (or any other measure appropriate for your business decision making) you are achieving in the target market. Markets that are yielding a high return on invested capital and are projected to continue to yield a high return generally encourage higher risk strategic initiatives than do low-return markets.

Once you have considered the impact on your market return on invested capital decision, you should be able to select the type of strategic initiative that is consistent with your market opportunity: BUILD, HOLD, HARVEST, RETREAT. (Note: PROBE strategies are selected only to test market assumptions and are temporary in nature.)

If all conditions were equally likely (they never are), this model would lead to the following outcomes:

Type of Strategic Initiative	*Frequency of Selection*
BUILD	9.4%
HOLD	37.5%
HARVEST	37.5%
RETREAT	15.6%

My business experience with well-run conglomerate companies would support the conclusion that they have, at most, 10—15 percent of their business in a BUILD-type strategy. Why, because they do not have the strategic market opportunities to warrant the investment in more BUILD strategies. BUILD strategies almost always drain resources from the company. HOLD and HARVEST strategies, when properly managed, are the cash providers to the company. RETREAT strategies are necessary to minimize company losses when you cannot defend a market position.

Adjusting Strategies to Market Maturity

Unfortunately, market battlefields are continuously changing as markets mature, necessitating periodic changes to strategies. As was shown in Figure 4-9, market battlefields are driven by market alternatives, market externalities and saturation to progress through five stages of market maturation over time: NEW, GROWTH, MATURE, DECLINE, and RESIDUAL.

Figure 5-2, "Type of Strategy vs. Market Maturity," describes how market maturity may affect your selection of a strategic initiative. Although there are no hard fast rules on selecting the most appropriate strategic initiative as markets mature, we offer some guidelines based on our experience with *Quick*Strategy users.

FIGURE 5-2
Type of Strategy vs. Market Maturity

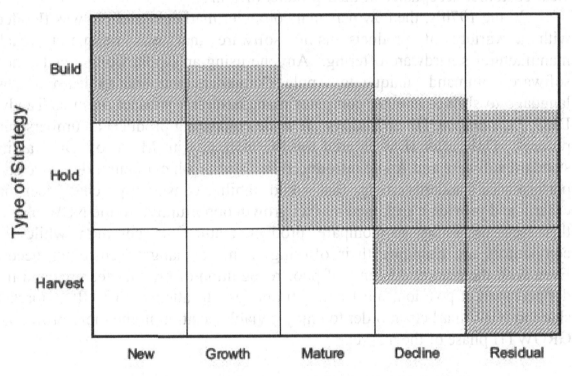

183

NEW Market Battlefields

In a NEW market battlefield, customer loyalty is usually not established and all competitors will be investing to gain market share by winning customers to their products and services from market alternative competitors. These investments will often generate near-term financial losses for all competitors but is the price of entry into NEW market battlefields. As we have seen, if you do not have a significant competitive advantage and few, if any, competitive disadvantages, you should not employ a BUILD-type strategy. It follows that you should not enter emerging market battlefields unless you have the requisite competitive advantage to try to gain market position. Unfortunately, in NEW market battlefields, most of your competitors will believe they have a significant competitive advantage. However, transient customers, characteristic of NEW markets, may not recognize the advantage. These customers have not established a firm price/performance criterion for purchase decision-making, forcing all competitors to build share without a clear customer acceptance of their product offering.

In the 1970's, the new personal computer market battlefield was flooded with a variety of products using software that was unique to each manufacturer's hardware offering. Anyone using an Apple Computer learned software commands unique to Apple Computers and had to learn a new language to shift to another computer manufacturer's product, such as Tandy, DEC, TI, Compaq, HP and others. It made comparing products a cumbersome process. Only after IBM entered the PC market, with Microsoft DOS as its standard software and Apple introduced the Macintosh computer, did price and performance standards emerge that would stabilize consumer purchase decision criteria and provide a sustained market growth opportunity. In the NEW phase, this lack of ability to compare product features is common while all competitors are changing their offering to meet changing customer needs. Even with the market dilemma of poor recognition of product features and ill-defined market position, most competitors have to attempt to BUILD market share in NEW markets in order to enjoy a viable position in the more profitable GROWTH phase of the market.

GROWTH Market Battlefields

In GROWTH market battlefields, market competition is usually more orderly as customer price/performance decision criteria become more established. Market leaders emerge, customer brand loyalties are formed, and competitors can define their market positions with more certainty than in NEW markets.

Most competitors will look for positive financial returns on their investment while holding or building market share, investing selectively as strategic opportunities arise. Growth will come either by holding market share in a growing market or investing selectively to build market share. Note, however, that many major companies supplying market alternative products or with perceived competitive advantages will enter markets in the GROWTH phase, not in the NEW phase, and aggressively BUILD share against the early market innovators.

They minimize their investment in product features by letting the NEW stage market competitors spend money to determine the customers' needs. They say the second bite of the apple is usually the sweetest.

In almost all cases, you will be forced into a HOLD strategy, holding market share gained in the NEW phase of the market, or a BUILD strategy, if you elect to enter the market in this GROWTH phase. In either case, GROWTH stage markets usually require an investment to achieve your strategic objective.

Tandy (Radio Shack) and DEC were unwilling to make the investment required to maintain their position in the emerging PC market after IBM entered the market. They dropped out and left the market to those willing to invest continuously in BUILDING or HOLDING market share in this GROWTH stage of the PC market.

MATURE Market Battlefields

When markets reach the MATURE stage, they are characterized by established customer loyalty, well-defined price and performance characteristics, and competitive equilibrium. Customers have had time to develop confidence in their suppliers and will change only if suppliers fail to adapt to their changing needs. Hence, there is a significant amount of customer inertia with only transient customers moving from supplier to supplier in search of special deals. Price and performance characteristics of products are clearly defined and compared in trade publications, consumer reports, and other media. A rational purchase decision is possible for each customer. The competitors have reached a more stable relationship (equilibrium); opportunities for building market share exist only when established competitors make a mistake or fail to defend their market position. Most threatened competitors will invest heavily to HOLD their market position and the market leaders often will realize significant financial gains.

The market leaders will be in control of the market, leaving room at either end of the market for niche price or performance competitors and little opportunity for any new market entrant to gain a significant market share as almost all growth in share has to come at the loss of a market competitor. Overall market growth is now limited by saturation, replacement by new market alternatives, or the impact of some external market factors.

As seen in Case 1, the fast-food burger market is a mature market with all of the above characteristics. McDonald's dominates the market with the largest market share followed by Burger King and Wendy's, leaving room for a handful of small niche competitors like Sonic, Bob's and Blake's. Only when McDonald's fails to meet changing customer needs will other competitors have a chance to take away their market share.

In the fast-food burger market, there has been little or no market growth for the last few years as market alternatives, like sub sandwiches and tacos, have taken customers from the market. There are few new location opportunities within the U.S. as most good street corners and off ramps have a fast-food burger outlet. There are external forces, like health concerns, that affect customer purchase decisions. All of these characteristics are typical of the MATURE stage of a market.

Some competitors, like Wienerschnitzel, have found the competition too difficult and have exited the fast-food burger market. It is difficult to say if they employed a HARVEST or RETREAT strategy, but clearly they could not find a winning strategy and found no profit opportunity in the fast-food burger market.

Customers in this market have established brand loyalties from years of advertising and satisfaction with product and service offerings. There is significant customer inertia. They decide they are going to have a McDonald's or Wendy's burger, not that they are going to have the lowest-priced fast-food burger. They expect to find the product offering consistent with their expectations and will only change if their preferred product fails to meet those expectations.

As Burger King found when they reduced the price of many of their products to 99 cents, McDonald's and the rest of the market responded with a vengeance with their own price reductions. Most competitors in this MATURE market will fight to HOLD market share.

DECLINE Stage in Market Maturity

The DECLINE stage of market maturity often brings intense rivalry for loyal customers with little product differentiation. This leads to severe price competition and a shakeout of all but the strongest market battlefield competitors. The market leaders may be able to realize an acceptable return on investment, but higher-cost competitors without a very strong niche performance position will be forced to HARVEST OR RETREAT from the market to minimize financial losses. It is very difficult to BUILD market share as product or price advantages are difficult to sustain and products or services tend toward commodity-type characteristics.

Market alternatives are often draining customers from DECLINE stage markets or external market forces are driving customers from the market.

Typically, successful strategies in declining markets are HOLD strategies for the well-entrenched niche competitors and market leaders. All other competitors are either in a HARVEST or RETREAT strategy to minimize their losses. Only extreme price competitors seem able to initiate a BUILD strategy in DECLINE stage markets.

The recent decline in the airline industry gives us some insight into the survival strategies of business in a DECLINE stage market. Market leaders American and United are fighting for their financial lives. Smaller "me-too" airlines like TWA have retreated. Some niche players, such as Midwest Airlines, are struggling to survive with premium service. The only airlines building share are the low-cost suppliers: Southwest Airlines and Jet Blue Airlines.

What caused the DECLINE in the airline market? Externalities like September 11, of course, were major factors. Market alternatives like conference calls and e-conferencing have driven away business travelers as service quality has declined in a price-driven market. Saturation has also served to erode revenues, as there are no un-served markets. Excess capacity for most classes of service is also a factor in the market decline.

RESIDUAL Stage in Market Maturity

The RESIDUAL stage in market maturity is often characterized by a more stable commodity market battlefield with surviving competitors having large market positions inclined to HARVEST their position. Niche competitors may be left as a sole-source competitor for their unique product offering with great profit potential. In these markets, most of the market alternative attrition that can take place has occurred and saturation has reached a point where replacement parts can be the driving force behind the recurring revenue.

However, there is no room for companies that develop significant competitive disadvantages in a residual market, as competitors will quickly react to force them to retreat from the business in the commodity end of the market. Most competitors are operating with minimum overhead and little or no investment and trying to extract cash from old residual phase markets to invest in better growth opportunities.

I spent time with a midwestern company in the early 1980's that had acquired vacuum tube manufacturing companies at ten cents on the dollar. The market for vacuum tubes was spiraling downward. In fact, semiconductor products had replaced 98 percent of the applications; but the owner knew there would be a few applications that could not be replaced and he could charge premium prices for those products. For example, if you owned an old multimillion-dollar radio station and one of your vacuum tubes burned out (as was often the case), would you replace the entire radio station or buy a new vacuum tube for $100, even if the tube only cost $2 to manufacture? This business was HARVESTED for some of the highest profit margins I have ever seen in industry.

Some commodity markets have been in a residual phase for many years, with no growth and little decline. These markets, like grain and dairy products, are characterized by fierce price competition and little or no profit potential. Most of the dairy farmers I know have RETREATED from the market, leaving it to the large corporate farms and niche specialty product farms.

Most light general aviation propeller manufacturers have experienced a residual stage market since major external market factors caused the annual production to drop to one-tenth the level of the 1970's. What caused this drop? The sharp increase in product liability insurance on the manufacturers and the subsequent increase in product pricing are blamed for most of the decline. Only recently has the industry realized any significant entry of new competitors as congress enacted legislation to limit aircraft manufacturer liability. Most competitors have either HARVESTED old aircraft designs or RETREATED from the light general aviation market entirely.

Market maturity stages (NEW, GROWTH, MATURE, DECLINE, and RESIDUAL) will impact the selection of strategic initiatives that offer the most profit opportunity for your business over the life of your products or services. The competitor unwilling to invest in NEW and GROWTH stage markets to BUILD or HOLD market share will be driven from these markets. The competitor who is well positioned in its markets as they reach the MATURE stage of growth will get to HARVEST cash from their investment. The competitor who has positioned its business to profit from a DECLINE stage market (like Southwest Airlines) can be very profitable and BUILD market share. The profit opportunities in RESIDUAL markets can be substantial in the niche performance end of the business and non-existent in the price end of the market. Continually repositioning your business to capitalize on the profit opportunity at each stage of market maturity is the essence of a winning strategy.

Translating Strategic Position and Changing Market Conditions Into a Winning Strategy

We have shown you how a winning strategy is any type of strategic initiative that will most benefit your business given your market position and stage of market maturity. If this leads to a BUILD type of strategic initiative, you will have to take share from direct competitors or market alternative competitors. If this leads to a HOLD type of strategic initiative, you will have to defend your market share against those competitors most inclined to attack your position. If this leads to a HARVEST or RETREAT strategy, you will need to defend your declining market share against those most aggressive competitors attacking your position. If this leads to a PROBE strategic initiative, you will have to select specific competitors against which you hope to test strengths or weaknesses. Notice that all strategies are executed against selected competitors to get maximum benefit from the resources you have at your disposal. Those competitors where you have a significant competitive advantage or minimal disadvantage are the most likely targets of your strategic initiative. Don't try to take on all competitors unless you are the clear market leader with unlimited resources.

Picking Your Target Competitors

For example, does Target Stores go after Neiman Marcus or Nordstrom's market position on the high performance end of the market? No! Do they go after K-Mart or Dollar General's position on the low price end of the market? No! Do they go after Wal-Mart or Sears' position? Yes! They could not possibly compete against all competitors from high-end stores to volume discounters and develop a winning position on the market battlefield.

How do you target competitors? You can choose the weakest competitor in the market if you can overcome their market weakness. You can pick strong competitors if you have a significant and defendable competitive advantage over them. You can target the market leader if you can nip off either a price or performance end of their business based on a real and defendable product or service advantage.

Picking off the weakest competitor is a viable strategic initiative only if it leaves you with a viable market position. For example, if you were to go after K-Mart's low price position, you might win the battle only to find you also were losing money at that end of the market battlefield. Maybe the reason a competitor is weak is that their market position is untenable. You must look carefully at the reason behind their weak market position and be able to compensate for their weakness in the same market position you have gained.

Picking strong competitors where you have a significant and defendable competitive advantage is a strategy that works. Well-managed companies qualifying for minority disadvantaged set-aside contracts can take on large well-entrenched government contractors and take away their market position. There is no way the strong competitor can react except to cede market share.

Market leaders are always vulnerable at their flanks, the extreme price end or the extreme performance end of their market position. Can Target Stores defend against Dollar General on the extreme price end of their market? Can Target Stores compete with Neiman Marcus on the extreme performance end of their market? It doesn't have the resources to defend against a flanking competitor.

Most strategic planners never consider the HARVEST or RETREAT strategic initiatives and how to develop a winning strategy in these market situations. A well-executed HARVEST strategy can yield substantial financial rewards, but you still must defend your position against specific targeted competitors or be driven into a RETREAT strategy with much lower return opportunity.

When you target competitors in a HARVEST strategy, limit your investment to defending against those competitors attacking your strongest market position where you can derive the maximum near-term financial returns.

Well-executed HARVEST strategies let you take as much cash from the business as possible while you exit the market battlefield. Invest vigorously to defend your proprietary performance position that will yield maximum financial returns; don't defend your marginally profitable product or service offerings or positions where your competitors are overwhelmingly advantaged.

As IBM HARVESTED its PC market, it fiercely defended its laptop business in which it had clear competitive advantages. It is still a significant player in the laptop portion of the PC market with a recognizable and profitable market share. (This may change tomorrow as the PC market redefines itself every few years.) It is not aggressively defending its position in the desk-bound portion of the market where COMPAQ, DELL and others were driving prices below IBM's breakeven costs, but maximizing its return on the piece of the market that it could defend. To do this, it would pick the competitors who were attacking it in the laptop portion of the market as its target competitors.

In a RETREAT strategic initiative, you are usually outgunned by one or more competitors and are trying to minimize your losses as you exit the market battlefield. You are doing things like liquidating inventory or selling services at cost while you restructure the business. Which competitor is most vulnerable to inventory liquidation or selling services at cost, the price competitor or the performance competitor? You still must pick your target competitors if you are going to sell product in the process of retreating from a market. Can you minimize your losses by selling off the product line to a competitor? Who is the target buyer? Who needs your market position most to supplement their position? Managing the RETREAT strategy against targeted competitors is the difference between coming away with your investment and losing everything.

In a PROBE strategic initiative, you do not have confidence in your market position, your strengths and weaknesses, your competitors' strengths or weaknesses, or how they would react to your initiative. You need to commit limited resources to determine if a more aggressive market opportunity exists. The Albuquerque Turkey Burger strategy is a probe of the fast-food burger market.

Setting Your Strategic Objectives

Once you have defined your target competitors and your relative strategic strengths and weaknesses, you can determine the strategic objective that maximizes your potential financial returns given your understanding of the market opportunity. Strategic objectives should be written in terms that are measurable against your target competitors; they are "not what you are going to do but what you expect to achieve." For example:

1. BUILD market share from five to ten percent over two years while holding a ten percent gross profit margin, investing less than $500,000 per year.
2. HOLD market share while increasing return on invested capital from 15—25 percent over a two-year period.
3. PROBE the market to determine if $500,000 per year per store revenue at ten percent gross margin is obtainable with an investment of less than $300,000 over twelve months.

4. HARVEST my position in the market over three years until we recover $1.5 million in investment; invest less than $200,000 to support product design changes.

5. RETREAT from the market within six months and keep losses less than $200,000.

Each of these objectives is measurable in both financial and strategic (market position) terms and identify the type of strategic initiative to be implemented. They set clear objectives to be used as a basis for your strategic plan.

Establishing the Strategic Plan

Again, a strategic plan is the "art and science of meeting your competitors in the market battlefield under advantageous conditions." That means the most advantageous conditions you can afford given the nature of the market, your position within that market, and the competitors you target. It is as simple as stating what strength you will focus against the targeted competitor in order to accomplish your strategic objective. It can be as simple as stating what weakness you will correct in order to hold market position against a targeted competitor. It can include a statement of anticipated reaction by target competitors and how you will respond. We leave the specifics of how we will implement a strategic plan to the tactical plan. Think in terms of:

1. Who will you attack?
2. What strength or weakness will be the focus of your strategy?
3. How do you expect your competitor to react?
4. Is this going to accomplish your strategic objective?

For example:

1. Use my significant (thirty percent) price advantage to take market share from competitor 'A.' No reaction is anticipated as it has significantly higher costs.
2. Overcome my performance disadvantage by introducing a new product line against competitors 'B & C' who are currently selling

two-year-old designs. Expect them to counter with new product introductions within eighteen months.

These are simple statements consistent with positioning your business on the market battlefield to meet your competitors under advantageous conditions. Too often, I see strategies written that include excruciating detail about how they will be implemented. Mixing strategy and tactics is a common mistake for even experienced strategic planners.

Establishing the Tactical Plan

I have read 200-page strategic plans that never tell you how they should be implemented and, hence, they never are implemented. The tactical plan is a detailed description of the specific actions that will be taken to achieve the strategic plan and its stated objectives.

My preference is to see a list of actions, when they will be completed, how much they will cost, and who will be responsible for the result. For example:

1. Decrease product size by 20 percent with a redesign costing no more than $150,000 to be completed by April 1, 2004. John Smith, Manager.
2. Launch new advertising program featuring 35 percent price reduction by June 10, 2003. Cost not to exceed $30,000 ad prep and $25,000 per month for ad space. Joe Smith.

Often, there are a series of tasks to be completed within the plan period to implement a strategic plan. All actions listed should be measurable in time and financial terms with outcomes clearly stated. Each task may have a different person responsible for achieving the specified outcome.

Measuring and Managing the Strategic Plan

The most resistance we find to implementing *Quick*Strategy plans is in the day-to-day management of the desired result. We recommend formal plan reviews with responsible plan and tactic managers every three months for most businesses; more for some fast-moving markets and less for slower markets.

Most plan reviews I attend become a discussion of why objectives were not met, what corrective action will be taken, and why more money is needed to achieve the objective. Occasionally, we find a manager who can manage to a strategic plan and the results are measurable and consistent with the market opportunity.

The most common mistake managers make in strategic planning is to promise performance that cannot be achieved given their markets, position in the markets, and the resources available. Too many managers want to justify large investments in their business and will promise financial returns at levels necessary to justify the desired investment. How do you measure strategic plan outcomes to differentiate the viable plans from the entrepreneurial dream?

When we measure strategic variables, we always measure market size. We look at history—at least three years—and we look at forecasted market size. This gives you a good indicator of the stage of market maturity the plan is addressing. I have seen hundreds of plans where the market size has been flat or declining for the last three years, but the plan manager is confident it is entering a growth phase and will grow twenty percent per year over the next three years. Why? Because that is the only way the manager can support his numbers or because of some real market externality that will impact the overall size of the market.

We then always measure the history and forecast of market share. As we have stated repeatedly, it is the primary measure of the success of our strategy. How well can you determine market share? It is an estimate at best in many markets, but a variable we continue to refine as we get more market data. Too often, we see a business with five percent market share attempting to go to twenty percent market share in one year, and we have to determine if the stated strategy and tactics will get the business to that position. Why have they only had five percent market share for the last three years? Is it a price market and their advantage focused on performance? The numbers have to track the reality of the strategic opportunity.

The remaining variables used in measuring the success of a business strategy are often tied to specific strategic or tactical objectives. For example:

1. In services businesses, we often measure the percentage of total hours paid that are billable to customers.
2. In low-cost manufacturing operations, overhead costs may be a critical variable.
3. In capital intense businesses, the rate of capital investment may be a critical variable and tied to ROI measures.

It is important that all involved in managing the strategic plan agree on the measurement variables and are held accountable for the measured results.

The Strategic Plan Summary

How can we summarize the strategic plan for each market segment of your business onto a single page? You need this plan summary to be a working document that translates the above concepts and ideas into a working document that you use in the day-to-day management of your business. The Strategic Plan Summary, *Quick*Strategy Form 2.0 below, is designed to accomplish this objective.

STRATEGIC PLAN SUMMARY   *QUICKSTRATEGY*™   Form 2.0

11. Your STRENGTHS vs. Competitor or Market Alternative	12. Your WEAKNESSES vs. Competitor or Market Alternative

13. Strategic Objective:

14. Type of Strategic Initiative:

15. Strategic Plan:

16. Tactical Plan:

17. History & Projections (performance measures)	Year-4	Year-3	Year-2	Last Year	This Year	Next Year	Year 3

Strategic Business Unit:	Plan Manager:	Date Prepared:
Company:	Strategy Advisor:	Date of Next Plan Review:

The first set of boxes in the form, (11) Your STRENGTHS vs. a Direct Competitor or Market Alternative and (12) Your WEAKNESSES vs. a Direct Competitor or Market Alternative is where you list those strengths and weaknesses your business has against these targeted competitors. These targeted competitors will be the focus of your strategy. The next two boxes (13) and (14) are where you clearly identify your strategic objective and the type of strategic initiative you plan to pursue. Box 15 is where you state your strategic plan as described above, and Box 16 is where you list the actions necessary to carry out the strategic plan against your strategic objectives, your tactical plan. Box 17 is where you enter the data you will use to measure the success of your plan and compare it to historical performance.

A detailed set of instructions for completing this form is found in Appendix B.

By using this format for all of your strategic segments, you will have a concise comparison of the business opportunities and problems your business is facing. You will also have a tool for measuring the success or failure of each business activity that is focused not on the wishes of your managers, but on the reality of the markets they serve and their relative position in those markets.

Chapter 6
Summary—Winning and Losing Strategies

You now have a unique way of looking at your businesses. What makes some businesses succeed and others fail? You can now use *Quick*Strategy methods and terminology as a tool to look at some of the winning and losing strategies we have identified. These examples should help you recognize market opportunities as you see the importance of properly positioning businesses on their market battlefields.

1. Loser: **ME-TOO Competitor**

Too many competitors enter established markets with the notion that they can copy the market leader and take market share. We call them ME-TOO competitors. They may survive briefly in NEW markets where customers have not established any product or brand loyalty, but in more mature markets they will only capture transient customers. They will never have the volume of repeat sales and economy of scale of the market leader and, consequently, never enjoy adequate profit margins.

In more mature markets where the second or third-tier player tries to copy the market leader to gain share, they will pay the ultimate price of decreased brand loyalty and margins. Burger King differentiated its product from McDonald's by offering a charbroiled product versus a fried product, while giving customers the option to have it their way with assorted toppings. Clear market differentiation of its product gave it the number two market position. Customers were either loyal to McDonald's or Burger King. Burger King felt it could imitate McDonald's program of attracting young families and children to its outlets by adding children's play areas. It also copied McDonald's ancillary products with minimum differentiation. It also initiated a price war to try to undercut McDonald's lower-priced products. Many of Burger King's franchises are now in financial trouble because of lower sales and profits. Burger King followed the leader instead of emphasizing their unique offerings, a ME-TOO strategy.

If your sales manager or marketing manager comes to you and says we are losing sales to a major competitor, do you then respond with the same product offering? Or, do you think of how you can offer a better or at least a differentiated product? Don't fall into the trap of copying the market leader's products in an attempt to gain market share; ME-TOO strategies don't work.

Market Maturity Factors: May work for a limited time in NEW markets, but fails as markets mature.

Market Shape Factors: ME-TOO strategies fail in Price, Value, and Performance markets, but fail faster in Price markets.

2. Loser: **Cheap Products Competitor**

How many competitors have decided to focus on the price end of a market and offered significantly inferior products to maintain profit margins? We call these CHEAP PRODUCTS COMPETITORS; most of the time, they fail as they neglect other customer needs.

In the 1960's, some of the U.S. automotive companies became so wrapped up in price competition and cost reductions to their products that they produced cheap products. If a car lasted three years, you were lucky. The market response to their cheap products was to import better-quality products from Japan and Germany. The car companies were failing to meet the consumers' basic need for safety and reliability. Are you old enough to remember when Ford Falcons rusted out in three years and the Chevrolet Corvair was under continuous assault by Ralph Nader for alleged safety issues?

Why is K-Mart having such a difficult time surviving in the discount department store market while TARGET is thriving in this market? Could it be that K-Mart has let its products and services drop below an acceptable level of performance to meet customers' minimum expectations?

Occasionally, government agencies will get caught up in reducing the cost of services at the expense of service quality. I co-owned an engineering firm supplying services to a federal government agency. They solicited bids for engineers and scientists at prices below our cost of payroll and benefits for our more experienced personnel. We lost the competition to a firm that recruited engineers and scientists willing to work without benefits. What do you think happened to the quality of service provided to the government customer? The better engineers and scientists went on to provide services to other market segments where they were able to earn a fair wage and receive reasonable benefits. The government got low price and low-quality cheap services.

Remember, Maslow said when a person succeeds in satisfying an important need, it ceases to be a motivator and the person will turn their attention to the next most important need. Once a product is priced at an acceptable level, we look for other performance. Also, if our minimum performance expectations are not met, we will not buy on price alone.

CHEAP PRODUCT or SERVICE COMPETITORS do not survive in most market battlefields.

Market Maturity Factors: May work in NEW or GROWTH markets to establish entry position, but must be converted quickly to Price competitor to survive as markets mature. This strategy tends to attract transient customers.

Market Shape Factors: If CHEAP PRODUCT COMPETITORS survive, it is usually in Price markets.

3. Loser: **Promisers**

PROMISERS are those competitors who enter markets promising more performance than they deliver. They will take market share and then fade away as the market catches up with their inability to deliver.

How many times have you found that some stores are typically sold out of the sale special by the time you get to the store? Do you go back to them when they advertise their next special?

In aircraft products, some competitors advertise aircraft speeds in their promotional material that lead you to believe they offer superior performance. Only when you read the aircraft manual do you find that those speeds are obtainable only when flown under very specific conditions and not under normal flight conditions.

In time, PROMISERS are discovered and discredited in most markets and fail to attract loyal customers.

Market Maturity Factors: Works at any stage of market maturity, but will usually attract only transient buyers; most often present in NEW markets.

Market Shape Factors: PROMISERS are less successful in Value and Performance markets, as there are fewer transient buyers.

4. Loser: **Coattail Competitor**

COATTAIL COMPETITORS hang onto another business entity to survive. They also cannot control their destiny or develop strategies for long-term survival.

I knew a baker in New England who positioned his bakeries next to new supermarkets. The strategy worked in the 1960's and early 1970's until supermarkets, seeing the profit opportunity, opened their own in-store bakeries. His businesses failed within two years.

I knew a supplier of machine tool services to a number of the U.S. golf club manufacturers in southern California. It had dramatic growth in the 1990's boom in high tech golf clubs. When golf club manufacturing was moved overseas, the company lost half its business. Its business was coattailing on the success of the golf club business and not competing for market share with the broader market for their services.

COATTAIL COMPETITORS are lulled into thinking they have a viable strategy, when in reality they may just be riding a temporary opportunity. How much of your business is dependent on a single customer? Are you competing in the broader market for your products and services or are you being lulled by a good relationship with one customer into thinking you can win in the wider market for your goods or services?

Market Maturity Factors: COATTAIL COMPETITORS can compete in most markets, but will usually find it progressively difficult to hold their position as markets mature and usually fail in the DECLINE stage of market maturity.

Market Shape Factors: COATTAIL COMPETITORS fail faster in Price markets.

5. Winner/Loser: **Captive Supplier**

Many big retail chains and manufacturers like to pull suppliers into their "Preferred Supplier Programs," making them the supplier's primary customer. This can be a bonanza for small suppliers by opening up their business to substantial growth opportunity. However, in most cases, the customer will also squeeze profit margins as they begin to dominate the supplier's output. Furthermore, they often insist on regular financial audits of the supplier business to ensure that they are getting a preferred price on the products they purchase.

I once acquired a specialty machining operation in the Midwest that made aircraft engine parts. They had an ability to manufacture large round parts to mechanical tolerances that their customers could not match with their in-house machining processes. The company had sales revenues of about $40 million and pretax profit of about $12 million—way above average for this type of business.

Its secret process was carefully guarded by the owner and he refused to divulge his process to his customers, even though they often insisted it was necessary under their government contracts. After we acquired the business and replaced the owner manager—the owner manager retired—our new manager told us the customer had selected them as a preferred supplier and their business should grow fifty percent in the next year. It did! But the profit margin dropped to six percent of revenue. The customer insisted on a detailed description of the secret manufacturing process and received it from the new manager. He said he had no choice but to cooperate as they were now sixty percent of his business. Was this a winning or losing strategy on the part of the supplier?

I worked with a company next to the Mexican border that made shade cloth for garden stores. One of the giant national hardware store chains placed an order that would double his volume, but at a lower profit margin. The next year they doubled his sales volume again. Now he was a CAPTIVE SUPPLIER. The giant hardware store ran into financial problems and stretched out his accounts receivable to 120 days. He borrowed against the receivable to pay his bills. When the giant hardware store filed for bankruptcy, the shade cloth supplier had no choice but to downsize and fight off its own bankruptcy.

One survival strategy for CAPTIVE SUPPLIERS is to harvest their captive position at every opportunity and keep costs variable to the extent that a loss of the captive position will not destroy their business. Monitoring the health of your customer is critical to anticipating major adjustments to business strategy. Never translate a captive relationship with one customer into thinking you can win in the wider market for your goods or services.

Market Maturity Factors: CAPTIVE SUPPLIER strategies can occur at any stage of market maturity. They are most vulnerable in MATURE markets as commodity pricing dominates purchaser needs.

Market Shape Factors: CAPTIVE SUPPLIER strategies fail most rapidly in Price markets.

6. Loser/Winner: **Prestige Competitor**

PRESTIGE COMPETITORS charge more for their products than the features of their product justify. This is a losing or temporary strategy in most markets and a winning strategy in very limited Performance markets.

In Price-driven markets, there is no place for a PRESTIGE COMPETITOR as the customers tend to need their price objectives satisfied before they are willing to consider product features or claims.

In Value markets, there may be a limited market position as some customers may migrate toward a product whose price is not justified by its performance. Some people will buy the limited edition automobiles offered in the midsize market.

In Performance markets, PRESTIGE COMPETITOR positions may be a viable strategy for some competitors. Jewelry can be acquired at the discount jeweler on 49th street in New York or at Tiffany's. Tiffany's is a PRESTIGE COMPETITOR; the box that holds the jewelry means more to some people than the item it holds.

Market Maturity Factors: PRESTIGE COMPETITORS thrive in MATURE markets where customers' needs are well established and the competitors' products are well defined.

Market Shape Factors: PRESTIGE COMPETITORS do best in Performance markets.

7. Winner: **Market Leader**

From the early 1960's, studies indicated that MARKET LEADERS, or those with the largest market shares, enjoyed significantly higher returns on investment than the smaller market competitors. They should have enough cash to defend their position and a cost advantage in most markets resulting from economies of scale. But market leadership position does not guarantee strategic success; you must manage against flanking competitors on the price and performance ends of your business or they will whittle away your market share. Look at the recent losses at McDonald's—a clear market leader that is losing money while the performance competitor, Wendy's, is making a profit.

Arrogant market leaders will overprice their product or fail to invest in new technology, only to lose to smaller competitors. RCA used to dominate the photomultiplier tube business. These vacuum devices were used to measure photoemissions in a variety of instrumentation. A Japanese competitor now owns the lion's share of the market because RCA did not invest in new research and development to keep their technology current. A performance competitor in a performance market can chew away the leader's position if they do not sustain their performance advantage. Market leaders cannot become complacent in their market position. If they do not defend their position at their flanks, price on one end and performance on the other, they can lose to an aggressive competitor.

As markets shift from Growth stage markets to Mature markets to Declining markets, customer needs change. A competitor that leans toward a performance strategy can dominate a growth market, only to lose to price competitors as markets decline. Will Southwest Airlines become the biggest passenger airline in the U.S. as the market matures?

The advantages the market leader has are lower overall cost, greater ability to invest to meet changing market needs, and better overall market awareness. The market leader who is not continually listening to changing market needs will not hold its dominant position in competitive market battlefields and enjoy the financial rewards of market leadership.

Market Maturity Factors: MARKET LEADERS should thrive in all stages of market maturity as long as they recognize changing customer needs.

Market Shape Factors: MARKET LEADERS should thrive in all markets.

8. Winner: **Vendor Qualified**

Many business opportunities are built around having a proprietary relationship with a supplier that uniquely qualifies their company to do business as a representative of the supplier company.

In Case #2, the complexity associated with installing wireless telecommunications equipment requires each EF&I supplier to go through training programs at the various supplier training centers. Without the training certificates, the customers for the cell towers will not consider you a qualified bidder.

I co-owned an engineering firm supplying engineers to a government agency that developed and tested nuclear weapons. Most contracts were awarded to suppliers having the requisite high level security clearance, an overwhelming competitive advantage. However, in the early 1990's the new administration decided to eliminate the requirements for security clearances and to open up competition to minority-owned and disadvantaged businesses.

A clear competitive advantage and winning strategy was eliminated and a new vendor qualification took over as the winning competitive advantage.

Vendor qualification can be a winning strategy, particularly if the vendor qualification is critical to your customer's decision process or the vendor limits distribution of goods or services to qualified suppliers. Without distribution limitations, you must monitor changes in customer requirements to understand the level of competitive advantage the vendor qualification provides in the eyes of your customer.

Market Maturity Factors: VENDOR QUALIFIED strategies work most effectively in GROWTH and MATURE markets where customer requirements are well defined. In DECLINE and RESIDUAL markets, most competitors will be vendor qualified.

Market Shape Factors: VENDOR QUALIFIED strategies work most effectively in Value and Performance shaped markets.

9. Winner: **Customer Qualified**

Oftentimes, customers will require that vendors have their products tested and meet rigorous customer specifications to qualify as a supplier.

In our weather instrument business, where we sell weather instruments to the National Weather Service, the FAA, and other government agencies, we must submit our products to rigorous testing against a government specification in order to qualify as a supplier to these agencies. Once qualified, we can enjoy a number of years as a supplier of this equipment to these agencies and it presents a substantial barrier to new entrants into this market.

I was once part of a company that invested heavily in a process for refining nickel-cadmium battery waste in raw materials that could be used as feed stock in other industries. However, the managers of this business found that industries that used raw material feed stock, like nickel and cadmium, spent years making sure that the trace impurities in their suppliers' feed stock did not upset the users' manufacturing process. The existing suppliers were CUSTOMER QUALIFIED and our raw material had trace elements in it that made its use risky to the prospective customer. We were not CUSTOMER QUALIFIED. Only qualified suppliers of feed stock were welcome at the customer's site. They had a preferred position and a winning strategy based on prior efforts to get their feed stock qualified for the customer's process.

<u>Market Maturity Factors</u>: CUSTOMER QUALIFIED strategies work in all stages of market maturity, although they become a less important differentiator as markets mature.

<u>Market Shape Factors</u>: CUSTOMER QUALIFIED strategies work best in Value and Performance shaped markets.

10. Winner: **Price Competitor**

True PRICE COMPETITORS are differentiated from CHEAP PRODUCT COMPETITORS in that they meet most of the customers' needs without sacrificing reputation. There is a very fine line between being a winner and being a loser on the price end of the market battlefield. Southwest Airlines and Wal-Mart are true PRICE COMPETITORS. They meet most customers' minimum needs, offering basic products at lower prices than many of their competitors. In my opinion, America West and K-Mart are losing market position as PRICE COMPETITORS because they fail to meet many of the customers' minimum needs.

<u>Market Maturity Factors</u>: PRICE COMPETITOR strategies work best in MATURE to RESIDUAL stage markets. They may fail in NEW or early GROWTH stage markets as the shifting performance requirements of customers may eliminate their ability to maintain the low costs required to remain profitable as a price competitor.

<u>Market Shape Factors</u>: Works best in Price-shaped markets. You knew that!

11. Winner: **Industry Standard**

INDUSTRY STANDARD competitors are the extreme end of Customer Qualified competitors. They have achieved industry recognition for the level of their product performance that can only be achieved through years of testing, certification, or experience.

For example, NIST, the government organization for maintaining national measurement standards, maintains the national standards for quantitative measurements. They will certify products that meet their standards and make them NIST traceable measurements. A rigorous program of certification and maintenance is mandated by NIST to make products NIST traceable, but they are then considered an industry standard.

Much of the success of Hewlett Packard's electronic measurement instruments can be attributed to their reputation as an INDUSTRY STANDARD. Leica cameras were once thought to be the standard of the industry, along with Zeiss optics. Metlar Scales and Balances are still considered by many to be a standard for weight measurement. Sears Craftsman tools are perceived by many as an industry standard because of their lifetime guarantee.

Market Maturity Factors: INDUSTRY STANDARD competitive strategies work best in late GROWTH stage markets as customer performance needs become well defined.

Market Shape Factors: INDUSTRY STANDARD strategies work in all markets, but work best in Performance-shaped markets.

12. Winner: **Last Resource**

The LAST RESOURCE competitor is the last available supplier of a particular product or service. They are typically working as a niche supplier of products or services in residual markets where the rest of the competitors have left the market.

I once studied a very successful supplier of replacement parts for DC3 aircraft. They had many used parts, along with the drawings and STC's (government approvals) to make new replacement parts. They were the last major supplier of these parts and were able to achieve very high profit margins, as many of these 1940's vintage aircraft were still in service.

As I mentioned earlier, I met with the owner of the last vacuum tube manufacturing company in the U. S. He was able to charge ten times the manufacturing cost for vacuum tubes that were used to keep vintage equipment in operation. It was a very profitable business, but with a limited life expectancy. When I asked the owner what he would do when the need for replacement vacuum tubes ended, he pointed me at several other product areas that met his criteria of critical parts needed for high value equipment where replacement of parts would be much cheaper than replacing the equipment. At the right time, he would buy them at ten cents on the dollar and harvest their residual business.

Market Maturity Factors: LAST RESOURCE strategies work in RESIDUAL stages of market maturity when most other competitors have exited the market.

Market Shape Factors: LAST RESOURCE strategies work in all markets.

Now You Know How to Use *Quick*Strategy!

These examples of winning and losing strategies are only a fraction of those we have identified over the years as guides to our strategic decision process. What is important is that *Quick*Strategy lets us identify and communicate what works and what doesn't work in the context of the market battlefield and a business position within the battlefield.

There are winning and losing strategies at each stage of market maturity.

- Is your business positioned poorly in your market battlefield so that you have to struggle every day just to survive?
- What strategy will work best for your business as you reposition it to compete in your market battlefields?
- Are you ready to adjust your market position as your market matures?
- How does your business strategy compare with the above examples of winning and losing strategies?

Now you have the tools to compare your business strategy to winning and losing strategies.

The Rest of the Story

*Quick*Strategy must be used on a day-to-day basis to keep up with rapidly changing market battlefields. Let's look at what happened to our three case study businesses of Chapters 1, 2, & 3 since we originally analyzed their markets and strategies.

CASE 1: Albuquerque Turkey Burger—three months later

Tony has been unable to find a suitable site for his first Albuquerque Turkey Burger outlet. He is still looking at the real estate market and he is determined to find the right location for his market probe. He found a store manager at a local national fast-food burger franchise who will join him when he gets the rest of his funding. This manager has been collaborating with Tony on his implementation plan. However, some of the investors are concerned that the three largest national competitors are revising their menu to address the low-calorie, low-fat customer needs and the competitors' financial performance continues to fall below their expectations.

McDonald's lost money for the fourteenth straight month in April with overall same store sales at restaurants open at least thirteen months down 0.8 percent. McDonald's has been changing over the last three months to fix its problems:

- The same store sales in the U.S. are on the rise.
- The introduction of entree-sized "premium" salads and improved food and service has commenced in the U.S., attributing to the U.S. improvement.
- Many McDonald's franchises dropped Big-n-Tasty from the $1.00 discount menu.
- McDonald's added wireless Internet access to outlets in San Francisco.
- McDonald's tests self-ordering kiosks that could eventually become a standard feature at its stores worldwide. These reduce cost and speed service while offsetting rising labor costs.
- Obesity lawsuits against McDonald's continue to be prepared by lawyers successful in suing the tobacco industry. McDonald's is fighting back and getting some claims dismissed in pending suits.

McDonald's is fighting to hold its market leadership position and demonstrating that it will make continuous improvements to its product and service offerings to defend its position.

Burger King continues to have financial problems at many franchises but is addressing complaints about animal cruelty by releasing its second report on audits of animal handling at its suppliers. It has introduced a new burger aimed at improving product quality, the "Great American Burger™." Burger King says it is a new fire-grilled sandwich that meets the growing demand among consumers for high-quality, "best in business" burgers. Research indicates a 6—1 preference by consumers to have flame-broiled cooking over other methods. With emphasis on improving product quality and new ownership, it seems likely that they will eliminate the 99-cent price war in the near future.

Wendy's same store U.S. sales for the June period that ended on June 29, 2003, declined two percent compared to a 10.2 percent increase in the same period a year ago. It has introduced three new lighter salad dressings, "Fat Free French," "Low Fat Mustard," and "Reduced Fat Creamy Ranch" and added a "Southwestern Chicken Caesar" salad to the menu. They are emphasizing their later store hours and promoting their low-fat salads in their recent advertising.

There have been highly publicized outbreaks of E. coli in Argentina that forced the closure of McDonald's and Burger King outlets and an outbreak of mad cow disease in Canada. Both of these externalities, along with an increase in the U.S. unemployment rate, have had a negative impact on the overall market for fast-food burgers.

How do these recent events impact Tony's strategy for a probe of the fast-food burger market for its Albuquerque Turkey offering? He should be aware of the new emphasis that the big three fast-food burger companies are placing on low-fat, low-calorie menu items. He should recognize Burger King is still offering 99-cent menu items while offering a new premium beef burger. This indicates that they are reacting to both ends of market demand for their products, price and performance. The biggest issues impacting Tony's strategy are the continued poor financial performance of all of the big three fast-food burger chains along with his continued difficulty locating a good outlet location. These issues are dampening his investors' enthusiasm for this business opportunity.

CASE 2: Georgia Wireless Constructors, "GWC"—three years later

Tim Murphy and the New York investment group met with Rhett Diener and his management in March of 2000 and completed their acquisition of the business. It did not continue to use *Quick*Strategy methods to keep GWC strategy current with the rapidly changing markets, and it brought in a telecom industry executive to run GWC along with several additional telecom acquisitions.

Rhett Diener turned over the day-to-day operation of his business to one of his subordinates and worked part-time marketing GWC services. He spent the rest of his time managing the investment of proceeds he received from the sale of his business.

By the end of 2000, the wireless telecom investment enthusiasm on Wall Street had ended—a negative potential market externality highlighted in the original market battlefield summary. GWC took little corrective action except to cut prices to meet more aggressive competition.

WFII, the largest competitor in the EF&I market, made its year 2000 forecast because it had long-term U.S. customer contracts. WFII estimated EF&I revenue of $150 million and was very profitable with substantial growth in its maintenance services segment that added more revenue. It showed little or no growth through mid-2003. In the second quarter of 2003, there were signs that its revenue and profits would improve and the price of its stock doubled, but remained below its peak prices achieved in prior years.

O2 Wireless Solutions, the second largest public competitor, completed its IPO and continued to lose money in 2000 and 2001. It was then acquired by an Israel-based engineering firm, Baran Telecom, and remains a competitor in the market at a reduced size.

LCC International's total revenue rose to $149 million in 2000, exceeding all forecasted performance, and generated an operating profit of $36 million. In 2001, its sales had fallen to $130 million and its operating profit to $1 million from continuous operations. By 2002, it lost $37 million on $67 million in total revenue. It continued to lose money in the first quarter of 2003 on $17 million in revenue. Some question its ability to survive in the new, more competitive market.

According to Rhett, GWC's two target competitors, O2 Wireless and LCC International, started bidding work below cost when their revenue started to fall in 2001. GWC's revenue and profit declined substantially in 2001 and 2002 with financial losses reported in both years.

In 2003, the New York investor group fired the corporate-level management hired to run their telecom business and sold GWC back to Rhett for a fraction of the price it paid for the business. He is now running the business at a profit with revenue one-fifth to one-tenth the maximum level he achieved the year he sold the business. He maintains that the wireless carriers are starting to invest in additional build-out as the financial markets gain confidence in their ability to eventually make a profit.

One major market externality, lack of third-party financing for continued build-out of the wireless telecom infrastructure, severely impacted the strategy of GWC. Could it have been anticipated? It was, but the company's reaction was too slow to compensate for the decline in revenue. WFII showed that a well-run business in this market, with adequate capital investment, could sustain sales through this downturn in the market by quickly and decisively reacting to market change.

CASE 3: Eclipse 500 Personal Jet—three months later

Eclipse 500 remains on schedule to deliver its first production aircraft in early 2006. Several events have occurred in the last two months that could have impacted the Eclipse 500 strategy:

- Flight tests with the temporary Teledyne engines were successful and are on schedule as are the rest of its development programs.
- Aviation safety issues with in-flight entertainment systems in commercial airline aircraft have created passenger concerns for flight safety.
- A recent commuter aircraft accident has been attributed to excess aircraft weight; average passenger weight exceeded standards.
- The State of New Mexico will invest $10 million into Eclipse Aviation and they raised an additional $77 million in equity financing.
- Eclipse Aviation announced it would partner with the FAA, Embry Riddle University and the University of North Carolina to develop a four-phase pilot training program specific to the Eclipse 500.

The management of Eclipse Aviation is keenly aware of their competitive market position and they are keeping up with changes in the competitive environment.

Their primary focus is on meeting the development and production schedule. Although I do not know the in-house strategy, I believe they have demonstrated an ability to adapt to whatever curves the market throws at them in pursuit of the Eclipse 500 objective.

Conclusion

In the above follow-up analysis, "the rest of the story," Cases #1 and #2 point out the importance of keeping *Quick*Strategy current in our rapidly changing markets. Case #3 has seen little change in its market battlefield in the last two months, but its markets are volatile enough to change dramatically over the next few years and must be closely monitored. *Quick*Strategy is a tool that lets you continuously reflect on the impact market changes will have on your business strategy and the adjustments necessary to meet your strategic objectives. Delays in implementing Albuquerque Turkey Burger's plan show how fast (three months) markets can change, dampening investor enthusiasm. Not anticipating the slowdown in wireless industry investment in Case #2 created significant losses for the New York investors in Georgia Wireless Constructors.

Charles Darwin observed:

"It's not the intelligent who survive
It's not the strong who survive
But those who adapt to change"

*Quick*Strategy is a tool you can use every day to keep your business favorably positioned, adapting it to continuously changing market battlefields. At www.quickstrategy.com, we track market data, provide on-line strategy analysis, and help keep your strategic plans current, thereby improving your ability to anticipate changes in your markets.

To survive and prosper, your business must anticipate and adapt to change.

Appendix A
The Market Battlefield Summary
(Form 1.0)

The Market Battlefield Summary form lets you translate the Market Battlefield model into a working one-page description of each of your market segments, providing the conceptual basis for a business strategy. It is divided into ten individual sections, which are required to describe each market segment.

1. Description of Product or Service (offered)
2. Customers
3. Customer Needs
4. Market Shape
5. Market Alternatives
6. Market Saturation
7. Market Externalities
8. Competitors
9. Market Size (History and Projections)
10. Market Maturity

This may look like a lot of information and you may believe that it is not readily available for each market segment of your business. Focus your efforts on succinctly describing each section; review the information entered with your strategy advisor and staff to improve its accuracy. The first draft is likely to leave you with more questions than answers, but you will at least know what you don't know and what you will need to find in order to assess your market position on the market battlefield.

Over time, the accuracy of the information entered on the form will improve and make the difference between developing a winning or losing strategy; but you must start with what you know now. Your first attempt at a rough strategy is better than no strategy. Have you properly segmented your markets? When you try to put the market battlefield together, you will discover what competitors are unique to the products and services offered to the identified set of customers.

The forms will help you with the segmentation process, so just get started filling them out and see what makes sense.

Section 1—Product or Service (offered)

This section requires a succinct description of the product or service offered in the market segment. This description will define the scope of your market battlefield. If it is too broad, you will not be able to focus on the appropriate set of customers and their needs and may find you are trying to compete against many competitors that you never see in the market you serve. If the description is too narrow, you will miss customer opportunities and competitor actions. It should include the products and services you currently provide and those to be added over the three to five-year forecast period. For example, if you owned a domestic airline:

1. Air passenger transportation service—too broad?
2. Scheduled air transportation passenger service—too broad?
3. Scheduled, coach class air transportation passenger service—too broad?
4. Regularly scheduled, coach class air transportation passenger service—too broad?
5. Regularly scheduled, coach class air transportation passenger service with average price of twelve cents per passenger mile—too broad?
6. Regularly scheduled, jet (turbine), coach class air passenger transportation service with an average price in excess of eleven cents per passenger mile—too broad?
7. Regularly scheduled, jet (turbine), coach class air passenger transportation service with average price in excess of eleven cents per passenger mile with full cabin meal service—too narrow?

How do you know when your product or service description is too broad or too narrow? First, does the description accurately describe your existing products or services? That is, does it exclude a significant portion of your existing products or services? If so, it may be too narrow. Does it include products or services that you do not supply or plan to supply in the forecast period? Then it may be too broad.

Think about your competitors—those taking customers from you or from whom you are taking customers. Does your product or service description include or exclude products or services used by competitors to take away business? Are these products "market alternatives" or just variations of the products and services offered in your market? If you're a niche, performance, or price competitor, you may tend to define your product or service too narrowly, concentrating on your niche and other related niche competitors.

Your description of products and services will define "market alternatives," those products or services that satisfy the same customer needs in a different way, by their exclusion from your description. For example, if we choose description #6 of a domestic airline market for a business "Regularly scheduled, jet (turbine), coach class air passenger transportation service with an average price in excess of eleven cents per passenger mile," market alternatives would then include:

1. Unscheduled air passenger service
2. Non-jet (piston propeller) air passenger service
3. Discount air passenger service (under eleven cents per passenger mile)
4. Rail service
5. Bus service
6. First class air passenger service

These and other passenger transportation services must then be monitored as "market alternatives." The market alternatives will not be analyzed as critically (except in New markets) as products and services in your description in Box 1 of the Market Battlefield Summary. The risk of too narrow a definition of your segment products or services is the exclusion of direct competition from your Market Battlefield Summary. Again, the risk of too broad a definition of your segment products and services is not being able to focus resources on specific customer needs.

If we choose description #1 of the domestic airline market: "Air passenger transportation service," market alternatives would then include non-air passenger transportation services such as buses, trains, automobiles, etc. You would have to monitor a much larger set of competitors to maintain your awareness of competitive actions. That is, all air passenger services including charter services, air taxi services, unscheduled air services, corporate air services, small piston propeller services, etc. As you can see, your market battlefield would become too broad to focus your resources on a specific set of customer needs.

Defining your product or service offering will always be a matter of judgment, which comes through experience. Remember, strategy is both the **"art** and science" of meeting your competitors under advantageous conditions on the market battlefield. It is not that easy. You must go through the process of looking at your market in the broadest sense (description #1 in the example) and the narrowest sense (description #7 in the example). Then look at the intermediate descriptions in order to choose the most appropriate one for your market segment. Spend time to develop the intermediate descriptions. Ask yourself:

1. Are my day-to-day competitors' products or services included in the description along with mine?
2. Can I collect relevant competitor data at trade shows and in industry publications?
3. Am I inadvertently including products or services that I don't supply and never intend to supply?
4. If I change the described product or service offered, what customers and competitors will react?

You will be using your best judgment in describing the appropriate scope of your product or service offering, which in turn will define the size and character of your market battlefield. You should plan to continually re-evaluate this description and refine it until it most closely correlates your market battlefield to the competitive actions you experience (or will experience) in your operation of the business.

Defining your customers too narrowly will result in missed market opportunities and competitor actions. In the airline example, transcontinental first-class air travel was the only market served by MGM Grand Airlines in the 1980's. It concentrated on serving the unique needs of first class air travelers between New York and Los Angeles. Unfortunately, the large domestic air carriers offered low cost first-class upgrades to frequent travelers. The economic downturn in the late 1980's also made air travelers more price-conscious and MGM Grand Airlines went out of business.

Although MGM Grand Airlines was able to focus (and do a great job) on the unique needs of the first-class transcontinental air traveler, it built its business strategy around too small a set of customers. The slightest competitive action (discount upgrades) and externality (economic slump) forced them out of business.

Look at your customers in the broadest and narrowest sense. Define the sets of customers in between the broadest and narrowest definition and then select the appropriate definition for your market. As with product definition, the scope of your customer definition will also determine the size and character of your market battlefield.

Section 2—Customers (served)

This section of the Market Battlefield Summary requires a succinct description of the customers served by your market. This description will limit the scope of your market battlefield to that set of customers served by you and your direct competitors, including those that will be served during the forecast period. For example, if your business was an airline, you may describe your customers as:

1. Air travelers
2. Domestic (U.S.) air travelers
3. East Coast U.S. air travelers
4. East Coast U.S. business air travelers
5. Transcontinental first-class air travelers.

As with product descriptions, if you define your set of customers too broadly, you may not be able to focus on satisfying their specific needs. If you define them too narrowly, you will miss market opportunities and competitor activities.

Defining your customers too broadly will require you to satisfy the most diverse set of customer needs. In the airline example above, description #1 "air travelers" requires that you address the needs of all air travelers in your strategic plan. If you are American Airlines or United Airlines, this definition may be appropriate. However, even these large airlines divide their customers into several market segments to better focus their services on different customer needs.

In Case #1, Albuquerque Turkey Burger, we talked about geographic segmentation of customers from the national market to the Albuquerque market, and then realized that customers for fast-food restaurants usually come from a ten-mile radius of where they live, work or shop. Too broad a definition would not let us focus on the unique regional tastes of the customers. Too narrow a definition would lead us to believe in an unrealistic market opportunity. Choosing the right geographic limitation on customers puts the market opportunity in perspective.

Section 3—Customer Needs

You cannot focus resources on customer needs until you have defined the customer in Section 2 above. Think about why the customers you have described will be motivated to purchase the products or services you described in Section 1 of the market battlefield summary.

As I summarized in Chapter 4, the generally accepted theory that leads us to understand human behavior based on need hierarchy was postulated by Abraham H. Maslow (1908-1970) and is based on the following premises:[*]

1. A person will have many needs.
2. These needs will vary in importance and, therefore, can be ranked in hierarchy.
3. The person will seek to satisfy the most important need first.
4. When the person succeeds in satisfying an important need, it ceases being a motivator for the time being.
5. The person will then turn his or her attention to the next most important need.

According to Maslow, individual needs can be ranked in order of importance from (most important) physiological needs, safety needs, social needs, esteem needs, and self-actualization needs. For individuals, he defined these needs as:

1. *Physiological Needs*—the fundamentals of survival, including hunger and thirst.
2. *Safety Needs*—concern over physical survival and ordinary prudence, which might be overlooked in striving to satisfy hunger or thirst.
3. *Belongingness and Love Needs (Social)*—striving to be accepted by one's family and others close to them.
4. *Esteem and Status Needs*—striving to achieve a high relative standing, including prestige, mastery and reputation.
5. *Self-Actualization Needs*—a desire to develop personal value systems that lead to self-realization.

---

[*] Abraham H. Maslow, Motivation and Personality (New York: Harper &Row, 1954).

So what does all of this psychological babble have to do with your business? We are talking about understanding the needs of your customers in a business environment. Their needs are different, but they still behave as Maslow described in his need hierarchy.

If your customer can't ship products and make payroll, you are not going to get their attention to sell them a new copier unless it solves this basic need. Try to understand your customer-need hierarchy. If you ranked your customers' needs in order of importance (most important first) from operational needs, regulatory and safety needs, customer acceptance needs, and status needs, would it look like this?

1. Operational Needs—the fundamental need of raw materials, trained workers, and utilities necessary to keep the lights on and the machines running.
2. Regulatory and Safety Needs—the basic need to comply with the rules, regulations, and reporting requirements imposed on business by acts or laws of governing bodies.
3. Customer Acceptance Needs—the need to be accepted by customers as a trusted supplier of goods and services.
4. Status Needs—the desire to be the biggest and best supplier of products or services.

What is the need hierarchy for your customers' business? Develop your own rank order for your customers and test it whenever the opportunity presents itself. For example:

- When I am working with government customers, can I ever get past their job security need in order to sell them on a new way of managing their workload?
- When my customer is a quality control manager, can I ever get past his need for high quality products to sell him a performance feature?
- When working with a design engineer to sell him a new instrument, if he has dollars budgeted, is he focused primarily on the latest product features?
- When selling fast-food burgers, if I deliver a product in twenty minutes instead of the expected three—five minutes, does an extra slice of cheese make any difference to the buyer?

Think about your customers' need hierarchy. Are you meeting their basic needs first?

Let's look more closely at the need hierarchy of the fast-food burger buyer in Case #1:

1. Physiological Needs: Minimum number of calories to satisfy hunger, served fast enough to avoid hunger pains (under five—ten minutes), tastes good, affordable price (if I can't afford it, I can't have it).
2. Safety Needs: Safe food, clean facilities, and healthy options.
3. Belongingness Needs: Courteous service with a friendly smile in a friendly environment.
4. Esteem and Status and Self Actualization Needs: Good reputation, high quality ingredients, great taste, consistent quality, and lots of options.

This is just a first pass at rank ordering the customers' needs. The case study did not rank order these needs and you can see how enlightening this would have been to Albuquerque Turkey Burger's strategy development.

If a customer's minimum number of calories to satisfy his hunger is not met with the product offering, the customer will not go forward looking to satisfy higher level needs, like "healthy options," a critical factor in Albuquerque Turkey Burger's strategy.

McDonald's is under heavy criticism for not meeting the customers' need for "healthy options." The new CEO has them focused on the basics of clean, safe facilities and consistent quality. Has he made the right decision?

Our point is: Understanding the need hierarchy of your customers is critical to your market battlefield understanding. Proper rank ordering those needs is what leads to truly great strategies.

Section 4—Market Shape

The collective customer needs define the shape of the market battlefield as described in chapter 4. If customers' needs are driven primarily by price considerations, the market is described as a Price Market. If the customers' needs are driven primarily by performance, the market is described as a Performance Market. If neither price nor performance considerations dominate the customers' needs, the market is described as a Value Market. The shape of the market battlefield plays a significant role in the selection of strategic alternatives. Strategies that are successful in Price Markets may not be as effective in Performance or Value Markets.

A classic mistake in strategy is for a Performance competitor to acquire a Price competitor in order to permit them to capture the low-price end of the market. I participated in such an acquisition in the 1990's as part of an engineering services company. We acquired a low-cost environmental services company when we saw the market mature and shift to a price driven market. (Most customers' needs were driven by cost considerations.) The acquired company did well for about six months until the acquiring company management decided that it was not carrying its fair share of overhead. They allocated additional costs to the acquired company, driving up its prices accordingly and driving it from the market. No amount of coaching could convince the acquiring company management that they were destroying the primary competitive advantage the acquired company brought to the combination.

I have also seen price competitors acquire performance companies in Performance markets and cut their engineering budgets, sales and marketing budgets, and product support until the performance competitor advantages disappeared due to the lower operating costs. A failed strategy often repeated in the acquisition of businesses shows that strategies that work in one type of market may not transfer to another type of market.

Section 5—Market Alternatives

Market Alternatives are those products or services that will satisfy your customers' needs but are differentiated enough to not be defined in the "Products and Services" section of the Market Battlefield Summary. They directly affect market maturity and, therefore, the growth (or decline) of your market. For example, with the fast-food burger market, market alternative products are:

1. Fast-food deli/sub sandwiches (+)
2. Fast-food tacos (+)
3. Fast-food take-out chicken (-)
4. Fast-food hot dogs (-)

When we list market alternatives on the Market Battlefield Summary, we also indicate the growth trend of the market alternative with a (+) for growing markets and a (-) for declining markets. It is also important to rank the market alternatives in order of those having the most impact on your market size. In the fast-food burger market alternatives listed above, the market for fast-food deli/sub sandwiches is growing rapidly and taking customers away from the fast-food burger market. The fast-food taco market alternative has also been growing and taking some market share from the fast-food burger market. The fast-food chicken and hot dog market alternatives have been declining in sales volume, losing share to the above alternatives and fast-food burgers. The overall impact of these market alternative products on the fast-food burger market is to stall its growth, with this year showing the first decline in market revenue. Declining markets are often an indication that customers are migrating to market alternative products.

In NEW markets, the primary source of customers is from the Market Alternatives. As we pointed out in Case Study #3 of the Eclipse Jet, they are growing this new business at the expense of the market alternatives. Until the market matures, most of the growth will come from business taken away from market alternatives: airline travelers moving to air taxi services, turboprop aircraft, and high-priced charter aircraft.

Section 6—Externalities (Market Externalities)

Externalities are those forces outside your market that cause the total market to rise or fall. For the fast-food burger market, externalities include:

1. Obesity litigation (-)
2. Poor economy (-)
3. City zoning laws (-)
4. Fast-foodborne illnesses (-)
5. Diet fads (+/-) (Atkins, high carbs., etc.)

These are forces unrelated to direct customer or competitor actions, but they affect the size and shape of the market. We also recommend a (+) or (-) to identify the positive or negative impact the identified externality has on the market. With the pending obesity litigation, the market for fast-food burgers is negatively impacted as customers identify fast-food burgers with obesity. With a poor economy, people spend less money eating out and more money on grocery store food. City zoning laws are limiting the property available to expand fast-food outlets. Fast-foodborne illnesses happen every few years.

When the media announces these illnesses, fast-food burger sales decline. Diet fads like Atkins diets affect the buying behavior of customers and may either add to sales or take away from sales of fast-food burgers.

Continuous monitoring of trends in market externalities is necessary to predict changes in the overall size of your markets.

Section 7—Saturation

Saturation is the percentage of customers in your market who have already acquired the products or services offered and have satisfied their need for that product for the forecast period (usually three to five years). Once purchased, if a product or service satisfies their need for the forecast period, the assumption is that the customer will not buy another product.

Another form of saturation occurs when there are more available suppliers of services than there is demand. This occurs in the hotel industry, the consulting industry, and the fast-food burger industry. As we identified in Case Study #1 on the fast-food burger market, when there is a fast-food burger outlet within a ten-mile radius of where people live, work, or shop, the market is saturated. (We also suggested that when 64 percent of the population is overweight, it generally can't eat any more food and the market is saturated.)

Some markets do not saturate over the forecast period. But when purchasers are buying all they need and they have available to them adequate means of supply, the market offers no growth. It is then considered saturated, with no additional growth opportunity.

Section 8—Competitors

Competitors are identified and analyzed in Section 8 of the Market Battlefield Summary. Each competitor should be identified and ranked according to size, their strengths and weaknesses, recent sales history (this year and last), and changes in market share noted as both dollar and percentage changes. This information will be used as the basis for selecting target competitors, the basis for developing your strategy.

We are often asked how do you get this information? It can be obtained legally and legitimately through public records and industry dialogue, such as:

1. Hire a market research firm that specializes in collecting customer information.
2. Log on to one of the customer survey web sites, such as www.epinions.com.
3. Talk to industry specialists.
4. Interview key industry personnel.
5. Attend trade shows and professional meetings (talk to salesmen).
6. Count cars in parking lots.
7. Talk to vendors and suppliers to your competition.
8. Talk to media consultants and ad space sales people.
9. Debrief your sales staff, asking for specific market-related information.
10. Ask distributors or sales reps carrying competing products.
11. Go to on-line public records for property, registrations, and credit information.

Few U.S.—based companies do a good job of masking their sales and marketing positions and strategies. Initially, your competitors' data may just be estimated. However, over time you should be able to precisely characterize your competitors.

Start by identifying your competitors. Ask your customers, your sales force, your sales representatives, or distributors about your competitors. You will often be surprised to find new or different competitors than you thought were in your markets. Talk to this same group of people about competitor strengths and weaknesses. Often, your competitors' customers will tell you their strengths and weaknesses. Survey customers about their level of satisfaction with their current supplier—it can be more objective than your sales force—then compare the results. Remember, in the end it is the customers' perception that counts with the sales force able to add value by their interpretation of the customers' perception.

Specific sales data is usually the most difficult information to obtain. However, trade associations often publish this information and sales people at trade shows are often proud to reveal their accomplishments (sales volume), although they are usually overstated. Ex-distributors, ex-sales representatives, and ex-employees frequently know the sales volume of their former businesses. Over time, you can develop a good information network to analyze the sales of your competitors.

The type of strategic initiative (BUILD, HOLD, HARVEST, RETREAT, or PROBE) is good to note for each competitor, but usually difficult to obtain. You may be able to look at external indicators to identify your competitors' initiatives:

1. What kinds of people are your competitors hiring and how aggressive are their hiring practices? Are they hiring engineers to develop new products or sales people to promote old products? Who are they laying off?
2. What does their advertising feature, volume discounts or performance features?
3. How are they paying their bills? Obtain a credit report or a Dun & Bradstreet report and look at their credit history.
4. Have inquiries been made about the possible sale of their business?
5. How are competitors reacting to competitive bids? Are they sacrificing profits to survive?

All of this information should be carefully gathered, stored, and used as a basis for evaluating your competitors' strategic initiatives. Remember, at best, most strategic data on competitors will be less than precise. However, it will aid in determining how they may react to your strategic initiative and it is better to have some evidence as to their behavior than just speculation.

Section 9—Market Size

Market Size is usually characterized by sales revenue dollars, best estimated in constant un-inflated dollars where inflation is a major factor. There are two distinctly different sets of data to be developed in characterizing market size. Historical data is developed using industry information or other collection techniques to monitor the cumulative revenue of your competitors. The historic size of the market should be the sum total of the revenue generated each year by the competitors identified in Section 8 of the Market Battlefield Summary.

Forecasted market size is more a function of how you believe the market will grow (or shrink) during the forecast period based on trends in market alternatives, externalities, and saturation.

We have found the most effective technique for forecasting the future growth (or decline) of your markets is "bracketing." First, look at all of those trends in market alternatives, externalities, and saturation that will tend to increase the size of the overall market and estimate their effect on future market growth. Forecast this best-case growth scenario based on these positive factors. Second, look at all of the trends in market alternatives, externalities, and saturation that will tend to decrease the size of the overall market and estimate their effect on market growth. Forecast this worst-case growth scenario based on these negative factors. Reality is somewhere between the best-case and the worst-case forecasts. You have "bracketed" the forecast market revenue. The amount of spread between these two forecasts is a measure of market uncertainty.

If the best-case forecast is only ten percent higher than the worst-case forecast, your estimate of future market sales revenue should be relatively accurate. If your best-case forecast is 100 percent higher than your worst-case forecast, you have a high degree of market uncertainty. In this case, your best estimate of future market size will be speculative and you should manage accordingly. You still must estimate the future of your markets as a basis for developing your business strategy. Look to history as a partial guide and how much market volatility has been experienced. I often see a market with declining sales for the last three years, only to see forecasted market revenue growing dramatically. Why, because that is the only way they can justify an investment in the business. This is usually the Wrong Answer! History is the starting point for your forecast and the best indicators of the future come from your analysis of market alternatives, externalities, and saturation, as they will impact the size of the future market revenue.

Section 10—Market Maturity

This section describes the current phase of market maturity, either New, Growth, Mature, Decline, or Residual as described in Chapter 4. You should indicate the phase of market maturity consistent with the history of the market and your forecast of changes in market size as shown in Section 9 of the summary.

MARKET BATTLEFIELD SUMMARY   *QUICK*STRATEGY™   Form 1.0

1. Product or Service:	2. Customers:

3. Customer Need: **4. Market Shape:**

5. Market Alternatives: **6. Saturation:**

7. Externalities:

8. Competitors	Strengths	Weaknesses	Sales $(000) Last Yr./This Yr.	Share (%)

9. Market Size (Sales Revenue $000)   Total

Year-5	Year-4	Year-3	Year-2	Last Year	This Year	Year 2	Year 3	Year 4	Year 5

10. Market Maturity _____ **Stage**

Strategic Business Unit:	Plan Manager:	Date Prepared:
Company:	Strategy Advisor:	Date of Next Plan Review:

231

Appendix B
The Strategic Plan Summary
(Form 2.0)

Once you have completed the Market Battlefield Summary, you can focus on developing a Strategic Plan. The Strategic Plan Summary (Form 2.0) helps you translate market opportunities into a plan of action to capitalize on those opportunities. It lets you convert your competitive position (advantages/disadvantages and strengths/weaknesses) into the most appropriate strategic initiative for your business. It helps you estimate competitive reaction to your initiative and how it will be affected by market maturity. It aids you in translating your strategic objective into a strategic initiative and then into a tactical plan of action to achieve your objective. It will also let you measure strategic success by achieving measurable financial results consistent with meeting your market objectives.

You can start the strategic planning process by studying the Market Battlefield Summary for your business and asking questions about your position in the market, such as how it may change in the future and whether you should change your current position. What are your market opportunities (Opportunity Questions)? How will they change over time (Timing Questions)? What can you do to alter your position (Resource Questions)? The answers to these questions should lead you to an achievable strategic direction, given the nature of the opportunity and your abilities.

Market Opportunity Questions:

1. Does my business have a significant competitive advantage? Against one or several competitors?
2. Can my business develop or acquire a significant competitive advantage? Against one or several competitors?
3. Is there an opportunity to combine with competitors to upset market equilibrium (given antitrust limitations)?
4. Is there a weak competitor, such as a large competitor spread too thin or an undercapitalized niche competitor?

5. Are customers loyal to suppliers or are they primarily transient customers? What percentage of my customers are first-time buyers versus repeat buyers?

6. Is market maturity forcing out competitors? What void are they leaving and who is filling the remaining market needs?

7. Is there a dominant competitor? Who manages the market (sets the standard for performance)? Will they aggressively pursue market opportunities and defend their weaknesses?

8. Is market demand shifting away from competitor offerings? For example, a Performance Market shifting to a Price Market as it matures.

9. Has any competitor lost its strategic focus? For example, a good niche competitor leaving its niche position to pursue a broader offering.

10. Can my business overcome a significant strategic disadvantage (competitive weakness)?

11. Can my business reposition its products or services to more closely match the market's needs? What customer needs remain unfulfilled?

12. Should my company counter new competitors or aggressive competitors with investments to defend my position or exit the market?

13. Are there new market growth opportunities in this market as customers migrate from market alternative products, or are market alternatives pulling customers from this market?

14. Do market alternatives represent a better investment opportunity?

15. Do market externalities threaten the near-term future of the market or my position in the market? Should my company exit the market?

Resource Questions:

1. Is there a critical resource necessary to sustain or hold my market position that is threatened by competitors or externalities?

2. What financial returns on invested capital are achievable in this market? Is it worth investing in this market?

3. Does my company have adequate (any) financial capacity to pursue a strategic objective? How much?

4. Does my company have the management resources to dedicate to a strategic initiative? Who and how much time?

5. Do competitors have the financial resources to defend against a strategic initiative? Which ones? How much?
6. Do competitors have the management resources to defend against a strategic initiative?
7. Do market leaders have adequate resources to take out marginal competitors with price wars? Would the market respond to discounting?
8. Does my business have the resources to project an overwhelming competitive advantage and inhibit competitor reaction?
9. Does my business have the ability to limit resources available to competitors?
10. Does my business have adequate financial and people resources, beyond the proposed strategic initiative, if it fails?

Timing Questions:

1. How fast can (will) competitors react to a strategic initiative by my business?
2. Are market changes creating strategic opportunities or limiting opportunities?
3. What is the current stage of market maturity? How fast is it changing and what force is driving the change?
4. Can my business complete a strategic initiative in time to capture a market opportunity?
5. How quickly might market alternatives, externalities, or saturation force a change in my strategic direction?
6. Can my business move so rapidly that it will gain market share before competitors can react?
7. How long will my business's competitive advantages last before being neutralized by competitors?
8. How long will it take for competitors to capitalize on my disadvantages? Does my business have time to fix them? Should I exit the market?

There are often no hard fast answers to these questions as you develop your first strategic plan, but each question should be contemplated in the context of your position on the market battlefield before you start the strategic planning process.

For example: Why bother to contemplate a Build strategic initiative if you have neither the money nor people to affect the strategy? That does not mean you do not need to develop a strategic plan to Hold or Harvest your business, but that your options are limited by your resources.

DEVELOPING THE STRATEGIC PLAN

The next step in developing a strategic plan is to target a competitor or competitors that will be the focus of your strategy. Then complete Sections 11 and 12 of the following form:

STRATEGIC PLAN SUMMARY				*QUICKSTRATEGY*™			Form 2.0
11. Your STRENGTHS vs. Competitor or Market Alternative				**12. Your WEAKNESSES vs. Competitor or Market Alternative**			

13. Strategic Objective:

14. Type of Strategic Initiative:

15. Strategic Plan:

16. Tactical Plan:

17. History & Projections (performance measures)	Year-4	Year-3	Year-2	Last Year	This Year	Next Year	Year 3

Strategic Business Unit:	Plan Manager:	Date Prepared:
Company:	Strategic Advisor:	Date of Next Plan Review:

Section 11—Competitive Strengths vs. Target Competitor(s)

Identify your business's competitive strengths (advantages) against your targeted competitors. List these competitive strengths versus each target competitor in order of their ability to attract customers. This means that customers must recognize these strengths in order for them to be of value in developing your strategic plan. For example:

Competitive Strengths vs. Competitor X

1. Three percent lower price
2. Fifty percent more sales outlets
3. More dedicated sales organization
4. Immediate product availability

Once you have identified your strengths versus the target competitor, test their value from the perspective of customer needs. In the above example #1, "Three percent lower price," is this significant to your customers? In some markets it could be very significant, in others it would be of no consequence. In the above example #2, "Fifty percent more sales outlets," how is it significant to your customer? It only addresses a customer need if convenient location is meaningful to the customer. More sales outlets are only a significant competitive advantage if this translates into ease of access to your products compared to the competition. If your outlets are all in the city, while the primary customer population is in the suburbs (Sears had this problem in the 1970's), then more sales outlets are not an advantage.

In the above example #3, "More dedicated sales organization," this is not a competitive strength as it does not directly address a customer need. The strength must be recognized by the customer and must be significant, relative to your target competitor, to be real. If this more dedicated sales organization was able to solve customer problems with greater efficiency than a competitor, it could be a competitive advantage. If this more dedicated sales organization was better trained to answer customer questions on product performance, it could be a competitive advantage. In the above example #4, "Immediate product availability" could be a competitive advantage in some markets; in other markets, the customer is willing to wait a reasonable time period for product delivery without affecting their purchase decision. If the targeted competitor also has immediate product availability, it is not a competitive advantage; it has been neutralized.

When listing competitive advantages, consider the type of market you are serving. A Performance Market is looking for improved products and/or services; a Price Market is looking for the lowest price. However, your business can target either end of the Market Battlefield; you can target the Price end of a Performance Market or vice versa. In all cases, the effectiveness of your strengths (advantages) is a function of how well they address the target competitors' customers' needs. If the target competitor operates on the Price end of the market battlefield, you are not as likely to attract their customers with improved product performance at a higher price.

Consider the significance of your business's competitive strengths relative to your target competitor. To be significant enough to gain market share, your strength must upset market equilibrium and take away your competitors' loyal customers, not just transient customers. This means it must change customer behavior. A three percent price advantage may be real to many customers and significant to others, but is it enough to get them to break their habit of buying from your competitor and change loyalty. It may take a ten percent price advantage to take loyal customers from targeted competitors. As we pointed out in Case #1, in a market where a market leader (McDonald's) can react to a discounted price by a significant competitor, they will neutralize the advantage. Significant competitive advantages upset market equilibrium and change customer behavior. Are the competitive strengths you have identified versus your target competitors enough to change the way your customer behaves in their purchase decision?

Where do your perceived strengths fit within the customers' need hierarchy? Remember once a need is satisfied, it no longer becomes the driving force in changing customer behavior. For example in Case #1, the fast-food burger market buyer, the majority of customers have accepted the $3—$5 price range as acceptable for a fast-food burger, fries, and a drink for a number of years. It is their standard purchase. Are they motivated by a price reduction, once they have accepted the $3—$5 price range as reasonable and acceptable for their standard purchase? (When Burger King dropped the price of a burger to 99 cents, you still had to add $2.48 to get the fries and soda, bringing the average meal price right back to the $3—$5 range.)

Price is a motivator if you don't expect to pay the asked price or you can't afford the product. Once a customer can easily afford a product and the price charged is consistent with their expectations, price is less of a motivator in the customer's need hierarchy.

How defensible are your business's competitive strengths? In many cases, a performance or price advantage is only a temporary advantage. We have all seen price advantages in air travel destroyed within weeks as competitors respond with similar price cuts. Can competitors react rapidly to neutralize your strengths? List your competitive strengths with an estimate of how fast your competition will neutralize those strengths, such as:

Competitive Strengths vs. Competitor X

1. Three percent lower price (three months)
2. Fifty percent more sales outlets (three years)
3. Immediate product availability (six months)

This gives a more complete assessment of the value of your competitive strengths over the life of your strategic plan. It highlights the obvious:
"A BUSINESS CANNOT BUILD A LONG-TERM STRATEGIC PLAN AROUND A SHORT-TERM COMPETITIVE ADVANTAGE."

Competitive strengths must address current customer needs, be directed at competitors' weaknesses, and be defendable if they are to be the basis for a strategic initiative.

Section 12—Competitive Weaknesses vs. Target Competitors

Identify your business's competitive weaknesses (disadvantages) versus your target competitors. (If in a defensive position, look at weaknesses versus those competitors attacking your position.) List these weaknesses against each target competitor in order of maximum exposure to your market position, most significant weakness first. As with competitive strengths, weaknesses (or disadvantages) are only relevant to your strategy as they are perceived by your customers and to the extent they fail to meet customer needs. For example:

Competitive Weaknesses vs. Competitor Y

1. Ten percent higher price (one year)
2. Thirty percent fewer sales outlets (three years)
3. Thirty day delivery (two months)
4. Fewer product features (be specific where possible) (one year)

As with competitive strengths, it helps to identify the estimated time to correct the weakness (in parentheses) should you decide to invest in a corrective action.

Once listed, each weakness should be evaluated for its impact on your market position. For #1, "Ten percent higher price (one year)," this may or may not be significant to your customers. If you are competing in a performance market, a ten percent higher price may not be significant to your customers. In a turbine engine overhaul facility that was breaking even, we were able to implement a ten percent price increase over a one-year period and maintain market share. In Price Markets like grain and salt, ten percent higher prices could destroy your market position in less than the one year required to fix the weakness. For #2, "Thirty percent fewer sales outlets (three years)," do your targeted customers recognize your outlet deficiency? This could be a major long-term (three year) investment; will your strategy be effective over this time period to justify the investment. For #3, "Thirty day delivery (two months)," how does this compare with your target competitor and customer expectations? As we saw in Case #1, the fast-food burger buyer is expecting three—five minute service, but will endure a ten-minute wait. In many industries, just-in-time delivery is very high on a customer's list of needs in order to keep their factory operating. Can you schedule to meet your customer needs, or do you have to fix the weakness immediately (two months) to hold market position? For item #4, "Fewer product features (one year)" is a general complaint often held by sales personnel. When you add those features, does your price increase accordingly? Are you positioned as a price competitor where additional features are not a priority to your customers' purchase decision?

Are you a performance competitor that has fallen behind the competition? The magnitude of the weakness is a function of how you are positioned on the market battlefield. Remember, unless you are one of the market leaders, you are unlikely to be able to straddle the market battlefield with product offerings from low price to high performance and have a winning strategy.

The fact that you have competitive weaknesses does not mean you have to correct all of the weaknesses to develop a winning strategy. Every salesman who has ever worked for me wants the lowest price and the most performance from our products and services. Unless your business is in a market leadership position, you cannot satisfy all customer needs and you cannot compete against all competitors. For smaller competitors, you must pick your market position on either the Price or Performance end of the market, and focus on correcting weaknesses of importance to your target customers and focus resources against targeted competitors. These targeted competitors may include market leaders if you are chewing away at their flanks (price end or performance end of their offering). Your weaknesses are only relevant on a competitor-by-competitor basis when developing your strategy.

Sections 13 and 14—Strategic Objective and Type of Strategic Initiative

A review of your target competitors and your business strengths and weaknesses relative to those competitors will give you insight into the type of strategic initiative you should initiate and help you establish an obtainable strategic objective. Again, "business strategy is the art and science of meeting your competitors on the market battlefield under advantageous conditions." The type of strategy you pursue should be directed to positioning your business to maximize your financial returns relative to your competitors. A common mistake in establishing strategic objectives is to set objectives that are driven by a desire to meet shareholder, owner, or your boss's financial objectives.

How often have you heard mandates like "you must grow your business ten percent per year and achieve a minimum twenty-five percent return on investment?" This is a promise someone has made to investors, not part of a strategic objective. The market battlefield and how you position your business within that battlefield will determine your growth opportunity and potential financial returns; your strategic objectives must be consistent with the market. Furthermore, the stock market knows that opportunity is as much a function of opportunity in the markets you serve as it is how you manage your business. A doctoral study by Benjamin King at the University of Chicago showed average stock price changes were correlated 49 percent of the time to public reaction to industry data (the markets you serve) and 20 percent of the time to company-specific information. We have recently seen the stock market retreat en masse to changes in the dot com market, the telecom market, and the electric power trading market. Wise investors understand that financial objectives are limited by the opportunities in the markets you serve. You should expect to set strategic objectives for your business consistent with the market opportunity.

A wiser corporate mandate would be to HARVEST or RETREAT from any business that does not meet the ten percent growth and twenty-five percent return on investment objective in order to redeploy cash to other market opportunities. Even this strategic objective would be inconsistent with the market opportunity in NEW markets and early stage GROWTH markets where low returns are consistent with the strategic objective of positioning your business for future financial returns.

Too many managers fail when they try to meet growth and financial objectives inconsistent with the strategic market opportunity. When you set strategic objectives, focus on maximizing the value of the strategic market opportunity, not meeting unrelated financial objectives.

As you have seen in the case studies and Chapters 4 and 5, in *Quick*Strategy there are only five types of strategic initiatives: BUILD, HOLD, HARVEST, RETREAT, and PROBE. These all relate directly to your market share strategic objective. A BUILD type of strategy means that you will build market share relative to your competitors. A HOLD type of strategic initiative means that you will hold your market share relative to your competitors. HARVEST and RETREAT strategic initiatives imply that you will lose market share relative to your competitors. A PROBE type of strategic initiative implies that you will gather information to determine if there is a strategic opportunity to change your market share. There are market conditions and market positions that are most suitable for each type of strategy.

BUILD—To invest in a strategic initiative to increase market share. This means that you are taking market share from a targeted direct competitor or, in some cases, a supplier of market alternative products or services. This strategy is most appropriate when your business has a significant competitive advantage, no significant competitive disadvantages, competitors unwilling or unable to defend their position, and an opportunity to achieve acceptable rates of return on your investment. To be successful, you must either have the significant competitive advantage or have adequate resources to develop one in time to take advantage of the market opportunity.

I have initiated many BUILD strategies with what I thought was an overwhelming competitive advantage, only to find out that it was only overwhelming in my mind, not in the customer's mind. This error has cost more money than I want to recall. If you are not sure of the significance of your competitive advantage, a PROBE strategy to verify the customers' acceptance of the competitive advantage may be appropriate. As in Case #1 with the Albuquerque Turkey Burger, rather than launching a national campaign, a smaller test (PROBE) against the national competitors in the local market will tell the owners and investors if the competitive advantage is real at a fraction of the cost of a national campaign.

Most managers want to initiate a BUILD strategy. Often, that is the only way they can meet their financial objectives or meet their bonus plan objectives. In a NEW or GROWTH market, you often don't have to gain market share to build the revenue of the business. A HOLD strategy in a NEW or GROWTH stage market can generate the desired revenue growth at a fraction of the cost of a BUILD strategy. To BUILD market share in a NEW or GROWTH market, when you have an overwhelming competitive advantage and no significant competitive disadvantages, your business must take share from a competitor and outgrow the market.

To initiate a BUILD strategy in a MATURE market, where there is little or no growth, the GROWTH is always at the expense of market competitors and should only be initiated if the market is expected to remain stable long enough to payback your investment in the BUILD initiative.

Typically, there are few opportunities to build market share in DECLINE or RESIDUAL markets, as financial returns can be too small to warrant the investment. However, sometimes an investment in consolidation at these later stages of market maturity makes economic sense.

More than half the strategic plans I review are focused on a BUILD strategy. To be successful, BUILD strategies require resources to support the strategic initiative. If you don't have the financial, people, and other resources needed to sustain a build initiative, can't counteract competitors' reactions to this initiative, and can't hold onto your gain in market share, don't waste your company's time and money. Most BUILD type of strategic initiatives that I review fail to achieve their objectives.

HOLD—To invest only in strategic initiatives that help retain and defend your business's market share. This is not an idle strategy where you sit back and observe changes to your market position. HOLD strategies often require continuous investment to defend your market position. In selecting target competitors, you must select those that are actively engaged in taking your business. Bolster your competitive advantages where possible and fix your competitive weaknesses against these competitors. Market leaders must defend both the Price and Performance ends of their markets against niche competitors.

Price and Performance competitors must defend against competitors attacking their niche positions. To HOLD market position, you must have a thorough understanding of the market battlefield and your competitive position, or you can over or under-invest to sustain your market share.

In Chapter 5, Figure 5-1, we showed how a Strategic Initiative Decision Model could be used to assist in deciding the market conditions that would lead to a HOLD strategy:

1. Significant competitive advantage, no significant competitive disadvantage, competitors unwilling or unable to defend market share, but return on investment too low to justify investment in BUILD strategy.

2. Significant competitive advantage, no significant competitive disadvantage, competitors willing to defend their position and block a BUILD strategy, even with return on investment opportunity adequate to justify investment in BUILD strategy.

3. Significant competitive advantage, no significant competitive disadvantage, competitors willing to defend market position, but not aggressively, with unacceptably low returns on investment.

4. No significant competitive advantage, no significant competitive disadvantage, competitors unwilling or unable to defend market position, and high return potential on invested capital.

5. Same as 4, but low return on invested capital where very little investment is required to HOLD market position.

6. No significant competitive advantage, no competitive disadvantage, competitors willing to defend market positions, and high potential return on invested capital.

7. Significant competitive advantage, a competitive disadvantage, competitors willing to defend market positions, and high return on investment opportunity.

8. Significant competitive advantage, a competitive disadvantage, competitors will not attack, and low potential returns on investment but little additional investment required to HOLD market position.

9. Significant competitive advantage, a competitive disadvantage, competitors that are not willing to defend their position or attack, but returns on investments to defend market position are high enough to warrant a defense to HOLD market position.

Understand that the rather simplistic decision model that leads to the above conclusions to HOLD market share is only one perspective on how to make a HOLD strategy decision. As you gain experience using the *Quick*Strategy model, you will develop more refined decision criteria for your strategic initiative decision-making. HOLD-type strategic initiatives are appropriate at any stage of market maturity. In the NEW stage of a market, it is difficult to know if you are holding market share as changes in competitor market positions are difficult to identify and most growth is from customers extracted from market alternative products and services.

In GROWTH stage markets, near-term low returns on investment may limit your options to a HOLD strategy. However, in the Growth Stage of market maturity, investments are often made to maintain market share in anticipation of higher returns in the later stages of a GROWTH market and as the market matures. In a MATURE stage of the market, HOLDING market share may represent the best strategic choice to generate high returns on invested capital before market declines limit your financial opportunity. In DECLINE and RESIDUAL stages of market maturity, returns on investment are often too low to justify anything other than minimal investment to hold market share and usually lead to HARVEST or RETREAT strategies. HOLD strategies for the market leader, or a well-defined niche position in the markets you serve, can produce good financial returns at every stage of market maturity and preserve capital to BUILD market share in other markets where there are clear opportunities.

HARVEST—To withdraw from a market battlefield making no additional investment and reducing existing investment when possible. This implies making an orderly and usually slow exit from a market by taking as much invested capital out of the market as possible for redeployment to other markets. Anticipating conditions that will necessitate a withdrawal from a market and implementing an orderly HARVEST is a way to maximize the returns on your prior investments in a market.

I have seen HARVEST strategies implemented over many years, producing what we once called "cash cows" by generating very substantial profits for our businesses. All too often, we try to hold onto a market position until our business is in a crisis, losing market share, losing money, and with little chance for recovery. Why? Few of us want to admit when it is time to exit a market and redeploy assets to another market opportunity or even give money back to investors where market opportunities do not exist (a novel idea for many companies).

Again looking at Chapter 5 Figure 5-1, the Strategic Initiative Decision Model gives us some perspective on the market conditions that should trigger your decision to harvest a market:

1. Significant competitive advantage, no significant competitive disadvantage, competitors that will aggressively defend their market position, and financial returns too low to justify any additional investment in the market.

2. No significant competitive advantage, no significant competitive disadvantage, competitors that will not defend their market position, but financial returns too low to justify any additional investment in market.

3. No significant competitive advantage, no competitive disadvantage, competitors who will aggressively defend their market position and limit business to a market share too small to allocate company resources to even if financial returns appear to be adequate.

4. No significant competitive advantage, no significant competitive disadvantage, competitors who will aggressively defend their market position, and financial returns on investment too low to warrant further investment to defend market position.

5. Significant competitive advantage, a significant competitive disadvantage, competitors that will not attack your market position, but return on invested capital too low to defend market position.

6. Significant competitive advantage, a significant competitive disadvantage, competitors who will attack your competitive position so aggressively that even high potential financial returns on investment are not adequate to justify defending your market position.

7. Significant competitive advantage, a significant competitive disadvantage, competitors who will aggressively attack your competitive position, and low potential returns on investment.

8. No significant competitive advantage, a significant competitive disadvantage, competitors who are not attacking your market position, and high potential financial returns that will let you extract significant amounts of invested capital as you yield market share.

9. No significant competitive advantage, a competitive disadvantage, competitors who will attack your market position, but not too aggressively to permit extraction of your investment as you yield market share.

These rather simplistic decision criteria are only offered as initial guidance to your decision to execute a HARVEST strategy. HARVEST strategies will be very difficult to implement in most organizations as the sales staff will often argue that discounting products or adding a few more features is all that is necessary to keep the business going and their commissions flowing. The design and engineering organization will always be a few months away from having just the right feature to secure your market position. It takes truly skilled and disciplined management to orchestrate a successful HARVEST strategy.

HARVEST type strategies are most commonly initiated in more mature market stages like the DECLINE and RESIDUAL stages of market maturity as potential financial returns on additional investment decline. However, being overwhelmed by the competition at any stage of market maturity may justify a HARVEST strategy. Even in GROWTH stage markets, where the competition was so aggressive in gaining market share that they drove the entire market into financial losses with little hope of recovery, I have executed HARVEST type strategies to preserve invested capital.

RETREAT—To exit the market battlefield as fast as possible while minimizing losses.

Retreating from the market battlefield is a type of strategic initiative that is executed when facing insurmountable competitive conditions in the market battlefield and financial losses or the near-term prospect of losses. As with the other types of strategies, Figure 5-1, the Strategic Initiatives Decision Model, gives us some direction in when to implement the RETREAT strategy:

1. No significant competitive advantage, a significant competitive disadvantage, competitors who are not attacking, but losing money or facing near-term financial losses to stay in the market.
2. No significant competitive advantage, a significant competitive disadvantage, competitors attacking where financial returns are adequate but unable to defend market position without investing beyond available resources.
3. No significant competitive advantage, a significant competitive disadvantage, competitors attacking aggressively, and low potential financial returns.

Whenever your business faces overwhelming competition that will destroy your market position without any hope of an orderly withdrawal from

247

the market battlefield, the RETREAT strategy should be employed. In a NEW or GROWTH market, you may not be able to keep up with the investment requirements necessary to maintain your market position. In a MATURE market, you may find investors willing to discount to gain market share and create near-term financial losses with little hope of recovery. In a DECLINE or RESIDUAL stage of market maturity, customers may shift so heavily to low price product or service alternatives that there is no profit potential for Performance competitors. A RETREAT strategy should be implemented at any stage of market maturity to minimize losses.

PROBE—To make a small investment in order to define potential market opportunities. It should be implemented against specific strategic objectives, over a well-defined and limited time period, and by investing a limited amount of resources. This strategy is used to test a perceived competitive advantage or to test the magnitude of a disadvantage in a targeted market or market segment. It can also be used to test a competitor's reaction to a market initiative in a limited market.

Financial resources and time spent executing a PROBE strategy should be limited and considered expendable, as most PROBE initiatives will not identify strategic market opportunities. It can be implemented at any stage of market maturity to minimize potential losses while verifying a strategic assumption.

You should have selected the most appropriate type of strategic initiative based on your analysis of the target competitors, your relative strengths and weaknesses, your position on the market battlefield, and the potential financial returns relative to the resources you have at your disposal. In Section 14 of the Strategic Plan Summary, Form 2.0, you should identify the type of strategy you intend to pursue, both now and in the future. Often, you will initiate a BUILD strategy in the near term followed by a HOLD strategy once an objective is achieved. Or you may HARVEST a business until financial returns diminish to a point where a RETREAT strategy is more appropriate. The type of strategy you have selected is the starting point for setting your strategic objectives in Section 13 of the Strategic Plan Summary.

Strategic Objectives in Section 13 should always be described in terms of a measurable strategic position to be obtained over a defined time period within defined financial limitations, such as:

1. Increase market share from five—ten percent over two years while holding ten percent gross profit margin, investing no more than $1 million. -BUILD Strategy-
2. Increase sales to price portion of market from $1 million to $3 million over three years, investing no more than $1 million while maintaining existing profit margins. -BUILD Strategy-
3. Hold market share while increasing return on invested capital from 15—25 percent over two years. -HOLD Strategy-
4. Determine if annual sales of $500,000 are obtainable in market segment X with a minimum potential return on invested capital of 25 percent. Complete within one year and spend no more than $100,000. -PROBE Strategy-
5. Exit the market over three years while harvesting $1.5 million through positive cash flow. -HARVEST Strategy-
6. Exit the market within six months limiting losses to $200,000.
7. -RETREAT Strategy-

Note that the Strategic Objective does not say "how" you will operate, but simply what you will accomplish.

Section 15—The Strategic Plan

The strategic plan is where you identify the competitors you will target, what strengths you will take advantage of, what weaknesses you will defend or correct, and how this will impact your market battlefield position. For example:

1. In Strategic Objective #1 above, your strategic plan may state: "Target competitors X and Y with emphasis on strategic strength AAA to accomplish strategic objective."
2. In Strategic Objective #2 above, your strategic plan may state: "Target competitors A, B, & C emphasizing Price strategic strength to accomplish strategic objective."

3. In Strategic Objective #3 above, your strategic plan may state: "Yield market share to competitors X, Y, & Z while defending competitive strength A and B to accomplish strategic objective."

4. In Strategic Objective #4 above, your strategic plan may state: "Focus competitive strength A on target competitors M & N to accomplish strategic objective."

5. In Strategic Objective #5 above, your strategic plan may state: "Yield market share to target competitors F & R defending competitive weakness Q only to the extent strategic objective can be achieved."

6. In Strategic Objective #6 above, your strategic plan may state: "Yield market position to competitors T & S without defending market position to accomplish strategic objective."

What is important to recognize is that the statement of the Strategic Plan is only a statement of what competitors will be the focus of your competitive strength or weakness to accomplish your strategic objective. It should be a simple declarative statement based on accomplishing your objective. It should tell how you are going to meet your competitors (targets) on the market battlefield under advantageous conditions (competitively advantaged), or how you will exit the battlefield. DON'T GO INTO DETAILS OF HOW YOU WILL IMPLEMENT YOUR STRATEGY. The Tactical Plan will get into the details and the steps you will take to capitalize on your advantage or defend/fix your disadvantage as you face the target competitors.

Section 16—The Tactical Plan

The Tactical Plan is a detailed description of what actions you will take to achieve the strategic plan and meet the strategic plan objectives. Where the strategic plan talks about who you will target and how you will leverage your competitive position, the tactical plan details how you will implement your strategy, who will be responsible for each tactic, and how much it will cost or return to your business.

To the extent possible, each element in the tactical plan should be measurable and assignable to a responsible party. For example, in the Eclipse 500 Strategic Plan for Building Market Share in a New Market, the tactics are directed at specific milestones that must be accomplished by certain dates. Specific investment levels for each task and the responsible person for each task was not available as public information, but should be added by the Plan Manager:

- Complete assembly and test of six prototype aircraft. Use temporary Teledyne Engines to facilitate airworthiness and performance testing. Two by --/--/02, two by --/--/03, and two by --/--/04.
- Continue to test, evaluate, and certify advanced flight controls and avionics. Complete by --/--/03.
- Continue to develop improved jet engines with Pratt & Whitney Canada for delivery by --/--/04. Complete aircraft certification with these engines by --/--/05.
- Continue to build market with air taxi operators, charter freight carriers, and charter medical emergency carriers to build order backlog to 3000+ aircraft by --/--/05.
- Continue to develop training simulators and a training program that will help pilots meet insurance and FAA requirements while ensuring a high level of flight safety. Complete the training simulators and the training program by --/--/04.
- Complete the friction-stir welding facility in Albuquerque and the production facility at Double Eagle Airport (west of Albuquerque) by --/--/04.
- Continue to work with the insurance companies to assure availability of insurance by --/--/04.
- Initiate production of ---- aircraft by --/--/06.

As you can see from the above tactics, after reviewing the Strategic Plan Summary for the Eclipse 500 we tried to be specific about key milestones that must be achieved to meet their strategic objective for a Build-type strategy in a NEW market.

- In the Georgia Wireless Constructors' Strategic Plan Summary, the tactical plan to build their market share from five-ten percent over the next two years via internal growth and to twenty percent with acquisitions, is the following:
  - Upgrade the project management system, adding a field accessible on-line project management center for each customer to reduce costs, provide real time customer support and status information by 06/30/00, Cost: $125,000, (responsible manager B.B.)

- Reduce overhead by reducing unbilled hours on direct labor. Improve employee scheduling, bill for contract delays, and set minimum billability requirements on all direct labor by 06/06/00. Cost $10,000, (responsible manager R.D.)
- Reduce costs by eliminating internal administrative overhead, contracting out payroll, benefits administration, and insurance to Adminstaff Services, and accounting to local independent accounting firm by 09/30/00. Cost: $40,000, (responsible manager R.D.)
- Initiate acquisition program (after securing financing) targeting selected regional EF&I suppliers to build additional $100 million in revenue over two years. Estimated financing required: $50 million, (responsible manager R.D.)

As you can see from this tactical plan, costs were assigned to each task and a responsible manager identified. The tasks tie directly to the strategy and strategic objective and are measurable actions. The Albuquerque Turkey Burger, Case Study #1, Strategic Plan Summary shows tactics supporting a probe strategy and are specific as to timing and responsible manager, but need to have costs identified for each tactic to manage activity, as follows:

- Recruit a trained fast-food store manager by 5/10 (TR, responsible manager).
- Research Albuquerque fast-food outlet locations and select location by 5/10 (hired realtor).
- Complete facility renovation and site improvements to house first Albuquerque Turkey Burger outlet by 7/10 (hired Contractor/TR).
- Schedule outlet opening by 7/10 (TR).
- Select advertising agency and develop advertising and marketing program by 5/10 (TR).
- Order and install all equipment, tables, etc. by 8/10 (store manager).
- Obtain necessary permits to open food service business by 8/1 (store manager).
- Recruit and train staff by 8/1 (store manager).
- Finalize initial menu by 6/1 (TR and store manager).
- Order initial food inventory with scheduled deliveries. Order by 6/15, initial deliveries by 8/15 (TR and store manager).

- Initiate advertising program for grand opening by 8/15 (TR).
- Open outlet, 9/1 tentative (TR and store manager).
- Commence customer surveys to identify sensitivity to competitive position by 9/15 (TR).
- Modify menu to react to initial customer input by 12/16 (TR).
- Introduce modified menu items by 1/15/04 (store manager).
- Revise marketing and promotion around new menu and customer response to survey by 1/15/04 (TR and store manager).
- Conclude test-marketing phase of plan by 5/10/04 (TR).
- Develop financial prospectus for national franchise or sell/close business by 6/10/04 (TR).

A detailed set of tasks involved in implementing the Probe strategy for the Albuquerque Turkey Burger shows how it will take just over one year to complete the Probe strategy, consistent with the strategic objectives.

As you can see from the above examples, the details of how a strategic initiative will be implemented is the Tactical Plan.

Section 17—History and Projections (Performance Measures)

The first line on the chart in Section 17 should be Market Size transferred from Section 9 in the corresponding Market Battlefield Summary. By dividing your sales revenue (bookings in some cases) by the market size, you can calculate your business market share, which can then be entered on line 2 of Section 17 on the chart. Enter sales revenue (or bookings, in some cases) on line 3. These three lines will tell you whether you are achieving your market share objectives and should be in all plans. Subsequent lines should contain measurements critical to monitoring the success of your strategy such as annual investment in the business, operating profit, return on investment, etc. This information is critical to reviewing a business's manager's ability to manage to the strategic plan and to make changes to the plan when strategic objectives are not met or expectations exceeded.

In these two pages, the Market Battlefield Summary and the Strategic Plan Summary, you have the necessary information to direct your business in rapidly changing markets. They are only snapshots of your strategic position and business strategy. They are not "fixed in concrete" and should be compared with actual day-to-day operating results to determine if market conditions have changed that would warrant revising the plan.

Appendix C
Glossary

This appendix provides a quick reference alphabetical listing of the definitions and the terminology used throughout the book:

Build Strategy: To invest in a strategic initiative to build market share.

Business Strategy: The art and science of meeting your competitors on the market battlefield under advantageous conditions.

Captive Supplier Strategy: A strategic initiative where a product or service output is dominated by one customer to the extent that the customer can dictate terms and conditions to the supplier.

Cheap Product Competitor Strategy: A low-price strategic initiative that also delivers poor product quality; does not lead to have repeat sales.

Coattail Competitor Strategy: A business strategy that depends on an often unrelated business's success to achieve its strategic objectives. Example: A shopping mall store may locate next to a supermarket and depend on the supermarket traffic to achieve its success. If the supermarket fails, the coattail business will also fail.

Competitive Advantage: A product or service performance or price advantage over competitors that is consistent with customers' needs and recognized by the customer.

Competitive Disadvantage: A product or service deficiency relative to competitors that is recognized by customers as not fulfilling their needs.

Competitive Strength: Same as Competitive Advantage.

Competitive Weakness: Same as Competitive Disadvantage.

Competitors: Those businesses or business segments that compete directly in the defined market for your products or services and are directed at the same set of customers.

Customers: Those people or businesses that purchase goods and services in the market you serve.

Customer Qualified Competitor: Those competitors who are qualified by the customer to provide services based on meeting some specific minimum customer criteria.

Decline Market: That stage of market maturity represented by a continuous long-term decline in the overall demand for products or services. This stage occurs between the Mature and Residual stages of market maturity. It is usually driven down by increased sales of market alternative products, external market factors, or saturation.

Growth Market: That stage of market maturity characterized by a continuous expansion in demand for products or services, usually driven by decreased demand for market alternative products. This stage occurs between the New and Mature stages of market maturity.

Harvest Strategy: To exit the market battlefield while investing only to maximize the near-term cash to be extracted from the sales of the product or service.

Hold Strategy: To invest only in those strategic initiatives that help hold or defend market position.

Industry Standard Competitor: A recognized (by the customers) supplier of the highest possible quality product or service in the industry.

Last Resource Competitor: A supplier of the last available product or service to customers. No other competitive product is available to the market.

Loyal Customers: Those customers who return to a given supplier based on their history of satisfaction with the supplier's product or service offering.

Mature Market: A stage in market maturity where demand for products or services has stopped growing, but has not started to show a significant decline in demand. This stage occurs between the Growth and Decline stages of market maturity.

Market Alternatives: Those products or services that fulfill the same or similar needs as those supplied to a market, but in a distinctly different manner. For example, a motorcycle is a market alternative to a car in fulfilling transportation needs.

Market Battlefield: A well-defined set of products or services delivered to a specific set of customers to satisfy a defined set of customer needs. Also referred to as Markets and Market Segments throughout this book. It includes a description of the forces that change the size and shape of the market, such as Market Alternatives, Market Externalities, and Market Saturation. It includes a description of competitors, their strengths and weaknesses, and the competitors' relative position in the market. This defines the total market size as the sum of all of the competitors' revenues. In combination, the information describing the market battlefield forms the basis for developing a business strategy.

Market Externalities: Those factors external to the market, and beyond the influence of competitors, that can change the size and shape of the market, such as government regulation, financial market shifts, etc.

Market Leader Strategy: To focus on supplying a broad range of customer needs, from Price needs to Performance needs, in order to capture the largest market share. The market leader defines the center of the market battlefield and other competitors are postured around the leader.

Market Maturity: The normal growth and decline of market demand for products or services driven by market alternatives, market externalities, and saturation.

Market Shape: Defines the dominant customer need in a market, either Price, Value, or Performance.

Market Share: The percentage of sales revenue (in most cases) a competitor has relative to all of the competitors in a market.

Market Size: The total sales revenue (in most cases) of all competitors in a market.

Me-Too Competitor: A competitor who imitates another competitor, usually the market leader.

New Market: The earliest stages of market maturity when all businesses are replacing market alternative products, competitors are not well defined, customer needs are not well defined, and rapid unstructured growth is common.

Performance Market: A market where most of the customers' needs are oriented toward product or service performance features and not price.

Performance Measures: The financial criteria against which a set of tactical successes will be measured in a strategic plan.

Performance Competitor: A supplier who has a unique and defendable competitive advantage that is recognized by customers as filling a defined need.

Plan Manager: The business manager responsible for controlling all input to a strategic plan.

Prestige Competitor: A supplier who charges more for his product than the underlying value of the product compared to other products in the market. Jewelry stores are typically prestige competitors.

Price Competitor: A supplier who meets most of the customers' minimum needs at the lowest possible price.

Price Market: A market dominated by customers needing the lowest possible price for the product or service they purchase.

Probe Strategy: To make a small investment to explore market battlefield opportunities, limiting the amount of investment and terminated at a specific date.

Product or Service Description: The specific product or service offered by each competitor in the defined market, usually including a specific price or range of prices to differentiate it from market alternatives.

Promiser Strategy: A supplier of goods and services to a market who promises more performance or lower prices that he can deliver; often a spoiling strategy to delay sales of a competitor's products.

***Quick*Strategy:** A method for rapidly analyzing and tracking business strategies as they apply to specific market battlefields (market segments).

Residual Market: That stage of market maturity characterized by a relatively predictable demand for products or services. This stage occurs after the Decline stage of market maturity.

Retreat Strategy: To exit a market battlefield as rapidly as possible, while minimizing losses without defending market position. No investment is made to defend market position.

Strategic Business Unit: The old name for market segment or market battlefield.

Strategic Initiative: The changes a competitor makes to reposition itself on the market battlefield.

Strategic Objective: A specific market share related target against a defined set of competitors to maximize your financial returns given the strategic options available.

Strategic Plan: The market advantage(s) or disadvantage(s) that will be used against a specific competitor(s) to accomplish a strategic objective.

Strategy Advisor: A third-party monitor or strategic plan activity that keeps the Plan Manager appraised of changes in the market battlefield that can impact a strategic initiative.

Tactical Plan: A detailed set of actions to be taken to implement the strategic plan and achieve its objectives. Each action, where possible, should include cost, what is to be accomplished, and the time needed to complete the objective.

Transient Customer: A one-time buyer of products or services who always searches for the slightest improvement in product or service offering.

Type of Strategic Initiative: The relative importance placed on gaining (or losing) market share and the investment to be made to achieve the desired objective. BUILD, HOLD, HARVEST, RETREAT, AND PROBE are types of strategic initiatives.

Value Market: A market that cannot be defined as driven either by the price or the performance needs of the customers.

Vendor Qualified Competitor: A competitor who relies on a unique or proprietary relationship with a supplier in order to offer their goods and services to a market. Distributors with an exclusive territory, or a supplier-trained workforce are examples of Vendor Qualified Competitors.

Appendix D
Blank Forms and Notes

Bruce R. Robinson

Bruce R. Robinson

MARKET BATTLEFIELD SUMMARY *QUICK*STRATEGY™ Form 1.0

1. Product or Service:	2. Customers:

3. Customer Need:	4. Market Shape:

5. Market Alternatives:	6. Saturation:

7. Externalities:

8. Competitors	Strengths	Weaknesses	Sales $(000) Last Yr./This Yr.	Share (%)

9. Market Size (Sales Revenue $000) Total

Year-5	Year-4	Year-3	Year-2	Last Year	This Year	Year 2	Year 3	Year 4	Year 5

10. Market Maturity _____ **Stage**

Strategic Business Unit:	Plan Manager:	Date Prepared:
Company:	Strategy Advisor:	Date of Next Plan Review:

STRATEGIC PLAN SUMMARY   *QUICKSTRATEGY*™   Form 2.0

11. Your STRENGTHS vs. Competitor or Market Alternative	12. Your WEAKNESSES vs. Competitor or Market Alternative

13. Strategic Objective:

14. Type of Strategic Initiative:

15. Strategic Plan:

16. Tactical Plan:

17. History & Projections (performance measures)	Year-4	Year-3	Year-2	Last Year	This Year	Next Year	Year 3

Strategic Business Unit:	Plan Manager:	Date Prepared:
Company:	Strategic Advisor:	Date of Next Plan Review:

Bruce R. Robinson

About the Author

The author was introduced to market focused strategic planning after he sold his electronic instrument company to a NYSE high technology conglomerate 1977.

He has expanded and refined the methodology over the last 26 years; applying it to 12 companies he and his partners have acquired and managed. As co-author of, "Strategic Acquisitions, A Guide to Growing and Enhancing the Value of Your Business", Irwin, 1995, he demonstrated the utility of market focused strategic planning in valuing business opportunities. He is currently part owner and Chairman of 5 companies and actively teaching seminars on the subject of strategic planning using his *Quick*Strategy methodology.

He lives with his wife in the mountains of New Mexico and enjoys, fly fishing and flying small airplanes throughout the southwest. He holds a BSEE and MBA from Rochester Institute of Technology.

Printed in the United States
By Bookmasters